KU-435-961

A REFLECTIVE APPROACH TO TEACHING PHYSICAL EDUCATION

Donald R. Hellison, PhD
University of Illinois at Chicago

Thomas J. Templin, PhD
Purdue University, West Lafayette, IN

Human Kinetics Books
Champaign, Illinois

Library of Congress Cataloging-in-Publication Data

Hellison, Donald R.
    A reflective approach to teaching physical education / by Donald
R. Hellison, Thomas J. Templin.
      p.   cm.
    Includes bibliographical references and index.
    ISBN 0-87322-311-X
    1. Physical education and training--Study and teaching--United
States. 2. Physical education teachers--Training of--United States.
I. Templin, Thomas J. II. Title.
GV361.H39 1991
796'.07'0973--dc20

90-20654
CIP

ISBN: 0-87322-311-X

Copyright © 1991 by Donald R. Hellison and Thomas J. Templin

All rights reserved. Except for use in a review, the reproduction or utilization of this work in any form or by any electronic, mechanical, or other means, now known or hereafter invented, including xerography, photocopying, and recording, and in any information storage and retrieval system, is forbidden without the written permission of the publisher.

Acquisitions Editor: Rick Frey, PhD
Developmental Editor: Christine Drews
Assistant Editors: Dawn Levy, Kari Nelson, and Julia Anderson
Copyeditor: Wendy Nelson
Proofreader: Pam Johnson
Production Director: Ernie Noa
Typesetter: Angela K. Snyder
Text Design: Keith Blomberg
Text Layout: Tara Welsch and Denise Lowry
Cover Design: Hunter Graphics
Interior Art: Mary Long and Gretchen Walters
Printer: Versa Press
Bound by: Dekker

Printed in the United States of America

10 9 8 7 6 5 4 3 2 1

KING ALFRED'S COLLEGE
WINCHESTER

375
796
HEL

0125444 8

Human Kinetics Books
A Division of Human Kinetics Publishers, Inc.
Box 5076, Champaign, IL 61825-5076
1-800-747-4457

Canada Office:
Human Kinetics Publishers, Inc.
PO Box 2503, Windsor ON N8Y 4S2
1-800-465-7301 (in Canada only)

UK Office:
Human Kinetics Publishers (UK) Ltd.
PO Box 18
Rawdon, Leeds LS19 6TG
England
(0532) 504211

Contents

Preface

We heard somewhere that there are two kinds of people: those who think there are two kinds of people and those who do not. In one sense, at least, there are two kinds of people: left-handers and right-handers. Both of us are left-handers, which may give you some hint of the direction of this book. There may be two kinds of teacher educators as well (Porter, 1988, all quotes from p. 4): those who characterize good teaching as being based on "general guidelines and predispositions that point teachers in productive directions" and those who characterize good teaching as being based on a set of prescriptions with "lists of micro-level detailed statements of effective teaching behaviors." These two kinds of teacher educators are accused, respectively, of "making good teaching too complex and idiosyncratic" and "oversimplifying what is involved in good teaching." We want to plead guilty at the outset of this book not only to being left-handed but to being the kind of teacher educators who believe more in principles than prescriptions and who see teaching physical education as a complex and idiosyncratic activity. We also believe, along with John Goodlad (1988, p. 109), that teaching involves

> a moral intention to develop a certain kind of human being . . . that the craft of teaching must be honed within the context of moral intention. Otherwise it is little more than mechanics and might be performed better by a machine. . . . No method

of impersonal theory relieves the . . . teacher . . . of the burden of judgment.

But if good teaching is more principle than prescription, more idiosyncratic than generalizable, more a moral activity than a mechanical one, how in the world does someone learn how to do it? The difficulty can be put this way: No one set of values, no one style, no one set of skills will fit all physical education teachers or their settings and kids. Of course, research on teaching can help. So can theoretical constructs such as Mosston's spectrum of teaching styles (Mosston & Ashworth, 1986). So can local input from parents and school officials. But these kinds of forces cannot substitute for teachers themselves being the chief decision makers, problem solvers, and evaluators in their own programs. It is our view that physical education teachers must be empowered to be just that, and the earlier the better, especially in the face of national and state mandates as well as the advance of a science of teaching that purports to give teachers answers before they have asked the questions.

This perspective on the empowerment of teachers should not be confused with a laissez-faire, do-whatever-feels-right approach. To become good at decision making and problem solving, teachers need to learn how to think and act reflectively. They need a fat bag of "tricks"—curriculum models, teaching skills, teaching styles, evaluation procedures, and so on—but that is only the beginning. They also need to develop and test for themselves their own sense of purpose and what the curriculum reconceptualists call their own "theory in action," and they need to go back often to the drawing board to rethink their purposes and their plans. Moreover, they need to problem-solve specific situations, to learn what works for them, with whom, and under what conditions, and to recognize clues for sizing up situations as they develop. And they need to be able to evaluate their programs, to ask themselves again and again whether they are working.

This book is based on our belief in the empowerment of physical education teachers to do these things with the understanding that teaching is not only an idiosyncratic activity but a moral one as well. We do not argue that this is the easiest approach to teaching physical education. We do argue that it respects the dignity of the teacher and recognizes the humanness of the gym to a greater extent than other approaches. It is not without difficulties, however. Some teacher educators agree with our philosophical position but say that it is impossible to effectively teach beginning teachers in this way. We agree that it is more difficult than giving preservice teachers a prescription, but we believe that there are some principles that can facilitate a reflective approach to teaching physical education. Perhaps more importantly (to us), our values dictate that we teach this way—and that, if we write a book on teaching, it be this kind of book. Valli and Tom (1988, p. 6) support our position:

The preparation of teachers is essentially an educational rather than a training enterprise. Competing explanations, perspectives, and theories that meet commonly accepted standards of scholarship must be presented. . . . "How to" questions . . . must always be presented in the context of and must be subordinated to normative questions of goals, purposes, values, and meanings. . . . Teacher educators can compare and contrast competing visions of good teaching and can emphasize that questions of values and goals cannot be adjudicated through empirical knowledge, and there is a fundamental difference between "what is" and "what ought to be."

A major obstacle to proposing such a book is the philosophical–theoretical heaviness of such key concepts as empowerment, reflective thinking, morality, and the idiosyncratic nature of teaching. However, there is nothing philosophically abstract about problems physical education teachers routinely face, such as large classes, low motivation, and conflicts between kids. Reflective teaching encompasses not only questions of what's worth doing in one's professional life but also, and importantly, how one's teaching can be made to work better. This book, then, is our effort to share some principles that are intended to empower preservice and perhaps even in-service physical education teachers to respond to this idiosyncratic and moral calling reflectively.

Acknowledgments

A few thank-yous are in order: First, to three University of Illinois at Chicago colleagues: Bill Schubert (1986), whose three curriculum commentators gave us the idea for our four experts (whom you will get to know quite well); Nick Cutforth, who wrote most of the games for the understanding section in chapter 6; and Sue Wilkinson, who offered helpful comments on chapter 5. Second, to Linda Bain and an anonymous reviewer, whose reviews of the manuscript strengthened it considerably.

Third, the senior author (especially when *senior* is defined in relation to aging!) wishes to dedicate this book to his former graduate students Mike Debusk, Tim Dunnagan, Nikos Georgiadis, and Bobby Lifka in recognition of their skills, their sensitivity, and their unswerving professional commitments and especially for breathing new life into an old veteran.

Fourth, the junior author wishes to dedicate this book to Leo Kratz for nurturing his interest and development in sport and physical education; to Shirley Cooper for opening a young mind when it was closed to some of the injustices that exist in society and in our schools and for showing him the real issues of teaching; to Dale Hanson for being a colleague and friend and for giving him a chance; to Sarah, Kate, and Andrew for their love, support, and patience; and to Dr. Nasty II for being a friend, colleague, and mentor whose wisdom, knowledge, and warmth are duly appreciated by all.

Setting the Stage

If we are going to write a different kind of teaching methods book than others on the market as we have described in the preface, we will need a format that facilitates this mission. Therefore, we assign you, the reader, 30 hypothetical students to teach, in case you are not working with kids as you read this book, and we will remind you throughout the book of your responsibility to figure out how you would teach physical education to these students if you could do whatever you wanted. We have also asked four expert physical education teachers to respond to our ideas in each chapter. Their responses should help you think more critically about our ideas. That, of course, is the whole idea behind a reflective approach to teaching. We have also asked the four to introduce themselves to you at this time.

Robin: I am happy to be a part of this book, but I must tell you that in my teaching, kids come first. I want my students to feel good about themselves and about physical activity. I value their opinions and try to put their suggestions into practice. Although it is difficult with large classes, I try to treat each student individually. In my gym it is not unusual to see kids engaged in different kinds of activities and different levels of challenges at the same time. I see myself as a helping professional, as a facilitator of my students' development, not only physically but emotionally and socially as well.

Pat: I'm not sure why you want my participation in this book or, to be perfectly candid, why you are writing this book in the first place. It seems to me that we already know what we need to know about how to do a good job teaching PE and that most physical education teachers are doing the best they can. People seem to be more and more critical of tradition, even though it has held up over time. What's wrong with cals, drills, tournaments, 3-week units, and so on? It's the way I teach, and it works!

Lynn: I'd be happier if you would write a book about effective rather than reflective teaching. From my perspective, becoming more effective as teachers ought to be our goal. By that I mean teaching motor skills to our students as effectively as we can. Fortunately, in the last few years there has been a lot of research to help us do just that. I've taken a number of classes and workshops that have changed the way I teach—how I start the class, cues and feedback I give to students, how to keep them on task, and so on—and I'd like to pass this information on to other teachers who might benefit as I have. I'll probably try to do just that in my comments about your ideas!

Chris: I'm sorry I accepted this assignment. I really don't have the time—I'm working a second job—or the interest. To tell you the truth, I quit trying to teach a few years ago.

Kids just aren't the same anymore. Their home lives, even in the relatively affluent area in which I teach, are all screwed up, administrators give teachers no support, we don't get paid much—the list goes on and on. I'd have quit a long time ago, but I've discovered how to keep kids busy and happy in my classes, I have summers off, and I'm through by 3:30 p.m. (I got out of coaching) so I can work a second job. But I'll respond to your ideas the best I can, since I said I'd help you.

We will be asking Robin, Pat, Lynn, and Chris to comment on our ideas in each of the following chapters. We hope they will provide some alternative perspectives that will in turn help you develop your own approach to teaching physical education.

We will also include a self-reflection section in each chapter to further help you sort through and evaluate the various ideas we have pre-sented. If we were to include such a self-reflection section in this prologue, we might ask you questions such as these:

1. What did you think of each of our experts? How did they differ? Were they alike in any ways?
2. Did you find yourself identifying with any of our experts?
3. Have you had any physical education teachers who reminded you of any of our experts? How did you feel about these teachers?

Finally, we will end each chapter with some suggested readings. Our intention is to provide some exemplars of the ideas described in each chapter as well as some sources that describe these ideas in greater detail. We have briefly annotated these readings to point out how they might be used.

Part I

Is Reflective Teaching the Best Approach?

Before we take on the task of helping you become a reflective physical educator, we need to convince you that reflective teaching is worth trying. Because it is not, at least for now, the "mainstream" approach to teacher education in physical education, it is important to describe what it is and why physical educators ought to do it.

Chapter 1

Reflective Teaching— Who Needs It?

We pointed out in the preface that this is a different kind of a book on teaching—that it does not reduce teaching to a set of prescriptions, that its purpose is to help physical education teachers become the chief decision makers, problem solvers, and evaluators of their own programs. These premises set this book apart from most others in the field.

WHAT IS IT?

Unfortunately, reflective teaching has become another buzzword in educational jargon. Therefore, we need to define what *we* mean by the term and why we think reflective teaching is your best bet for a rewarding career as a professional physical educator.

In essence, reflective teaching means to think about your teaching and especially to ask yourself two questions throughout your teaching career: What's worth doing? and Is what I'm doing working? These questions can take an almost endless variety of specific forms. The first is philosophical and requires reflection concerning your beliefs and values. For example: Is fitness more important than sportsmanship? Does sexism deserve attention in my class? The second concerns your choice of subject matter, your instructional strategies, how

you solve problems that arise. For example: Does playing this game really lead to skill improvement? How can I individualize this activity so both the highly skilled and the low-skilled are challenged? How could I have better handled the argument between Karen and Chester yesterday?

Nonreflective teaching simply means not thinking about these kinds of issues. If you are nonreflective, you may allow others to make your curriculum decisions. You may teach basketball in the winter because ''it's always been

Reflective teaching involves thinking about the political, moral, and social implications of what and how we teach.

done that way." You may teach the way you were taught without thinking about what is best for your students. You may rely on the same teaching strategies year after year without reflecting on their effectiveness. You may believe teacher educators like us because we are supposed to know what and how to teach.

Physical education scholars have contributed to the conceptualization of reflective teaching (e.g., Kirk, 1986; Tinning, 1985), but much of the conceptual work has been done outside of physical education. The following snippets give some indication of the various interpretations in the literature. For John Dewey (1933), reflective teaching involves the analysis of one's beliefs, monitoring the effects of one's actions, and certain attitudes such as open-mindedness. Van Manen (1977) divides reflective teaching into three parts: the instructional techniques necessary to achieve the objectives; the relation of educational principles to educational practice; and the ethical, social, and political implications of practice. Schon (1983) sees reflection in terms of problem framing, implementation, and improvisation. Fenstermacher (1986) argues that teachers need to reflect on the premises of their practical judgments. Hustler, Cassidy, and Cuff (1986) focus reflection on the consequences of the teacher's actions. Henderson (1988) has his preservice teachers reflect autobiographically upon their past experiences, "their prejudg-

ments concerning professional development, and their reasons for pursuing a teaching career" (p. 14).

Although this peek into the literature gives something of the flavor of the various conceptualizations of reflective teaching, it masks the conflict among contrasting conceptualizations. Of particular interest to us is the conceptualization that emphasizes thinking about the political, moral, and social implications of what and how we teach *versus* the exclusive focus on the teaching event itself, often in relation to the scientific knowledge available to help solve an instructional problem (Gore, 1987; Ross & Hannay, 1986). Figure 1.1 shows the range of conceptualizations of reflective teaching.

Our own conceptualization of reflective teaching, which provides the framework for this book, involves both ends of this continuum, but perhaps insufficiently to satisfy proponents of either end. The following four reflective questions represent our conceptualization of reflective teaching and form the basis for this book. In these four parts of the book, we provide ideas, concepts, and strategies designed to help you, the reader, answer the questions.

1. Is reflective teaching the best approach?
2. How should you respond to the larger issues of society?
3. What's worth doing and how should you do it?

| Ethical, social, and political issues | Values and goals | Assumptions and consequences of the teaching act | Analysis of teaching strategies |

Figure 1.1. Continuum of conceptualizations of reflective teaching.

4. How can you solve discipline and motivation problems and implement the ideas suggested in this book?

It should be obvious by now not only that this is not a typical "methods" textbook, but also that it draws on much more than the recent scientific research on teaching for its insights. Philosophy is central, of course—not the kind of academic philosophy that seems to dominate physical education in higher education, but the practical kind that Miller (1984) calls for and that many practicing physical educators deem important (Bandy, 1987), that is, a critical analysis of the whats, whys, and hows of conducting a good physical education program. Some analysis of social forces is also important if we are to make any sense of the context within which we teach, and psychology plays a role as well in understanding the human drama of the gym. However, research on teaching isn't left out of this process. Although Wildman and Niles (1987, p. 30) found in their work with teachers that "the research evidence we laid on the table became simply one small piece of the puzzle, and not one of unusually high priority at that," recent research on teaching motor skills (see chapter 5), fitness (see chapter 7), and concepts (see chapter 8) can help teachers make better decisions about their teaching. We have drawn on relevant research related to teaching but always with one goal in mind: to bolster, not circumvent or substitute for, the physical education teacher's decision-making responsibilities.

WHY BOTHER?

From our perspective, reflective teaching offers the best opportunity for both preservice and in-service teachers to learn how to teach well. Our case rests on four convictions. First,

teaching is a complex and idiosyncratic activity. Certainly there are some principles that hold up in most situations—principles derived from research and theoretical constructs and a certain level of knowledge about the community, the school, the students, and oneself. But the application of those principles in a specific setting requires insight, even artistry (see chapter 13). So much of good teaching depends on the uniqueness of the teacher, the students, the setting, and the moment.

Our second conviction is that teaching is an intensely personal process (Lampert, 1985). Whether one believes in an essentialistic approach (everyone ought to teach the same way) or an existential approach (all teachers ought to "do their own thing") to teaching, the "believing and cherishing" on the part of the teacher cannot be ignored (Greene, 1986). We contend that the commitment essential to good teaching resides in a teacher's teaching from, standing for, and living out his or her own values and beliefs. It follows that we need to help teachers sort out and analyze their values, to determine to what extent they hold up to scrutiny, and then, making modifications as necessary, to learn to teach from them.

Our third conviction is that, despite tradition and a typically narrow range of experiences in physical education, there is little agreement about what constitutes a good physical education program. In 1986, yet another blue-ribbon task force, the National Association for Sport and Physical Education Outcomes Committee, was commissioned to determine what constitutes a physically educated person. Yet the results of their deliberations look much like the lengthy list of goals that most school programs espouse. This is the "do everything" approach to teaching physical education, most often represented by the multiactivity model (see chapter 4). The truth (according to us) is that most programs don't have nearly enough time to do everything, that a wide variety of specific curriculum models are available (also in chapter 4), and that, as Siedentop (1987) has argued, a good physical education program is one with a specific purpose (but not necessarily the same purpose as other programs), a teacher committed to that purpose, and administrative support.

Our fourth conviction is simply something Socrates said a long time ago: The unexamined life is not worth living. We believe that thinking is important, perhaps especially in a field with the stereotype of brawn over brains. Of course, there needs to be something to think about, and there needs to be action at the end of the thinking. But technical training and implementation make no sense unless they are accompanied by reflection. Perhaps this ought to be especially so at a university.

WHY NOT DO IT?

Perhaps the most frequently cited argument against reflective teaching is that preservice teachers (those of you who are now preparing for a career in teaching) need one solid way of teaching so they can survive their first year. Later they can learn to reflect. A few of our colleagues also argue that public schools aren't ready for thinking teachers—they won't survive the system—or alternative curriculum and instruction programs. They want a perpetuation of the status quo, and they say it is our job to provide it. From our perspective, whether to perpetuate the status quo ought to be a choice, and teachers new and old need to do some thinking about it!

Another common complaint is that reflective teaching is not a linear, step-by-step, scientific process. Perhaps unfortunately, neither is being human! Vulnerability often accompanies reflective teaching. As Wildman and Niles (1987) learned, teachers realize that reflective teaching "has a great potential for failure" (p. 26) and that in reflective teaching "basic beliefs and personal dilemmas about teaching are often laid bare" (p. 28). We can only reply that vulnerability is part of what being human is about and therefore part of what learning to

Teachers must decide what is most important to teach and how to best teach it.

teach (as well as teaching itself, as we point out in chapter 13) is about. There just aren't any certainties about teaching; vulnerability comes with the territory. We aren't going to improve as teachers without experiencing some vulnerability. (This is one of the ways being a teacher differs from being a computer operator.)

Because the reflective process is subjective, it is open to the vagaries of human psychology and therefore, some believe, cannot be trusted. If it is true that we all rationalize who we are, what we feel, and what we believe, and that we try to protect ourselves from our insecurities and justify our desires, then true reflection about human values—about what is best for students—may be out of reach. In one sense, this is a rather cynical, even dismal, portrayal of what it is to be human. However, the subjectivity of human perceptions, and the importance of perceptions in each of our lives, underscores the vital role of psychology in any discussion of human values.

So far we have alluded to the psychological dimension of values by stressing the importance of your beliefs and your identity—i.e., what you want to stand for, what values you want to represent you. There are other factors important to the psychology of reflective teaching, however. For instance, reflection could be a thin disguise for rationalization. To be truly reflective, one must ask the tough questions and not settle for defensive maneuvers such as blaming others. One must reach deep inside oneself to risk discovering unsettling, often contradictory, things. This takes courage and persistence. What's at stake are one's illusions and the certainties that have provided the building blocks of one's life. We suspect that reflection also requires a belief in cognitive activity as a significant source of information. Physical educators have been accused of being nonthinkers, but based on some 30 collective years

of working with physical education majors and teachers, we don't agree. However, for the most part, physical educators are doers who trust their bodily senses more than their minds. They are likely to know with some certainty what physical education is and what it does for kids, but they are less likely to be able to clearly articulate why, to provide a defensible case for their argument. In our view, they need to develop this capacity, as a supplement to, rather than a substitute for, their own ways of knowing.

Another intrusion of psychology into the creation of one's own model involves the comfort of doing what is familiar. If you have always led calisthenics as a Marine Corps drill instructor might, you will feel insecure in doing it another way, even if you truly believe that a regimented, militaristic approach is not what you want to stand for and not in the kids' best interests. It takes courage to risk teaching outside the mainstream, in part because most of us feel a need for approval at one time or another. If all the other physical education teachers in your school or district use the drill-instructor approach, you risk their disapproval by trying something different. If your students are used to a certain way of doing physical education—say, playing games all the time, as in organized recess described in chapter 4—you risk their disapproval, and especially the disapproval of the motor elite, by making changes in your program.

It takes tough thinking to be a reflective physical educator, and it takes courage, especially if your thinking leads you outside the mainstream concepts and practices of school physical education. All we can offer you is encouragement and support: encouragement because we believe that reflective teaching is a major road to good teaching, and support in the sense that our reflective thinking has led

It takes courage to try new methods.

us outside the mainstream, and we feel quite comfortable out there.

WHAT ABOUT ACCOUNTABILITY?

We are in an age of accountability. Government and other reports on the status of teaching in the United States are receiving more attention than they have in the past. The result has been dissatisfaction with the product of American education and a shift toward "top–down" dictates—teachers being told what to do and how to do it by the feds, states, boards of education, school administrators, and even, heaven forbid, teacher educators. More and more, teachers are being perceived as technicians, carrying out a blueprint created by someone else. Of course, this state of affairs hasn't been without its backlash, and as we go to press it is unclear what ultimate impact this trend will have on teaching. What is clear, however, is that teachers are being required to become more accountable for what they do. The issue becomes whether teachers will demand respon-

sibility for specifying just what they are to be held accountable for or whether they will allow others to do this job for them.

Of course, there are many problems with holding teachers accountable for student learning, not the least of which is that some of the social and cultural forces discussed in Part II obstruct student learning no matter what the teacher does. Nevertheless, the question remains: Do you want to have some say, one would hope a lot of say, in specifying what goals, strategies, and evaluation procedures you will be held accountable for, or do you want someone else to decide this for you?

We have been asked more than once, "What about those teachers who won't assume this responsibility, who won't engage in a reflective process?" Our answer is simple: Those are the teachers who need the top–down guidance; they are the ones who need to be "teacher-proofed." But instead of reducing everyone to the lowest common denominator, let's individualize the process! Then each of us can choose whether we want to be teacher-proofed or to play an active role in specifying our accountability.

WRAP-UP

Teaching is a complex, personal process, and physical education subject matter offers little guidance about how to teach it best. Despite the subjectivity of the process, there is no substitute for learning to reflect upon one's teaching—upon the larger social and ethical issues, upon one's beliefs and values, upon the act of teaching itself.

Human life is a process; as a Nike poster says, there is no finish line. In the same way, one's own model of teaching is never finished, always in need of modification. Once it's started, the reflective process can't be turned off very easily; moreover, it ought not be. However, the illusion of certainty, the dream of perfection in teaching and coaching, are casualties of this process. In their place will develop a certain openness to new ideas, to alternatives, to improvement. In this way, both one's model of teaching and the constant struggle to put that model into practice will be continuously challenged. And in our view, that's a lot of what good teaching is about.

THE EXPERTS RESPOND

Because we have invited four experts to participate in this book, it is only fair to see what they have to say about the reflective process that caused us to invite them in the first place.

Lynn: I think reflective teaching as you define it deemphasizes the role of research in helping teachers become more effective and, as you admit, substitutes a very subjective process of introspection. From what I can tell, most of the improvements in teaching physical education in recent years have come not because physical educators have become more reflective but because they have learned how to teach better. I for one want to know what the research says, not so I can think about it but so I can do it! I'm getting the feeling—although I'll hold my judgment for now—that this book will be more fluff than substance.

Pat: I would tend to agree with Lynn, *if* tradition were substituted for science. We pretty well know how to teach—we've learned how by trial and error over many years, and the best has survived. You seem to be asking me to reinvent the wheel. In my opinion, we need less philosophizing, less emphasis on thinking teachers, and more emphasis on doing what we already know how to do.

Robin: I can relate to teaching being complex and idiosyncratic. Every day there is some new situation I haven't quite figured out, so I spend considerable time reflecting. However, I can't always sort out being reflective from just being defensive, so I hope that this book can help me do it better.

The kids certainly bring into the gym the results of what you call social forces. That's okay. I enjoy being more than a gym teacher. Again, I've tried to think about this—what it means to be more than a gym teacher—but I'm not sure I'm fully living my values in the gym.

Chris: You know what I think? I think you've created a big scam just to make a splash and maybe sell some books (although why anyone would spring for any book on teaching I can't imagine). I could write a book on how to be a PE teacher; it would have about one chapter.

It's just not that hard to get kids to play games. Maybe I would add some chapters on administrators and pay scales, but all this stuff about being the chief decision maker in your gym? What's to decide? Whether to do soccer or kickball? Talk about making a mountain out of a molehill!

We are having some second thoughts about our selection of experts. We wanted reflection and got considerable deflection!

SELF-REFLECTION

This whole chapter has been about reflection, but we do have a few questions for you.

1. In your opinion, right now, how important is reflection to becoming a good teacher? Is Lynn right, that knowing the science of teaching is more important, and that being reflective is just too subjective a process? Is Pat right, that tradition is more important? Is Chris right, that teaching is just not that big a deal? Try to get a fix on your perspective—it will condition everything you read from here on out. (If you have to read this book despite your reservations about reflective teaching, remember that our experts will be with you every step of the way, so you won't be without support.)

2. Let's go back to those 30 hypothetical kids we have assigned you. Are you willing, at this point, to take a reflective approach to teaching them? Or do you already have the answers, what you need to do to get them to go where you want them to go? Or are you willing to opt for survival—finding something, anything, that has been proven to work—to get you through the experience?

3. Interview a physical education teacher or coach you know. Try to find out what role reflection plays in his or her job—in the role of physical education in the larger social issues, in developing goals and strate-gies, in dealing with discipline and motivation problems. How does he or she make decisions about teaching? What role is played by tradition? Science? His or her values and beliefs? Does his or her ratio-nale for program goals and strategies seem full of defensive arguments?

SUGGESTED READINGS

Gore, J.M. (1987). Reflecting on reflective teaching. *Journal of Teacher Education*, **38**, 33-39. (Critiques and offers modifications to two different approaches to reflective teacher education.)

Kirk, D. (1986). A critical pedagogy for teacher education: Toward an inquiry-oriented approach. *Quest*, **5**, 236-246. (Advocates a critical theory–based reflective approach to teacher education in physical education.)

Ross, E.W., & Hannay, L.M. (1986). Towards a critical theory of reflective inquiry. *Journal of Teacher Education*, **37**, 9-15. (Describes two approaches to reflective teacher education; advocates a critical theory–based approach.)

Tinning, R. (1985). *Student teaching and the pedagogy of necessity*. Paper presented at the AIESEP International Conference on Research in Physical Education and Sport, Adelphi University, New York. (Perhaps the first physical educator and teacher educator to advocate reflective teacher education; compares reflective teaching to other approaches to teacher education.)

Wildman, T.M., & Niles, J.A. (1987). Reflective teachers: Tensions between abstractions and realities. *Journal of Teacher Education*, **38**, 25-31. (A friendly description of the problems encountered in trying to teach teachers from a reflective perspective.)

How Should You Respond to the Larger Issues of Society?

The debate over the conceptualization of reflective teaching described in the last chapter is especially relevant in determining where to begin the reflective process. In line with our conceptualization, we begin by investigating the relation of large social issues to physical education instruction. We then work our way to questions of purpose and strategy and finally to the "nuts and bolts" questions of discipline and implementation in the "real world." There is some danger in this approach. By starting with questions that are not directly connected to physical education—questions one might more likely find in a sociology textbook—we run the risk of alienating some of our readers right off the bat. We are going to take that risk because we believe, first, that the larger social, political, and moral issues of our society are connected to teaching physical education and require some serious reflection (and action), and second, that it makes sense to work our way from societal issues to questions of purpose and then to instructional strategies and finally to implementation.

Part II consists of two chapters. Chapter 2 reviews some of the more important social and cultural trends in American society from both functional and critical perspectives. Chapter 3 focuses on what has become a major, perhaps *the* major, social, political, and moral issue in American society: equity.

The Influence of American Social and Cultural Trends on the Practice of Physical Education

This chapter analyzes some of the major social and cultural trends that affect the conduct of physical education programs. By understanding the context within which physical education operates, you will be able to examine your assumptions and reflect upon program practices that result from these trends or from the failure to take these trends into account.

TWO LENSES FOR VIEWING THE WORLD AROUND US

None of us is objective or value-free when we observe and try to analyze what is going on around us. We look at ideas and events through what we might call a lens (or more than one lens) that filters and distorts what we see and how we think about it. A variety of lenses have been described in the literature—for example, Bain's (1986) application of three research lenses to studying teaching in physical education and Coakley's (1986) three sociological lenses for studying sport. However, for our purposes, two lenses depict accurately enough the choices we have when we view the events around us. One of these lenses is the functionalist perspective, which takes for granted the social order—that is, the way society is structured, the way its institutions, such as schools and family, function—and looks at events as being either functional (contributing to the continuation of an orderly society) or dysfunctional (disrupting the social order, the way things are). The other lens is the critical perspective, which views the social order as being socially constructed—that is, created by people, based on their subjective judgments of what's best for them in a particular place and time—and therefore open to analysis, criticism, and change.

These two lenses contrast sharply. Functionalists tend to see teachers as transmitters of the culture, whereas critical theorists tend to see teachers as the changers of the culture. Functionalist teachers tend to work from a given curriculum that represents dominant societal values. Critical teachers tend to view the curriculum

15

as "contested terrain" (Lather, 1985). Functionalists tend to embrace tradition, advocating change only for those trends that appear to be dysfunctional; they tend, for example, to embrace a say-no-to-drugs approach to the trend of drug abuse. Critical theorists tend to embrace social change in the direction of wider distribution of power and equity for the disenfranchised; they tend to look for the root causes of drug abuse in the ways society is organized and in the unequal distribution of power, wealth, and opportunity.

This description greatly simplifies these two perspectives, ignoring their nuances. Functionalists range from hard-core conservatives to moderates who generally support the liberal ideology of individual development in a meritocratic society. Critical theorists range from hard-core neo-Marxists to proponents of modifying the liberal ideology toward greater individual autonomy and empowerment. However, we purposely use these two labels to encourage you to think about your own lenses—how you tend to view the world. We might add that most physical educators tend toward some form of the functionalist perspective (Hellison, 1973) and that we, your authors, tend toward some milder form of the critical perspective.

Current social and cultural trends can be viewed from various angles within either lens. The question we want to raise throughout this and the next chapter is: To what extent *should* these trends be perpetuated or changed *in the gym*—in the practice of physical education? We will take a moderately critical perspective in presenting these trends (and in the equity discussion in the next chapter). We want to bring to your attention trends that may require reflective thinking and perhaps some action. Like us, you may be critical of some of these trends and may decide to do something about them in your gym. Or you may take a more functional per-

spective, viewing them as healthy aspects of American society worthy of being perpetuated. It is our hope that our brief explanation of the two lenses will help you identify your own lens and perhaps encourage you to look through both lenses before passing judgment.

FITNESS AND SPORT IN AMERICAN SOCIETY

Bain (1988) provides an excellent critical perspective on fitness and sport in American society. As she points out, both fitness and sport are dominant forces in our society.

Fitness-Related Issues

Fitness has become a form of preventive medicine and is now a major factor in the "wellness" movement. However, concerns have been voiced about a number of fitness-related issues (Carlyon, 1984; Ingham, 1985; Minkler, 1983; Vertinsky, 1985). Fitness is usually promoted as an individual responsibility, ignoring social and political factors that contribute to health problems, especially for the poor. Health clubs that primarily promote fitness are expensive and therefore exclude the poor, and they tend to try to keep their clients enrolled, thereby discouraging individual responsibility (contrary to the promotion of fitness as individual responsibility). In fact, responsibility is often defined as adherence to a list of dos and don'ts—reduce fat in your diet, exercise regularly, and so on—rather than as empowerment to make choices based on personal needs and values as well as knowledge. The fitness movement is sometimes called the "cosmetic fitness movement" for its promotion of thinness and sexual attractiveness rather than, or perhaps in addition to, health. Its promoters have sometimes been accused of propaganda—basing their promotions on limited or even contrived evidence—for example, the typical percent-body-fat recommendations (15% for men and 23% for women), which are averages based on a young, fit population. Finally, at least some fitness devotees become compulsive, narcissistic, guilt-ridden exercisers, not exactly models of good health.

The fitness movement has made significant inroads into American society mostly among upwardly mobile, white, middle-class individuals in the 20 to 40 age range; American youth and the poor have not been swept up in it. Several studies have shown a decline in the performance of American youth on fitness tests (Carey & Taylor, 1987; Ross & Gilbert, 1985; Updyke, 1984) and an increase in body fat (Ross & Gilbert, 1985). In one study (Updyke, 1984) only 36% of 6- to 17-year-olds were able to meet minimal fitness standards, and in another (Carey & Taylor, 1987), 40% of boys ages 6 to 12 could do no more than one pull-up.

The fitness movement has not reached American youth.

Moreover, Heitmann (1988) cited a study in which over half of the youth had at least one coronary heart disease risk factor. It is estimated that by the time kids reach adulthood, 80% will experience some form of lower back pain, most of which can be attributed to a lack of flexibility and strength (Heitmann, 1988).

Sport-Related Issues

Unlike fitness, sport has been central to mainstream American culture for several decades. A quick glance at the number of pages devoted to sport compared to other topics (say, international affairs) in newspapers across the country, including the *New York Times*, attests to its popularity. "Sport influences clothing styles, language, and concepts of the hero" (Bain, 1988, p. 135). Despite its popularity, at almost all levels sport has become increasingly professionalized—that is, increasingly bureaucratized with increasing doses of commerce and politics. Although playground sport may be alive and well in the inner-city, it is a thing of the past for many American kids. In its place, "age-group everything" is offered, and it is often costly. Playing to win has become more important than playing for fun, and young athletes often receive much adulation. Cheating and corruption are now routinely associated with big-time intercollegiate sport, and the low graduation rates of football and basketball players at many highly competitive universities are cause for alarm. Sexism and racism, treated extensively in the next chapter, have been repeatedly linked to big-time sport practices. So has drug abuse.

The good news, from a critical perspective, is that sport opportunities have proliferated. There are more sports (e.g., soccer) and more female sports, although this growth has occurred within the trend toward professionalization.

Playing for fun has been replaced by playing to win.

Also, sexist, ethnic, and racial stereotypes—for instance, that dance is for females and basketball is for males, that blacks don't play tennis, that soccer is a foreign sport—have softened, at least around the edges, although they have by no means been eradicated.

What do these sport practices mean for the physical education student? As a result of the popularity and bureaucratization of sport, some students become the motor elite of the class, school, or city; others get cut out somewhere along the way. Some receive help in "play for pay" programs outside the school; others receive help inside school because they are athletes. Still others take drugs to become more competitive (or perhaps different drugs to forget that they haven't been competitive enough!). In addition, despite the "softening" of sex and race roles mentioned above, certain sports are associated with a specific gender and/or racial or ethnic group so that stereotypes are perpetuated. Playing for fun has not been

eradicated, but these trends have taken their toll on the play ethic.

Has PE Successfully Taught Sport and Fitness?

What role does physical education play in the development of motor skills so that more children and youth can experience success in the highly salient sport world? Evidence of student learning in physical education (Siedentop, 1983) suggests that students are not improving their motor skills very much in physical education programs. Graham (1987) cites two studies of motor skill acquisition among children that show less than satisfactory developmental gains.

What about student knowledge about fitness and motor skills? Do they know enough to learn on their own? Data from polls and observations by physical education scholars (Corbin & Lindsey, 1980) suggest that, although today's youth no doubt know more about wellness than in the past, their understanding of physiological, biomechanical, and motor learning concepts is limited.

LIFE OUTSIDE THE GYM

In our work with physical education teachers, we often hear older teachers say that "kids aren't the same any more." Although sometimes these teachers are using this statement to excuse their own problems or justify their organized-recess approach to teaching, the statement has considerable merit.

Changes in Kids

Kids aren't the same any more, because the world isn't the same any more! In general, kids receive less guidance as a result of one-parent families, working parents, parents whose personal goals and lifestyles do not focus primarily on their kids, and anonymous neighborhoods that no longer help raise children as they did in the past. Both child abuse and child neglect seem to be more prevalent these days, and many children are both abused and neglected. In addition, more kids are raising kids; every day in the United States 40 teenage mothers give birth to their third child (Duckett, 1988).

This weakened role of appropriate guidance authorities is coupled with an increase in choices, due primarily to the influence of television and other media, the increased influence of peers who have filled the guidance void, and the increased availability of drugs and other options. Teenage statistical trends in drug use, gang membership, suicide, homicide, and pregnancy, for example, have escalated markedly over the past couple of decades (see Figure 2.1). Subtle forms of intimidation, manipulation, and abuse have also accelerated; it is estimated that approximately one in seven schoolchildren is either a bully or a victim (Roberts, 1988). Today's youth often "cruise in neutral" or at an early age become "couch potatoes," a form of dropping out that is less drastic than absenteeism from school, going to school stoned, or suicide but still reflects an absence of commitment to anything. Dropout itself has become a major issue, with nearly half of the teenagers in major cities dropping out of school. Youth culture for many has become a mall culture; participants are consumers with few opportunities to make positive contributions to society. The following statistics illustrate some troubling trends (Children's Defense Fund, 1989):

- Every 8 seconds of the school day, an American child drops out (500,000 a year).
- Every 26 seconds, an American child runs away from home (1.2 million a year).
- Every 47 seconds, an American child is abused (675,000 a year).
- Every 67 seconds, an American teenager has a baby (472,000 a year).
- Every 53 minutes, an American child dies because of poverty (9,855 a year).

Csikszentmihalyi and McCormack (1986, pp. 416-417) argue that young people today "lack meaningful goals [which] most likely accounts for the unprecedented surge of social pathology in the U.S. over the past 30 years." It isn't fair to characterize the goals of all teenagers as sex, drugs, and rock and roll, or to say that all that young people are interested in these days is making "a buck," but these trends and social problems suggest that the choices many kids are making these days require attention.

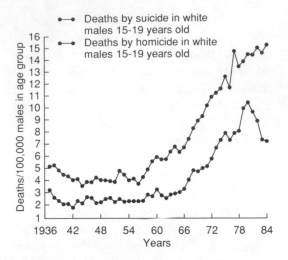

Figure 2.1a. Changes in the rates of homicide and suicide among white males, ages 15 to 19. *Note.* From Larry P. Nucci, *Moral Development and Character Education,* © 1989 by McCutchan Publishing Corporation, Berkeley, CA 94702. Permission granted by the publisher.

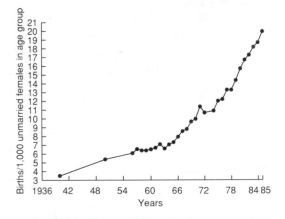

Figure 2.1b. Changes in the rates of illegitimate births among whites, ages 15 to 19. *Note.* From Larry P. Nucci, *Moral Development and Character Education,* © 1989 by McCutchan Publishing Corporation, Berkeley, CA 94702. Permission granted by the publisher.

Students' Goals

What are students' goals in school these days? Having fun and socializing head the list, although passing their classes is often mentioned as well. Picture trying to teach junior high school students how to head a soccer ball when their hormones are zinging around in high gear! Self-image management must also be high on their lists, although they are not likely to confess this, and this is especially true of teenagers who are very conscious of their appearance and belonging to certain groups. In fact, peer pressure appears to have become more important as adult influences shrink. On the other hand, many kids are content to set their goals at just avoiding embarrassment and negative attention. Whatever the student goals are, they are often more powerful than teacher goals; one study showed that the teacher's goals of cooperation, helping, and democracy conflicted with, and were overpowered by, student goals of segregation and stratification (Wang, 1977).

Increasing Minority Populations

Minority populations are growing, especially in the cities, and many minority children in the major cities come from families below the poverty line. These kids have few enrichment opportunities; and, as minority families who have achieved in education and employment move to more affluent areas in the city or surrounding suburbs, minorities who remain in poverty areas have few if any role models to help them better their situations. Common teen and adult role models in many of these communities are welfare participants, teenage mothers, drug dealers, and prostitutes (Wilson, 1988). One popular role model, the professional basketball player, is particularly damaging, with the odds at about 65 in 10 million of ever becoming even a fringe player in the NBA (Leonard & Reyman, 1988). Moreover, even those minority students who are not poor tend to drop out of school more than nonminority students who are not poor (Fernandez, 1988). Meanwhile, the number of black teachers has decreased, and blacks are predicted to comprise less than 1% of the teacher population 10 years from now (Oliver, 1988).

What the Changes Mean

As a result of these kinds of trends, youth today have more to cope with, and teachers have a tougher job. One teacher writes: "If I tried to meet their needs I'd be arrested!" (Breinin, 1987). Schools are asked to take on responsibilities that were formerly the province of parents, yet at the same time are being attacked by right-wing "back to the basics" advocates for trying to carry out their increased responsibilities. Currently, as perhaps in no other time in American history, schools are being pulled in several directions at once, and teachers are feeling these cross-pressures. School reform and school restructuring efforts are attempting to respond to these problems, but whether they will significantly change the traditional school will not be determined for some time.

THE ROLE OF PHYSICAL EDUCATION IN RESPONDING TO THESE TRENDS

These trends raise many questions, among them these: Should the current wellness movement be modified in some ways? Should cosmetic fitness be promoted? Should youth fitness be emphasized more in schools? Should the professionalization of sport be encouraged,

or should kids be encouraged to play for fun? To what extent should physical education contribute to sorting students into the haves (the motor elite) and the have-nots (everyone else)? Should motor skill development be emphasized more in schools? To what extent should physical education perpetuate societal racial-ethnic and sex stereotypes? How should physical education be changed to better meet the needs of today's kids who experience less guidance and more choices? Should physical educators try to do something about drug abuse, teen pregnancy, gangs, suicide, and other current social problems? What should physical education do, if anything, to help poor (often minority) students?

From a functional perspective, most of the above alleged trends are either integral parts of American culture or exaggerated versions of what is really occurring. A few are truly dysfunctional and require attention; certainly drug abuse and teen pregnancy fall into this category. On the other hand, someone from a critical perspective will identify more problems in the trends and want to take some kind of action. Taking action, however, may seem to be an overwhelming task. It is discouraging to look at the "big picture"—social and cultural trends at the societal level—from a critical perspective. Most of us don't operate in political circles that influence the big picture. However, all of us who teach do exert influence in our own gyms; these gyms are our microsocieties, and in them we can promote certain trends and counter or downplay others. One of your authors works with kids who live in poverty and a myriad of daily negative influences, and he gets depressed when he looks at the big picture—the statistics, incidents of violence, child abuse, crime, and on and on. But when he looks at the kids in the gyms where he works, he has an entirely different feeling, a feeling of hope,

To what extent should physical education perpetuate sex stereotypes? Other stereotypes?

of making a small contribution to these kids' lives.

Perhaps the overriding question in this brief survey of social and cultural trends is just this: What do kids *need*? The importance of meeting student needs has been a central premise in most arguments for changing curriculum or instructional strategies or for school reform or restructuring. But our question is a loaded one: What you see as student needs depends on the lens you look through. One of your authors worked in a school in which parents strongly believed that what their elementary school children, especially the boys, needed was a highly competitive physical education program in which their kids could learn to be competitive in life. Other parents in other school districts feel just as strongly that their kids need self-esteem—to feel good about themselves. Even if we agree on the facts, we may disagree about what to do. For example, there is ample evidence that American kids are not very fit. Some use these data to argue for more focus on fitness in physical education classes. Others acknowledge the problem but argue that other things

are more important—say, learning to play for fun, or motor skill development, or knowing how to take care of one's body later in life, or learning to be cooperative. The point is not that kids' needs are not important; they are. The point is that trying to figure out what these needs are is tricky, subjective business. The lens through which we view the world will interpret those needs for us. Our values and beliefs provide the basis for the lens with which we view the world and are central to the development of a physical education program, which is why we will spend considerable time in this book helping you explore your values, their defensibility, and how to implement them.

WRAP-UP

By now you should have some insight into the question Part II raises: To what extent and in what ways should your physical education program respond to the larger social, political, and moral issues of society? Your program—think for a second about those 30 hypothetical students we assigned you—*must* respond, either by perpetuating what currently exists in our culture or by making modifications through what you teach and the ways you teach. The lens through which you view these trends, whether functional or critical, will help you interpret these trends, setting the stage for making curriculum, instruction, and, eventually, implementation decisions.

THE EXPERTS RESPOND

Pat: I'll go first, because I have some definite opinions about what you have just said. First off, I'm a functionalist and proud of it. I'm all for the popularity of fitness and sport in our culture. I prefer a sport-oriented curriculum, because it is time-tested—it has worked for a long time—but I promote fitness when I can, conduct cals every period, and have even stuck in some short fitness units.

However, we do need more discipline in schools. There was a time when physical education set the tone for the school, when the PE teacher was relied upon to "take care of" problem kids. We need to return to that era with a heavy dose of no-nonsense discipline. I believe that once we do that—once we put the fear of God back into our students—the traditional approach to physical education will be able to do the job for us, giving kids enough experience in a wide variety of activities that they can develop both fitness and motor skills.

Lynn: I couldn't disagree more. I don't know whether I'm a functionalist or a criticalist (I made that up!) or whether it matters. What does matter is that the important answers to questions about teaching physical education are now available from the research that has been conducted over the past few years. We now have a science of teaching that tells us how to improve everyone's motor skills [see chapter 5], which ought to increase the number of students who can enjoy activity, but it's certainly not the traditional cals–demonstrate–drill–play approach to teaching physical education. We also have data-based classroom management skills: We have skills for preventing discipline problems (such as minimizing waiting and management time) and for intervention to handle discipline problems (these skills range from ignoring the behavior to developing contingencies for appropriate behaviors) [see chapter 11]. Kids bring more problems to the gym these days, but research has kept up with these changes.

Robin: I guess I take a critical perspective, because I see lots to dislike in the trends. Gym class is often motor elitist, sexist, and even, like a lot of other classrooms, racist. Physical education doesn't pay enough attention to the individual person and his or her social relationships. I've been struggling to do physical education a different way, but without a model it is really hard!

On the subject of discipline, it seems clear to me from what has been expressed in this chapter that we need more than classroom management and certainly something other than discipline based on fear. We need to put kids—their feelings, their values, their total development—at the top of our priorities, ahead of fitness, ahead of motor skills, ahead of sport and fitness knowledge. The social problems our students have to navigate through demand our attention. These kids aren't bodies; they're people! We need to help them become better people, not more perfect bodies!

| Chris: | This chapter's list of social problems and a bunch of others that aren't discussed—like teacher salaries—are exactly why I roll the ball out. I don't see all these problems in my classes, because my students are having fun playing games. And because of this participation, they are getting fit and practicing skills. We don't need all this science to figure out what to do, and we certainly don't need these long-winded analyses of current social problems!

SELF-REFLECTION

Our experts are off to a fine start, disagreeing (heatedly, some might say) on just about everything. We hope their differences of opinion will help you to clarify your own views concerning the trends we have described and what, if anything, to do about them. Here are some additional reflection questions that might help:

1. Are you more functionalist or more critical in your views of current trends? On a separate sheet of paper, redraw the continuum that follows and check the space that best represents your perspective:

   Functional _ _ _ _ _ _ _ **Critical**

   Why do you choose this lens to look at the world?

2. Which of the following trends do you believe need some modification?
   - Fitness as preventive medicine
   - Inattention to the poor in fitness promotion
   - Cosmetic fitness
   - Fitness propaganda
   - Exercise compulsion and obsession with the appearance and performance of one's body
   - Competitive sport

   - The professionalization of sport
   - Gender and ethnic-racial stereotypes in sport
   - The increased number of sports now available
   - Lack of guidance for youth
   - Lack of meaningful goals for youth
   - Social problems such as dropout, drug abuse, teen pregnancy, gangs, suicide, and delinquency
   - Increased peer pressure
   - Lack of available help for minorities

3. Go back to the list in Question 2. Of those trends that you agreed needed some modification, how many of them can be modified in some way, even some tiny way, in a physical education class? Can you give an example of each one that you think can be modified in a physical education class?

4. Evaluate our description of youth today by doing your own research into the lives and values of today's youth. Your younger brothers, sisters, kids you have coached or taught, kids in the neighborhood—do they fit the picture we have drawn? Try interviewing a junior high student. Ask about his or her goals and commitments, leisure time activities, peer pressure. To what extent do your interviews square with what we have described?

5. Find someone who disagrees with you on the direction of the fitness/wellness movement. Interview that person (don't pick an argument!) to determine how well his or her argument and rationale compares to your own. Do the same thing for someone who disagrees with you about the direction of sport in America.

SUGGESTED READINGS

Bain, L.L. (1988). Curriculum for critical reflection in physical education. In R.S. Brandt (Ed.), *Context of the curriculum: 1988 ASCD yearbook* (pp. 133-147). Washington, DC: ASCD. (Describes sport, fitness, and physical education from a critical perspective.)

Coakley, J.J. (1986). *Sport in society* (3rd ed.). St. Louis: Times Mirror/Mosby. (A sociological analysis of sport from both functional and critical perspectives.)

Csikzentmihalyi, M. & McCormack, J. (1986). The influence of teachers. *Phi Delta Kappan*, **67**, 415-419. (Excellent analysis of youth today and recommendations for teachers who want to influence youth.)

Duckett, W. (1988). Using demographic data for long-range planning. *Phi Delta Kappan*, **69**, 166-170. (Interview with Harold Hodgkinson in which he discusses current statistical trends concerning American youth.)

Vertinsky, P. (1985). Risk benefit analysis of health promotion: Opportunities and threats for physical education. *Quest*, **37**, 71-83. (An in-depth critical analysis of the fitness movement.)

Chapter 3

Teaching in the Heterogeneous Gym

If we were to characterize some of the kids in your class of 30, perhaps we would see the following:

Billy wants to be there, Mary doesn't. Suzi is an exceptionally skilled athlete, Joey has difficulty with any physical activity. Danny is back in school after two suspensions, Karen has a perfect attendance record. Pam is epileptic, Larry is learning disabled, and Dave has a congenital heart defect. Tom constantly complains, and Don brings the teacher an apple every day. Andrew is a 4-foot, 5-inch ninth grader, and Jack is a 6-foot, 5-inch ninth grader. Kay's father is the CEO of one of the country's largest companies, and they live in the suburbs; Sue lives with her divorced mother in the inner city, and they are on welfare.

Of course, the descriptions could go on and on, but perhaps the picture is clear enough—the students you teach will be a heterogeneous lot. Although you may teach students that at first appear all alike, in most settings you will find that you interact with a myriad of students. You may finally understand the meaning of individual differences. The illusion of homogeneity will be replaced by the reality of understanding a wide range of student skills, interests, attitudes, and backgrounds. This is the challenge, and how you meet this challenge depends on your ability to draw upon your knowledge and skills in meeting individual differences. Equally, it depends upon your having an attitude that accepts the differences among students—an attitude that reveals an openness and willingness to teach all of your students, not just the best skilled, or the best looking, or the most affluent, or the haves versus the have-nots. Equal opportunity should be expected by all students, and you must try to meet this expectation. Further, you must recognize that this calls for varying pedagogical approaches to meet individual differences. As Swisher and Swisher (1986, p. 35) suggest, "Equity at times requires different treatment according to differences in background experiences and potential. Recognition of differences and why they exist is essential to providing equal opportunity."

As a prospective teacher, attempt to examine this chapter and your work with students from a critical perspective as you reflect about curricular and instructional processes. As implied earlier, this perspective assesses the criteria a teacher uses in deciding what opportunities students will have. This perspective looks at student opportunity relative not only to the normative curricular and instructional processes of schooling, but also to those norms that are dominant in culture. That is, issues related to race, gender, socioeconomic status, achievement, and other differences may very well carry over to the way you interact with students and the opportunities you provide them with. It is reasonable for you to ask what dominant views prevail in a particular setting and how such views influence the instructional process. One should ask why some students have particular advantages over others and the implications of such advantages for equity in the gym. Furthermore, it is reasonable for you to contest those views that appear to limit student opportunity. This is the "sticky" part of being a teacher, but it is critical to your effectiveness.

Hence, keep a critical perspective in mind as we review selected issues related to heterogeneity and equity in the gym:

- Teacher expectations
- Sex equity
- Cultural pluralism
- Students with disabilities
- Ability grouping
- At-risk youth

TEACHER EXPECTATIONS: INFLUENCES ON BEHAVIOR

The research over the last decade by Martinek (1989) provides a very important, simple, but powerful lesson that is confirmed by countless other research studies: Teacher expectations and perceptions of students can predict or affect teacher–student interaction and, consequently, student achievement. This is a familiar self-fulfilling prophecy, and this lesson is easily linked to a critical perspective of teaching.

Do you remember the student who was the "teacher's pet," or the one who was constantly in the doghouse? Do you remember who received more attention from the teacher and which students seemed to be neglected? Do you remember why some students were always se-

lected to lead exercises or to captain teams? Why some students were always praised and others scolded? Do you remember how the teacher treated you in comparison to an older brother or sister ("So you're the little sister of Susy! What can I expect from you?!")? Why do events like these occur? What is the self-fulfilling prophecy all about? Martinek (1981) provides a model for us to examine this process (Figure 3.1).

The model suggests the following (Martinek, 1989):

1. Teachers form expectations about their students' future performance from perceptions gained through a number of impression cues related to student characteristics. Cues are either static (such as gender, age, or race) or dynamic (such as behavioral disposition or performance).
2. Teachers' expectations ultimately affect the quantity and quality of interaction between the student and teacher, which in turn influence student growth.
3. Students perceive and interpret the interactions and may or may not perform in ways consistent with the original expectations.

Does this sound familiar? Can you illustrate this process through your personal experiences in physical education or other subject areas? Martinek and his colleagues have studied the PE settings closely and have concluded the following:

Students With Disabilities Versus Students Without Disabilities. Elementary school physical education teachers have lower expectations for students with disabilities, regarding their social relations with classmates.

Gender. Activities requiring strength, speed, or endurance are perceived as inappropriate for females.

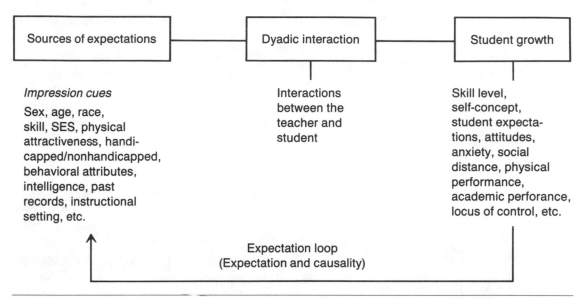

Figure 3.1. A model for the study of Pygmalion effects in physical education. *Note.* From "Pygmalion in the gym: A model for the communication of teacher expectations in physical education" by J. Martinek, 1981. This figure is reprinted with permission from the *Research Quarterly for Exercise and Sport,* **52**. The *Research Quarterly for Exercise and Sport* is a publication of the American Alliance of Health, Physical Education, Recreation and Dance, 1900 Association Drive, Reston, VA 22091.

Attractiveness. Highly attractive students are expected to do better in PE and to be more socially adept with their peers than less attractive students. As children get older, attractiveness becomes increasingly related to student performance expectations.

Effort. Teachers expect more from students who demonstrate greater effort.

Student Ability. Physical education teachers have higher expectations for highly skilled students engaged in activities considered individualized or competitive. Low-skill students are expected to do better in cooperative activities. Teachers give more technical feedback, more praise and encouragement, and more attention to the highly skilled than to the low-skilled. Low-skilled students receive more criticism, more directions, and less information, and teachers look for more misbehavior from these students.

It is easy to look at each of these areas separately, but think also of the interactions among them. What effect will a combination of student characteristics have on you as a prospective teacher? How will you react not only to the unattractive student, but also to the unattractive student with low skill and some type of disability? Make up various combinations of student characteristics and forecast your behavior.

You should realize that whatever your expectations of students, students will not be affected in the same way. Students will react variously to the expectancy messages you send to them. Students will also differ in how (or whether) they perceive the links between your expectations and their outcomes. For example, students may attribute success or failure to themselves, to you the teacher, to the nature of the tasks performed, or to a combination of factors. One must be careful to avoid a

How will you react to students with different
characteristics and abilities?

"What's the use?" response from students.
Students who perceive that the teacher always
interprets results in the same way, no matter
what degree of effort they expend, will be less
likely to care about PE or what's expected of
them. In essence, as the teacher you will have
to be sensitive to what students attribute success or failure to and how you respond to success or failure. You have to be sensitive to how
your expectations are communicated to and
perceived by your students.

Finally, however normal it may be to have
expectations for others, it is particularly important that you be flexible in adjusting your
expectations and perceptions. When you expect
a student to do poorly, how will you react when
the student succeeds? Will you think the performance was a fluke? Will you think the student
cheated? Will you make the student perform
again? Or will you accept the performance and
readjust your expectations and praise and encourage the student? Teachers don't like to say
they are wrong or that they have made mistakes, but remember that teachers are human,
too. Teachers make mistakes. Teachers can

show their students this human quality and use
expectations to the students' advantage rather
than disadvantage. What do you think you will
do the first time you have misjudged a student?

GENDER AND THE TEACHER

A closely related topic is student gender and its
influence on the physical education teacher.
See the work of Griffin (1989a) for excellent
examples of sex inequity in the physical education setting. In this section we discuss some of
Griffin's findings.

In 1972, Title IX, a federal law prohibiting
gender discrimination in our schools, was en-
acted. This law prohibits the segregation of
physical education classes by sex. The purpose
of the law is to promote equity within our gymnasiums and athletic fields—to give girls and
boys equal opportunities for instruction and
participation in all physical education and sport
activities. It was assumed that such a law would
guarantee equity and that, regardless of gender, students would benefit in numerous ways
through coeducational activity.

Unfortunately, the intended outcomes of Title IX have not been produced in all physical
education settings. We have learned that one
cannot assume that sex integration within PE
means sex equity. In reality, in many settings
sex inequity is alive and well, as evidenced by
various studies (Griffin, 1989a):

• Teachers interact differently with girls and
  boys. Boys are praised for performance,
  girls for effort. Boys receive more instruction, praise, control, management, and
  criticism than do girls.
• Activities (wrestling, dance, gymnastics)
  perceived as inappropriate to teach in sex-
  integrated classes have been dropped, so
  choices are limited.

- Teachers group students within classes by sex.
- Classes remain sex-segregated.
- Male teachers complain about teaching female students.
- Female teachers complain about teaching male students.
- Teachers remain unconcerned about equity among sexes in relation to play opportunities.
- Boys often leave girls out of game interactions.
- Girls and boys perceive boys to be more highly skilled even when they aren't.
- Students separate themselves by gender.
- Students tend to participate more seriously in events traditionally appropriate for their sex.
- Boys limit girls' opportunities to learn by hassling them.
- Girls limit their own opportunities to learn by accepting boys' hassles.
- Boys limit their own opportunities to learn by hassling girls.

What are you thinking? Perhaps if you are a male you are saying, "Not this women's liberation stuff!" Or if you are a female reader, you are saying, "Yeah, right on, that's exactly what we are talking about, and what are you going to do about it, Mr. Macho Man?" These responses may be perceived as somewhat extreme (or are they?) and perhaps as making fun of a very serious situation, but that is not our intent. The intent is for you, the prospective teacher, to realize that sex inequity is real and that you must take it seriously. What strategies do you suggest for promoting gender equity in physical education?

Let's draw from Griffin's (1981) research and wisdom. First, let's look at what might be considered simple and immediate solutions to sex inequity. (Of course, these solutions could be applied to other forms of inequity as well.) Griffin suggests the following:

Awareness of Sex-Stereotyping Patterns. "He thinks he's so macho." "What a fem!" "He throws like a girl." "This is for the boys, because it's too dangerous for girls." These statements all involve stereotyping. We must be aware of how we stereotype and how these stereotypes blur our vision.

Instructional Strategies. You will need to think about and plan your classes in ways that eliminate gender inequities.

Class Organization Strategies. Use a broad range of instructional styles (refer to chapter 12) to meet individual differences regardless of gender, monitoring and balancing out student opportunities by gender (e.g., opportunities to actually play, to be a team leader, to lead exercises, etc.). Use ability grouping, which promotes gender integration.

Teacher–Student Interaction. Monitor balanced participation patterns and the use of non-sexist language, and discourage sex stereotyping. Such practices should become normative in physical education.

Role-Modeling. Have boys and girls actively participate in activities traditionally associated with the opposite sex.

What other strategies would you suggest to eliminate sex inequities in the gym? Do you think methodological changes are enough? What about your attitudes and conceptualizations about gender? What about the pervasiveness of male domination in our society, including in physical education and sport? We are in agreement with Griffin (1989a, p. 228) when she states that we must reflect on "how teachers conceptualize gender and the role of physical education and sport in gender construction." In other words, the issue of equity is much larger than the use of sexist language or assuring that gender equity exists when monitoring playing opportunities, important as these are. It is a societal issue that teachers must address and consider as important to their personal growth. In the end, a personal commitment to equity is essential; without it, the inequities will endure.

CULTURAL PLURALISM

We live in a multicultural society, and it is important that you recognize, as suggested in our discussion of teacher expectation and gender, that the issue of culture is no different when it comes to providing equal opportunity to learn. Regardless of cultural origin (Asian, African-American, Chicano, Native American, etc.), all students deserve the chance to become physically educated. To facilitate this opportunity, it is essential that the teacher be well-enough informed about varying cultures to be able to instruct with a multicultural perspective. This requires not only learning about the values in other cultures but also being aware of the dominant views in society related to culture and how such views inhibit or promote equitable learning opportunities. For example, examine stereotypes that have been established between race and physical activity. Should some activities be linked to particular races? Should a teacher expect a student to excel in an activity because of ethnic background and expect another to fail for having a different ethnic background? Should students be allowed to group according to race? These and other questions should be addressed in assessing the relationships between curriculum and instruction and a student's ethnic background. Remember that your learning, conviction, and application of equal multicultural opportunity should be linked to students' learning the same lesson. That is, students should learn many valuable lessons about equal opportunity as they gain a multicultural perspective—a perspective intended to end prejudicial behavior and injustice in the gym and school.

All students deserve the chance to become physically educated.

In promoting this lesson, Freischlag (1977, p. 22) suggests that the physical educator should

- build and enhance the self-concepts of culturally different young people,
- help young people develop positive feelings toward other ethnic groups,
- break down cultural and ethnic stereotypes,
- build an atmosphere of trust in relationships with all young people,
- help young people dispel myths about the physical, intellectual, and behavioral inferiority or superiority of ethnic groups, and
- foster positive intergroup relationships.

Swisher and Swisher (1986) suggest additional practices that promote sound pedagogy in multicultural settings. For example, learning and being able to pronounce student names is very important when teaching students of varying cultures. Asking a student for help in the pronunciation of her or his name should be routine and will help prevent embarrassing situations as well as communicate to the student that you care. Also, accepting the language patterns of non-English-speaking students or the cultural nuances of English-speaking students is important. Further, a teacher should be flexible in using varying teaching methods sensitive to cultural differences. For example, one should prepare for and sense the responses of students to group- or individually structured activities. How will students respond to teaching by command or to self-directed activity? Equally, creative assignment of culturally diverse students to groups or teams will show an interpersonal sensitivity to students. Finally, as Swisher and Swisher (1986, p. 39) say, "What teachers can do is to accept a culturally flexible view about students for whom they are responsible. Accept students without conditions and communicate that differences are not problems to be remediated."

There is much to be accomplished in these areas within physical education, and you can play a key role. Naturally, any improvement in the promotion of cultural pluralism and humanism will depend on your commitment to such ends. It calls for a true sensitivity to one's cultural roots and the promise of positive multicultural settings. Where do you fall on the "sensitivity" scale? Perhaps completing the index in the self-reflection section of this chapter will give you some indication. It is a measure we believe all prospective teachers should

assess as they prepare for culturally diverse students.

STUDENTS WITH DISABILITIES

How prepared are you to teach the child with Down syndrome, or the student with muscular dystrophy, or the kid with a congenital heart defect, or the hyperactive student? What are the rights of these students or any other students with disabilities? Do you want to teach these children? Are you legally obligated to teach them? Should they be mainstreamed into your class?

Certainly, entire texts (see suggested readings at the end of the chapter) have been devoted to special and adapted physical education, and it is our hope you have taken or will take a class specifically designed to prepare you to teach children with disabilities. Nonetheless, we feel it is necessary to highlight some of the facts and our beliefs related to teaching these students.

Legislation

What is the major legislation concerning educational opportunity for students with disabilities? Public Law 93-112 and Public Law 94-142 are the two laws intended to guarantee the rights of individuals with disabilities to educational opportunity and protection from discrimination. We emphasize the word *intended* because we suspect that these rights (like the rights under Title IX) aren't always guaranteed or protected.

The Rehabilitation Act of 1973 (P.L. 93-112) is grounded in the Fifth and Fourteenth Amendments (due process and equal protection) to the U.S. Constitution and states that individuals with disabilities shall not be "excluded from participation in, be denied the benefits of, or be subjected to discrimination" in any setting receiving federal financial assistance. In all likelihood, the school or school system in which you teach receives federal support, and hence, the law will apply to your setting. It requires that

- A student with a disability cannot be discriminated against by being excluded from participation in a school program provided in the "least restrictive environment."
- A student with a disability cannot be discriminated against by being denied benefits of participation in those programs conducted in a least restrictive environment.

This means that individuals with disabilities must be accommodated to receive a program as effective as that provided for individuals without disabilities. It should be noted that "accommodation" doesn't mean that the teacher must treat all students alike or that students will achieve equally; it does mean that the teacher must provide equal opportunities for students to achieve. How will you accommodate the students you will teach?

In 1975, the Education for All Handicapped Children law (Public Law 94-142) was legislated. French and Jansma (1982, p. 42) highlight the major components of this law:

- All children with disabilities between the chronological ages of 3 and 21, no matter how severe their disabilities, are to receive a free public education.
- All children with disabilities are to be educated in the least restrictive environment.
- A pupil with disabilities (where appropriate) and the pupil's parent(s), guardian(s), or surrogate parent(s) must be actively involved in the educational team

that makes decisions and develops an Individualized Education Program (IEP) for each child.
- States are under mandate to find all children in need of special education services so that their educational needs can be properly addressed.
- Each state must develop a system of comprehensive personnel development of regular and special educators and support personnel.
- The federal government will provide funds to local education authorities to assist them in meeting the full service goal.

Mainstreaming

With the legislation described in mind, let's return to the concept of "the least restrictive environment." This concept is linked to the term *mainstreaming* and suggests that when it is in the best interests of the student with disabilities, the student should be placed, or mainstreamed, in classes along with students without disabilities. If the student's needs cannot be addressed through mainstreaming, then special and segregated classes may be conducted. As discussed in the opening of this chapter, teacher expectations may play a role in how the teacher relates to the idea of mainstreaming. The teacher who has a "problem" about teaching students with disabilities, for whatever reason, is going to have trouble with mainstreaming. That teacher will probably encourage segregation, diminishing the disabled student's prospects of receiving sound educational programming. Of course, one's personal preference is irrelevant to the requirements of law. One doesn't have the option not to mainstream simply because one is personally offended by having to teach students with disabilities. Perhaps the best principle to keep in mind is the following (AAHPERD, 1978, pp. 4-5):

> Putting individuals in programs or activities for which they are not ready is cruel; to keep [them] out of these same programs and activities when they are ready and can participate is criminal.

For teaching students with disabilities, a "noncategorical approach" (French & Jansma, 1982) is suggested. Students with disabilities can be mainstreamed or accommodated by the teacher by using a sequence of skills and activities from easy to difficult, by modifying rules and strategies, and by employing other alternatives that not only take into account the needs of students with disabilities but meet individual differences regardless of one's physical, emotional, or intellectual status. In essence, students are taught according to individual differences rather than according to how they are labeled or stereotyped or whether they are mainstreamed or not. Inclusion instead of exclusion is the key.

Finally, when teaching students with disabilities (or any student, for that matter!), know who they are, study their disabilities, talk to the students' parents, communicate with special educators, and develop IEPs (Individualized Educational Programs) to meet their needs. This will not be easy. Admittedly, a real problem with the legislation discussed earlier is the difficulties facing a teacher who is expected to write IEPs and still focus on other students. However, there is no alternative—IEPs must be developed and implemented as you teach the other students in your class. Perhaps the best strategy is to develop individualized programs for everyone. By so doing you will be addressing the needs of not only your students with disabilities but everyone in your class. Refer to chapters 6 through 9 for additional specific strategies for meeting this goal.

ABILITY GROUPING

Faced with heterogeneity, a teacher might believe that the best way to instruct is to group students according to certain characteristics—gender, skill level, socioeconomic status, physical stature, disabilities, and so on. It should be clear that we are not advocates of grouping, which leads to stereotyping and prevents students from achieving their potentials. This is particularly true when students are grouped by ability, for this may intensify the problem of teacher expectancy. If ability grouping brings about preferential treatment for high-ability groups versus low-ability groups, the students "tracked" into the low-ability groups suffer the consequences. The best get better, the poor get poorer. It appears we have enough evidence (even though some is conflicting) to suggest that low-ability students do not benefit from this strategy (Berliner, 1985; Lockhart & Mott, 1981; Nixon & Locke, 1973). Ability grouping may be useful only to the extent to which the teacher can effectively interact with different groups and to the extent that the teacher is able to reassess students' placements and is flexible enough to reassign students after initial placement. If this can be accomplished, grouping will prove to be advantageous, and students will develop more positive attitudes about themselves and physical education (Slavin, 1987).

AT-RISK YOUTH

Another type of student you are likely to meet in the heterogeneous gym is the problem kid.

These kids are referred to in educational jargon as the "at-risk" youth because their experiences—such as low academic achievement, juvenile delinquency, drug and alcohol abuse, teen pregnancy, running away from home, suicide attempts, neglect and abuse at home—place them in jeopardy (or at risk) of dropping out of school, being unemployable, damaging their health, harming others, and being inarcerated. We pay a good deal of attention to at-risk students in this book by emphasizing the social problems of today's youth (chapter 2), suggesting discipline and motivation strategies (chapter 11), and describing in some detail a variety of social development models that focus on helping at-risk (and other) youth (chapter 9). The presence of at-risk youth in your program—perhaps 1 or 2 in the group of 30 hypothetical students we assigned you at the beginning of the book—once again contributes to the heterogeneity of the class, rendering more obsolete than ever the old "shoot the middle" approach (that is, teach to the middle student in hopes of also addressing the needs of most of the rest of the class).

At-risk youth differ from disadvantaged youth in important ways. Disadvantaged students come from low-income backgrounds and are often members of minority groups, and their parents usually have little formal education. They typically do not receive educational reinforcement and enrichment outside of school, and they may have difficulty practicing the kind of deferred gratification that is required to achieve long-term goals. However— and this is a big however—disadvantaged students often assume incredible family responsibilities at an early age, may come from a very stable family environment, and may not find themselves in any of the at-risk categories. Of course, they are at greater risk of dropping out,

and perhaps some of the other at-risk activities, than advantaged students as a result of being disadvantaged, but many disadvantaged youth do *not* become at-risk youth.

The usual prescription for at-risk youth begins with primary prevention, which in physical education means good teaching (see the section "Prevention" in chapter 11). The second step is secondary prevention, which means focusing on students with problems (see chapter 2). The third step is diversion of the student into a special program or school. This step is taken when it is clear that the problem or problems cannot be effectively solved in the gym or school, when mainstreaming doesn't work.

Often (and unfortunately), at-risk students are left to "rattle around" in the system until they quit coming to school; then someone decides it is time to do something different. Diversion programs vary widely, from individualized basic skills programs to vocational programs. Physical education is often based on the organized-recess model (especially when the teachers don't often have a physical education background), although the social development background), although the responsibility model has been used (Hellison, 1986). The final step is a detention facility, designed to incarcerate and perhaps to attempt rehabilitation.

What alternatives do you have if one or more at-risk students show up in your class? You will need to develop your own version of prevention and, if necessary, intervention strategies based either on some discipline–motivation model (see chapter 11) or a social development model— or both—or neither, if you can come up with something else that works for you. You will also need to learn about the referral system in your school—whether there is one, whether it works, what diversion alternatives exist for these kids. You may need to develop your own referral system by establishing a progression of some sort that starts with time out and eventually leads to calling the parent and then to suspension proceedings.

WRAP-UP

It should be quite apparent that the physical education class is a heterogeneous setting when considering the variation in student backgrounds, interests, abilities, and yes, even their attitudes toward physical education. Your ability to engage in critical inquiry and define and assess the influence of the diversity that exists will determine your effectiveness as a teacher. Contesting dominant views that constrain student opportunity presents a great challenge to you, but one that may benefit your students immeasurably.

This chapter has addressed the diversity that will greet you upon your arrival to a public school. Are you really prepared to confront such diversity head on? If not, it's time to do your homework and learn as much as possible relative to the heterogeneous gym. This chapter is a start, and so is further reading and research on the chapter's various topics. Beyond this, it's time to search your own values in relation to your intellectual, philosophical, and ethical stance about diversity or pluralism. Should not all students have an equal opportunity to learn? That is what this chapter has been all about.

THE EXPERTS RESPOND

Robin: There's nothing more important than treating our students with dignity and complete impartiality! This means physical educators must recognize individual differences and teach accordingly. We must be able to challenge those views that promote inequity.

Chris: Once again, the true idealist, Robin. Fair this, fair that! Look, when I have 50 screaming zombies in my class, the last thing I worry about is Title IX or some public law or who goes in this group or in that group. Get real!

Lynn: No, you get real, Chris. Students deserve our best efforts, and that means planning in a systematic way to promote student equity and achievement regardless of who they are or how fast they can run or whether they have one leg or two or are a girl or a boy.

Pat: Although I agree with you to some extent, Chris, equity is the name of the game in the '90s. As much as I dislike teaching girls, it's required, and we have no choice. It's a real pain, but if that's what the big shots want, what are we going to do?

Chris: Hey, wait a minute! I'm not saying I'm going to give the kids the shaft, but I'm not paid enough to do an IEP for every kid every night or to think about how I'm going to help this kid in this group or that kid in another group. Just let them play and everything will be cool. That's all the kids want anyway.

Robin: I can just see you trying to figure out how to teach special education or at-risk students. Your organized recess will really help those kids who need special attention. I suppose you'll adopt Pat's ''fear of God'' and sexist approach as well.

| Pat: | We've been over this at-risk youth stuff already. If fear is what it takes, what's wrong with that? They won't get out of hand.

| Robin: | Your argument for using fear belongs in the Stone Age. These kids have needs: that's why they act out!

| Lynn: | But our job isn't to meet their needs, Robin. That's the counselor's job or perhaps the diversion program's. I don't think fear is the answer, but research-based discipline strategies are what every teacher needs.

| Chris: | All right! I surrender! I know deep down inside you are absolutely right, but how am I going to do all this stuff and hold a second job? It just seems impossible.

| Robin: | Chris, that's what teaching is all about. Trying to make that which seems impossible, possible.

What do you think? An impossible challenge or not? It's time to think about who you will teach and just how prepared and interested you are to teach in the heterogeneous gym.

SELF-REFLECTION

The following exercises (we aren't talking about push-ups here) may assist you in reflecting about this chapter. They ask you to examine some very sensitive issues, but we feel these issues are critical to your development as a teacher.

1. Observe a junior or senior high school physical education class and try to assess whether the teacher has any biased behavioral tendencies toward certain types of students. First, interview the teacher and ask the teacher to identify the best students (the most skilled and/or those with the best attitudes), and then ask the teacher to identify the worst students (the least skilled and/or those with the worst attitudes). Then observe the teacher's interactions with these students. Can you draw any conclusions about the teacher's interaction?

2. Interview one male and one female teacher from both a junior high and a senior high (four total) and ask them about their feelings about teaching students of the opposite gender. (Do they like teaching students of the opposite sex, and what are the implica-

tions of doing so?) What do you feel about teaching students of the opposite sex?

3. Develop a questionnaire that addresses teacher expectations and equity in the gym. Address the influence of impression cues and the consequences of such cues. Interview five junior high school and five senior high school students and assess how their responses relate to the conclusions of Martinek and Griffin. How would you want your students to respond to such questions?

4. Consider your 30 students and, on a sheet of paper, rate yourself on a scale of 1 (low) to 10 (high) for each item below (Knutson, 1977):

   • I help my students accept each other on the basis of individual worth regardless of sex, race, religion, or socioeconomic status.

   • I help my students recognize clearly the basic differences among all members of the human race and the uniqueness of every individual.

   • I help my students value the multicultural character of our society and reject stereotypes, caricatures, and derogatory references to any segment of our community.

- I help my students recognize prejudice as a wall that blocks communication, interaction, and mutual understanding and respect.

- I help my students understand the influences and pressures—historical and contemporary, environmental, social, political, and economic—that have been instrumental in generating group differences, progress, and antagonism.

- I help my students to analyze intergroup tension and conflict with honesty and a will to resolve them, and to seek resolution on the basis of fairness and cooperation and affirmative action.

- I help my students appreciate the contributions of all groups—such as sexual, racial, religious, social-class, and nationality groups.

- I help my students become motivated to uphold their responsibilities as good citizens by working and striving to achieve a democratic society with injustice for none and with equal rights and opportunities for all.

- I help my students by carefully evaluating all curriculum materials—books, pamphlets, films, and so on—to ensure fair and balanced treatment of all groups.

- I help my students learn the art of good human relations by providing a living model in my own treatment of people—each and every child, all members of the staff, from administrator to custodian, every parent, and other members of the community without exception.

Assess your response to each question. How sensitive are you? Do your responses call for a reassessment of your attitudes and behavior?

5. Interview one male and one female teacher from both a junior high school and a senior high school. Ask the teachers about their feelings and approaches to teaching students with disabilities. Ask them if they are satisfied with the concept of mainstreaming and what policies are in place to address mainstreaming in their schools. How do their responses compare to your feelings and approaches to teaching students with disabilities?

6. Observe a junior high or senior high and try to pick out an at-risk student. What does he or she do during PE? How would you deal with the student? After class, ask the teacher whether the student you picked is really at risk in any way.

7. Visit an alternative school (a nonpublic school for at-risk students). Interview the director (usually these programs have a very small staff). Do they offer PE? What is the role of PE (if they offer it) in the program? To have fun? To let off steam? To learn to work and play together? What would you have as the major goal if you taught PE there?

SUGGESTED READINGS

French, R., & Jansma, P. (1982). *Special physical education*. Columbus, OH: Merrill. (A helpful guide to understanding the world of atypical children and their instructional needs.)

Griffin, P. (1981). One small step for personkind: Observations and suggestions for sex equity in coeducational physical education classes. *Journal of Teaching in Physical Education*, Introductory Issue, 12-17. (Excellent article providing ideas for addressing sex inequities in physical education.)

Griffin, P. (1989). Gender as a socializing agent in physical education. In T. Templin, & P. Schempp (Eds.), *Socialization into physical education: Learning to teach* (pp. 219-232). Indianapolis: Benchmark Press. (A critical view of the influence of gender in society and in schools.)

Hellison, D. (1978). *Beyond bats and balls: Alienated (and other) youth in the gym*. Washington, DC: AAHPERD. (A monograph to share the author's experience in teaching alienated youth and the application of a responsibility model in the instructional process.)

Kneer, M. (1982). Ability grouping in physical education. *Journal of Physical Education, Recreation, and Dance*, **53**(8), 10-13. (A journal article that provides various strategies for ability grouping.)

Martinek, T. (1981). Pygmalion in the gym: A model for the communication of teacher expectations in physical education. *Research Quarterly for Exercise and Sport*, **52**, 58-67. (An article describing the influence of student characteristics on teaching behavior and research on the Pygmalion effect.)

Martinek, T., Crowe, P., & Rejeski, W. (1982). *Pygmalion in the gym: Causes and effects of expectations in teaching and coaching*. Champaign, IL: Leisure Press. (A book describing the Pygmalion effect and its influence in schools and physical education programs.)

Sherrill, C. (1986). *Adapted physical education and recreation: A multidisciplinary approach*. Dubuque, IA: Brown. (A useful text addressing the instruction of atypical students in schools and recreation settings.)

Slavin, R. (1984). *Cooperative learning*. New York: Longman. (Addresses issues related to cooperative learning in mixed-ability school settings.)

Swisher, K., & Swisher, C. (1986). A multicultural physical education setting: An attitude. *Journal of Physical Education, Recreation, and Dance*, **57**(7), 35-39. (Understanding and being able to equitably and effectively instruct culturally diverse students is the focus of this paper.)

Part III

What's Worth Doing and How Should You Do It?

In our view, "What's worth doing?" is perhaps the most important question you can ask yourself as you begin planning your physical education program. We try to help you answer this question by describing a variety of curriculum models that, alone or in some combination, could provide some direction for your program. Each of the models we describe in chapter 4 suggests a different purpose for teaching physical education. You may find yourself more interested in fitness or in motor skills instruction or in helping kids feel better about themselves. These are your values, your priorities in teaching. Your first task is to determine what your values are and whether you can defend them—whether they can be justified as the basis for a physical education program.

Your second task is to identify instructional strategies that will put your purpose—your answer to "What's worth doing?"—into practice. Chapters 5 through 9 describe a variety of instructional concepts and strategies based on the curriculum models in chapter 4. Chapter 5 focuses on teaching motor skills, chapter 6 on teaching games, chapter 7 on teaching fitness, chapter 8 on teaching concepts, and chapter 9 on teaching for personal and social development (e.g., self-esteem, cooperation). Chapter 10 provides some strategies for putting together your own model of teaching.

Curriculum Models in Physical Education

You have just been given the assignment of teaching physical education to 30 kids, 5 days a week, 40 minutes of activity time a day, for an entire year. (If you read "Setting the Stage," you know that!) The question is: What are you going to try to accomplish with them? You may set some lofty goals for yourself, but chances are that you will do to and for these students what was done to and for you when you took physical education classes. Maybe you'll try some of the ideas you've learned as a PE major, but that is not very likely. It is more likely that you will just try to survive the experience. What is most likely is that you won't have the energy or the luxury or perhaps even the awareness to ask what we feel is the most important (although not the only) question in teaching physical education: What's worth doing?

Alan Tom (1984) argues that teaching is a moral craft, not because teachers teach sportsmanship, cooperation, or other values, but because any decision a teacher makes affects kids' lives. We agree, and that is why "What's worth doing?" is such an important question. Moreover, Maxine Greene (1986) makes the point that no approach to teaching can afford to ignore the "believing and cherishing" of the teacher. Greene's point, that a teacher's beliefs and values play a central role in teaching, is amplified by others. "Morale is intimately re-

lated to being able to do one's work in a manner consistent with one's standards and values" (Mertens & Yarger, 1988, p. 35). Several teachers with whom we have worked agree. They say that every day they are faced with decisions that need to be based on a clear understanding of why they teach what they are teaching, what their long- and short-term goals for their kids are, what their strengths and weaknesses are, what their kids need and what their interests and backgrounds are, and the relationship of all of these things to what goes on in the school in which they work.

Returning to the 30 students we have just assigned you, the central question has just been put in several ways: How do you want to influence their lives? What standards and values do you believe in and cherish enough to promote in the face of sometimes reluctant, unmotivated, or even hostile students who are often more interested in each other, rock music, hanging out at the shopping mall, and whatever else happens to be popular, than in physical education? Do you know why you have chosen certain activities and certain goals? Can you defend them? In short, what's worth doing with these 30 students?

The answer to this question is complex; not only your values but also your strengths and weaknesses, who your kids are, and the nature of your school must be part of the equation.

43

However, without knowing anything about the 30 students we have assigned to you, you can make some preliminary judgments, a working hypothesis, about the focus of your new program. We haven't forgotten about your students' needs and interests or the situation in which you will work, but we are setting these factors aside for the moment to help you explore your own beliefs and values.

The truth is that whether you have thought about it or not, you do have priorities, some personal values about physical activity. You came into physical education perhaps because you were "into" fitness and wellness or perhaps because you love competitive sports (particularly certain ones) or perhaps just because you want to help kids. Or maybe even because you want to help the world become a more peaceful place and you believe that teaching cooperation is one way to accomplish this. Or maybe . . . . The list of possible motives goes on and on. We want you to get in touch with your motives and values and then examine them to determine whether they hold up under scrutiny and particularly whether they are relevant for others besides yourself—for example, for the students assigned to you.

Lots of people are ready to answer this "What's worth doing?" question for you. Teacher educators like us have some very clear ideas of what you ought to do. So do the physical educators at the school or in the district in your hypothetical assignment. So do the parents of the 30 kids. And don't forget your principal's input or that of the school board and, especially recently, the state's requirements. But remember the premise of this book: You are or should be the chief decision maker and problem solver for your program. Insofar as possible, don't let others do your thinking for you!

Many people have some very clear ideas of what you ought to teach.

What's worth doing emphasizes the *what* of teaching—what subject matter you are going to teach—and the *why* of teaching—your rationale for what you have chosen. The *how* of teaching is also important, and we want to deal with that at some length. However, in our view, the what and why come first. The what and why of teaching are often referred to as curriculum, whereas the how is often called instruction or teaching methods.

Here are some of the dominant curriculum models (Jewett & Bain, 1985; Lawson & Placek, 1981; Siedentop, Mand, & Taggart, 1986). Ask yourself which of these, if any, makes the most sense to you as the major purpose for your program for your 30 students. Then see whether you could defend such a focus in front of parents, the school principal, and other teachers. Keep in mind that whichever model you choose, it need not become your entire program; it will, however, be the major theme of your program and the one that will receive the most attention when the effectiveness of your program is evaluated. (You may want to pick two or three models, but if you do, be certain to rank-order them. We are going to ask you to do that anyway toward the end of the chapter.)

MOTOR SKILL AND GAME MODELS

Although they are substantially different from each other, several models share a similar focus: motor skills, sport, games, and play.

Organized Recess ("Rolling Out the Ball")

Although most curriculum books do not treat organized recess as a legitimate program focus, it is in fact reasonably popular among physical education teachers. It involves organizing a game for the students and then officiating or playing or monitoring from the sidelines (for unsafe and off-task behavior). Proponents argue that the kids like this approach, that it is easy to implement, that it keeps students active, and that students "let off steam" so that they can pay better attention during their academic classes. At a recent program-development workshop for secondary school physical educators from six school districts on the east coast,

> the major focus of their discussion was recreation and fun. These teachers felt that a major purpose of secondary physical education . . . ought to be stress reduction and relaxation rather than the continuation of an academic day filled with pressure to achieve. (Veal, 1988, p. 156)

Critics of the organized recess model point out that organized recess is recreational rather than instructional in nature, that not all kids enjoy playing group games (although those who don't tend to be less vocal), that some students are not very active in group games (a few dominate), and that the let-off-steam hypothesis has not been supported very well by research.

The Multiactivity Model

The multiactivity model is also very popular at both the elementary and the secondary levels. In this program, students experience a wide variety of physical activities in short (usually 2- or 3-week) units. The goals of the multiactivity model are exposure to many different activities and active participation in general (rather than participation in a particular activity). Its proponents argue that this kind of program reduces student (and teacher) boredom because of its diversity and the novelty of a new units every 2 or 3 weeks. They also emphasize that this approach is flexible because units can be added or subtracted without affecting the rest of the program. For example, a unit on frisbee could replace a flag-football unit.

Critics of the typical multiactivity model cite the low level of improvement in a 2- or 3-week unit, the lack of progression from year to year in the same activity (e.g., the volleyball unit in the seventh and eighth grades are virtually the same), and the tendency to introduce a few drills followed by organized recess or a tournament in the designated activity. According to Hoffman (1987, p. 128), the multiactivity model requires "the ability to teach a broad range of skills at the introductory level in environments that promise little hope of success."

Three modifications of the multiactivity model address these criticisms to some extent.

One variation that has been relatively popular in larger secondary schools is the elective program, which, proponents argue, gives students the opportunity to choose their activities and thereby enhances both motivation and self-responsibility. Another variation is to extend each unit, giving more time for instruction and learning. This is popular with those who contend that the multiactivity model does little more than expose students to a lot of activities (which is sometimes cynically referred to as the "dab" approach), but extending the units to 5 or 6 weeks cuts down on the number of activities that can be offered in a given year. The multiactivity model therefore becomes less multiactivity in this variation, although by vertical curriculum planning—that is, planning activities over a number of years—the multiactivity characteristic can be retained. A third variation is to offer a mixed curriculum, which means teaching more than one activity at a time. If students are going to do more than play, however, both classroom management (see chapter 11) and self-responsibility (see chapter 9) need to be employed, coupled with individualized instruction (see chapter 5).

The Sports Education Model

Traditionally, much of physical education has been sport-related, and the recently popular elementary physical education skill themes model (Graham, Holt/Hale, & Parker, 1987) strongly suggests that sport is the eventual goal of physical education. However, proponents of the sports education model would argue that neither organized recess nor the multiactivity model has provided a complete sport education for students.

The sports education model is intended "to help students become skilled sports participants and good sportspersons . . . to teach them to be players in the fullest sense of that term" (Siedentop et al., 1986, pp. 186-187). To do this, as many of the institutionalized aspects of sport as possible must be incorporated into the physical education program. Units are replaced by seasons in the sport education model. Students belong to teams that practice together and play together (although sometimes the team is represented by only some of the team members, as in three-on-three soccer). A formal competition of some sort is conducted during the season (e.g., round-robin format), culminating in an event such as a championship. Records are kept (preferably team records, so that individual performance does not occupy center stage). The teacher becomes the coach of all teams, at least until students can coach each other, and the season begins with more practice and fewer competitions and then progresses to more competitions with less practice, as in organized sport. Sports and drills are modified so that they are developmentally appropriate for the age of the students.

Critics of the model have suggested that, with the current abuses evident in organized sport, students need less, not more, activities based on the professional sport model. However, proponents counter that one of the fundamental tenets of sport education is that sport is an integral part of our culture and therefore that good sport helps to enhance the health and vitality of the culture. Physical education, they argue, ought to teach good sport and good competition rather than deemphasize sport and competition because of the abuses in organized sport. Critics also complain that sports education advocates exclude health-related fitness from the physical education curriculum, relegate it to health education, and limit fitness to preparation for specific sports. They also point out that in small schools, where most students are on varsity teams, such a model is redundant.

The Competitive Achievement Model

Those who criticize the sports education model because of its potential for condoning or even further popularizing the abuses of organized sport have a "field day" with this next model. Competitive achievement is not typically found among those physical education curriculum models discussed in the literature, but it is surely alive and well in many public school gymnasiums, no doubt because of its close association with organized sport.

The competitive achievement model emphasizes the ends rather than the means of competition, the product rather than the process. Simply put, it emphasizes winning and winners. In the extreme, this emphasis results in rules violations and worse. Competitive

The competitive achievement model emphasizes winning but neglects nonathletic students.

achievement is a strong strand in the ethos of American society and American social institutions (not just sport), more so than in most other societies, although it is by no means supported by everyone. Of course, sport has provided a very visible vehicle for the promotion of competitive achievement, and it is no secret that sport is big business, even outside the professional arena. Slogans exemplifying the competition achievement ethic abound—e.g., "Nice guys finish last," "Defeat is worse than death because you have to live with it," "Show me a good loser and I'll show you a loser."

Proponents usually cite the American competitive tradition and the need for competition in our society. Critics (including us!) question the impact on losers and more generally the kind of survival-of-the-fittest environment provided by this model.

What does it mean for a physical education class to be driven by the competitive achievement model? Obviously, it means using heavy doses of competitive sport and lectures on the importance of winning. But there are other less obvious indicators of a competitive achievement model in operation, among them: giving attention to winners, either formally or informally, in combination with posting those with the highest scores, those who hold the class record, and so on; holding required tournaments (rather than optional tournaments, as is the case in life outside mandatory physical education classes); and using elimination games.

THE FITNESS MODEL

The fitness/wellness movement in the United States has left its mark on physical education programs. Support for a fitness focus has come from national fitness tests that show that American youth are generally unfit and from studies that suggest that a sedentary lifestyle beginning in childhood contributes to the risk factors associated with cardiovascular disease. In the past, calisthenics were part of the daily physical education lesson, but critics note that the overload and interval criteria necessary for fitness improvement were not being met in those programs. For example, aerobic development requires medium-intensity rhythmic exercise for 20 to 60 minutes three to five times a week, and strength development requires regular overload of the specific muscular system. The associated learning argument—that fitness is developed while students work on motor skills and play games—is problematic when these criteria are being used to define fitness. Fitness proponents contend that these arguments support aerobic, flexibility, strength, and body-fat-control activities as the central focus of physical education. Critics point out that meeting the criteria for fitness development requires a substantial amount of time, so other aspects of the physical education program have had to be sacrificed. They also cite evidence of eating disorders and overuse injuries as indicators of an overemphasis on fitness. They also point to recent evidence that suggests health-related fitness can be achieved by regular participation in low-intensity activities.

Fitness testing has accompanied the growth of the fitness focus, and currently at least four national organizations offer separate batteries of fitness tests with various awards for fitness performance. Not only are these tests being contested, but concerned educators fear that testing itself can demotivate students. For example, students who don't do well on tests may discount the importance of fitness to protect their self-esteem (Fox & Biddle, 1988). As a result, recommendations that effort, improvement, and individual goals supplant or at least supplement norm-referenced testing have been built into some of the test batteries.

PERSONAL–SOCIAL DEVELOPMENT MODELS

Personal–social development refers to a large category of loosely connected concepts such as self-image, motivation, cooperation, and sportsmanship; it has often been referred to as the affective domain. Unlike the other perspectives we have discussed so far, personal–social development as a central purpose for physical education cannot stand alone. Instead, these models provide a framework for the subject matter of physical education; sport, fitness, dance, outdoor skills, and so on must still be selected. The difference is that this subject matter is selected to facilitate the development of certain personal and social qualities. For example, some personal–social development proponents use volleyball, because, unlike many sports, volleyball can be played properly only if team members cooperate (and because it includes a net between teams!).

Coaches and physical education teachers have made many claims about the personal–social development benefits of organized and instructional physical activity, but these claims have not been substantiated very well by research. However, recent studies in which specific personal–social goals and strategies have been employed have shown more promising results, suggesting that personal–social development does not happen automatically (again debunking the associated learning argument) but must be specifically planned and taught.

Several personal–social development models have been advocated.

The Self-Esteem Model

Self-esteem is often viewed as a primary indicator of a person's emotional adjustment and mental health and therefore often appears as a curriculum objective in school programs. The nature of self-esteem is still under investigation (e.g., Fox, 1988), but it appears that everyone possesses a global self-esteem—a general feeling that "I am OK" or "I am not OK"—that is composed of a number of more specific feelings about various aspects of the self (e.g., myself as student, myself as friend, myself as athlete). Four components—sport competence, physical strength, physical condition, and attractive body—contribute to physical self-esteem (or body image), which in turn contributes to global self-esteem. Those qualities and activities a person values weigh more heavily in the self-esteem equation, so that, for example, the physical self-esteem of someone who does not play golf well will not be affected very much if that individual does not value golf competence. Social influences play a major role in this valuing process, although people can customize their self-esteem priorities to some extent.

People also possess an outside self, composed of what others see (appearance, behaviors, and so on), and an inside self, composed of personal feelings, perceptions, aspirations, and problems. The outside self is like the tip of the iceberg: It's what everyone sees, but it comprises only a small part of the whole. This conceptualization helps to focus teachers' attention on what they don't see rather than exclusively on student behaviors.

Proponents of the self-esteem model advocate strategies such as positive reinforcement, redefining success so that improvement and effort count, remedial support for those who perceive themselves to be unskilled or unfit, and attention to the inside self in the form of listening, conferences, and choices. However, critics point out that self-esteem, because it is perceptual and subjective, is difficult to plan for. In addition, they wonder whether elevated self-esteem isn't just a setup for failure in the real world and whether arrogance, as expressed particularly by some of the motor elite, doesn't require a downward adjustment of self-esteem instead.

Moral Education Models

A recent line of research (Weiss & Bredemeier, 1986) suggests a different model of personal–social development: moral education. Two different approaches are described. One, based on social learning theory, utilizes modeling and reinforcement to teach predetermined moral values, such as playing fairly and winning graciously. In the other, the Built-In Dilemma/Dialogue (BIDD) model (Romance, Weiss, & Bokoven, 1986), students are routinely confronted with moral dilemmas related to fairness in games. One way to do this is to ask students whether the game they have just played is fair—did everybody get turns, did everybody have fun, and so on. Another way is to create moral dilemmas in game situations. A third way is to have students create their own games by following fair-play guidelines, such as that everyone participates and everyone has fun. Again, this model does not dictate the subject matter, but some physical activities such as team sports are better suited to moral dilemmas.

Critics question the allotment of time given to discussion, although some evidence (Romance et al., 1986) suggests that time may not be an important factor.

A third approach to moral education is organized around cooperation. Orlick (1978a) provides a theoretical framework for this model, primarily arguing that America's major social problems can be solved by embracing a "cooperative ethic." To implement his cooperative ethic in physical education, he provides a wide variety of cooperative games (Orlick, 1978b). Critics complain that this approach demeans healthy competition, changes cultural games (which are the focus of the sports education model), and is ineffective in combating media and other persuasive influences in American society. Proponents counter by citing evidence of changes in kids as a result of this model (e.g., they are more cooperative, more helpful, less aggressive in games, and more interested in good sportsmanship) (Orlick, 1978a).

The Responsibility Model

A third model of personal–social development focuses on teaching self- and social responsibility by empowering students to take more responsibility for their own bodies and lives in the face of a variety of barriers and limitations, and by teaching students that they have a social responsibility to be sensitive to the rights, feelings, and needs of others (Hellison, 1985). In this approach, a loose developmental progression of four goals either formally or informally provides the framework for the physical education program. The goals are sufficient self-control to respect the rights of others, participation and effort, self-direction, and caring about and helping others. Several

Cooperative games build helping and sportsmanship skills.

processes—learning the goals and rationale for the goals, invitations and opportunities to experience the goals, personal decision-making and group problem-solving, and self-reflection, for examples—are employed to help students interact with the model's goals on a regular basis. Advocates claim that this approach combats students' feelings of powerlessness and alienation, as well as inadequate adult guidance and peer pressure, by causing students to feel empowered and purposeful, to experience making responsible commitments, to strive to develop themselves, and to understand their essential relatedness to others.

Critics object to shifting authority from the teacher ("Whatever happened to the old-fashioned idea that teachers know what they are doing?"), worry about the ensuing chaos of such an approach, and wonder whether children and youth are capable of handling such responsibility. As with other personal–social development models, critics are also concerned about the deemphasis on the physical education subject matter, such as motor skills and fitness.

Other Personal–Social Development Models

Outdoor pursuits and adventure education emphasize competition against oneself or nature, challenge and risk, and mutual dependency. Some research (Segrave & Hastad, 1984) has shown that personal–social development occurs as the result of wilderness sport activities, especially among youth at risk. Although some of these activities can be brought into the gym in the form of adventure education activities, critics point out that many of these programs require travel, a different time frame, extra financing, and special training compared to traditional physical education.

Another example of a personal–social development model is Griffin's (1989b) equity model, which emphasizes inclusion and accommodation. Griffin argues that physical education should be coeducational and that stronger, more athletic students—often the males—need to learn to adjust to make games fair. After-school sport, she contends, is the place for highly competitive activities.

THE CONCEPTS MODEL

Teaching concepts to students emphasizes the how and why of movement, not just the doing of it. This model has a strong cognitive component in addition to the usual emphasis on psychomotor activities in physical education classes. The conceptual model is most common in fitness education where, for example, overload is explained to students so that they understand why they are to do as many push-ups as they can and so they can use this concept in their daily lives. Motor learning concepts such as practice and feedback, and biomechanical concepts such as leverage, spin, and rebound, can also be taught. Sometimes students are asked to problem-solve and then to discuss and discover the underlying concept, for example by trying to figure out what one must do to break down one's opponent in wrestling. Like personal–social development, the conceptual model does not dictate subject matter and therefore can be combined with the multiactivity model, sport education, or fitness. However, it does take time and planning.

Proponents argue that a student who does not have conceptual knowledge is not truly physically educated. Critics counter that knowing about is not the same as knowing, and that teaching concepts takes away from doing the activities.

THE EASTERN APPROACH

The Eastern approach offers an alternative to the ancient Greek sound-mind-in-sound-body perspective (i.e., that physical activity develops a sound body, which helps the mind to function better). Arguing that most models promote a mind–body dualism, this model draws on Eastern philosophies such as Buddhism and Taoism, which in different ways advocate the abandoning of self, the unity of mind and body, and flowing with the experience rather than trying to control it. The Eastern model finds its perhaps most well-articulated expression in the inner game of tennis (Gallwey, 1976), which involves specific drills designed to unify one's mind and body in a tennis game. Other books describe their own versions of the Eastern model: *The Zen of Running* (Rohe, 1974) advocates progressing by doing less (!) and running for enjoyment rather than pain; *Zen in the Art of Archery* (Herrigel, 1953) includes teaching tips such as letting the arrow shoot itself; and *The Ultimate Athlete* (Leonard, 1974) describes quarterback John Brodie's apparently mystical experiences in football. Ken Ravizza's (1973) research on peak experiences in sport describes those moments when athletes enter into a "zone" in which they feel totally at one with the experience.

Proponents are critical of the "Westernization" of physical activity, which to them means an overintellectualizing of the experience. Concepts advocates of course argue the opposite, that conceptualization enhances the experience. Other critics simply discount this model as mystical or science fiction.

WRAP-UP

The purpose of this chapter was to help you become aware of, and to reflect upon, the major curriculum perspectives currently in the literature and to some extent in practice in the United States. A few of these models—such as organized recess, the multiactivity model, and competitive achievement—are probably familiar to you, because you have experienced them and perhaps even taught according to them. Others—such as fitness and sport education—are based on familiar concepts even if they aren't very much in evidence in most physical education programs. Still others—such as the concepts model and the various personal–social development models—take somewhat new or alternative approaches to teaching physical education. Finally, the Eastern approach builds its case on Eastern rather than Western philosophy and therefore falls well outside typical conceptions of physical education.

Sifting and sorting through these ideas to find the best fit for you (or that nothing fits) is an essential first step in planning. All lesson plans and their delivery in the gym are based on some kind of intention, some set of values. Unfortunately, these intentions and values are often hidden so that the teacher has difficulty in explaining them and therefore in justifying the lesson. An important aspect of reflective teaching is to ask what's worth doing in one's gym . . . and why.

Which of these models, if any, most interested you? Did one or two of them make more sense than the others? What are the assumptions of the model that most appeals to you? Could you defend your choice? Could you combine two or even three of these approaches in a way that would make sense in teaching the 30 students we assigned you for the year? Maybe asking the opinion of our experts will clarify things for you.

THE EXPERTS RESPOND

Pat: I'll go first because the answer is easy. The multiactivity model has withstood the test of time, and the kids like it. The only drawback I see is that the teacher has to know something about a lot of activities, but then that's our job, isn't it? I'd include a 3-week fitness unit, I'd do some fitness testing in the beginning and end of the year so that the students get some idea of how fit they are, and I'd sprinkle in some competitive achievement—after all, even though the authors of this book don't like it, it has withstood the test of time too. Those are the only things I'd take from the other models.

Lynn: First of all, any approach that has a lot of teacher talk in it—such as the conceptual model—detracts from students doing the motor skill in the day's lesson. Research shows that if we want kids to learn a motor skill, we will have to get them to practice that skill over time—with appropriate feedback, of course. The same goes for the multiactivity model: not enough time to learn skills. (I won't even dignify organized recess or competitive achievement by discussing them; one doesn't teach anything, the other excludes people.) So I'm sort of left with either the fitness focus, which doesn't teach motor skills at all, or sport education, which might work okay in combination with the skill themes model in the earlier grades. My other choice is to modify the multiactivity model so that each unit is longer—say 6 or 7 weeks. That might best meet my needs; then I wouldn't have to fool around with teams and records and all that sport education stuff.

Chris: Spare me! There's no question that what you call (in a demeaning way it seems to me) "organized recess" makes the most sense, although I could live with the multiactivity model as long as it was light on drills and heavy on play. All the others are too much work for too little reward. Oh, yeah, the competitive achievement model seems okay, too, except it's too much work organizing formal tournaments and posting the names of top performers. Gotta go (to my second job).

Robin: I sort of like the personal–social development focus, because it's the only one that puts kids—whole kids that is—first. Most of the others reduce kids to bodies or movers or else neglect kids as people altogether (oops . . . the conceptual approach does recognize that students have heads). Or, as in the case of competitive achievement ("jock-itis," I call it), dehumanize the whole process. (I can't figure out the Eastern approach.) I am particularly interested in helping kids feel better about themselves and get along better with each other, so some of those personal–social development models helped me to reflect on my program and whether I am doing enough of that stuff. Some of the ideas sounded too structured for me, but maybe I need a little more structure to really do what I say I do. I can see that I could focus more on this. I also like the fitness idea of reducing emphasis on testing and of focusing on effort, improvement, and goal setting. And the idea of kids coaching their own teams in the sport education focus—it was sort of implied—fits well with personal–social goals. I can see that I've got some work ahead of me if I really want to do what I say I'm doing.

SELF-REFLECTION

As you can see, our experts don't agree. Chris is happy with, and a bit defensive about, the organized-recess model. Pat likes the multiactivity model. Robin favors some version of personal–social development. Lynn seems to support either sport education or a modification of the multiactivity model. Each argues from his or her own beliefs, values, and commitments.

1. What models made the most sense to you? Take out a sheet of paper and rank these purposes in terms of your personal preferences:

   _____ Organized recess
   _____ Multiactivity model
   _____ Sport education
   _____ Fitness
   _____ Competitive achievement
   _____ Self-esteem
   _____ Moral education
   _____ Responsibility
   _____ Outdoor pursuits and adventure education
   _____ Concepts
   _____ Eastern approach
   _____ Other _____

2. Write a brief paragraph that explains your reasons for each of your first two choices and perhaps a paragraph to explain the reasons for your last choice. This isn't busy work (if it seems that way to you, don't do it); you need not only to begin to make these kinds of judgments but also to gain some insight into the reasons for your choices.

3. After you have ranked these models and reflected upon your reasons for your choices, take a moment to trace the origins of your reasons. Did your own interests and values form the basis for your choices, or did you take into consideration what you have learned as a physical education major, the values of a coach or teacher you admire, or what you perceive to be the needs of youth today?

Many factors can influence these decisions. In this chapter, we are most concerned with the influence of your autobiography in this process. In our view it is perfectly valid to *feel* strongly about a particular curriculum purpose. In fact, that will enhance your commitment and enthusiasm, which are so important in teaching. But you do need to be aware of this autobiographical influence and to temper it with additional knowledge, experiences, and, most importantly, reflection. In the end, you not only must believe in your goals; you also must be able to defend them.

SUGGESTED READINGS

Jewett, A., & Bain, L. (1986). *The curriculum process in physical education*. Dubuque, IA: Brown. (Describes the theoretical–philosophical bases of several physical education curriculum models.)

Lawson, H.A., & Placek, J.H. (1981). *Physical education in the schools: Curricular alternatives*. Boston, MA: Allyn & Bacon. (Contains a critique of several curriculum models.)

Siedentop, D. (1980). *Physical education: Introductory analysis* (3rd ed.). Dubuque, IA: Brown. (Devotes a chapter to describing the Eastern approach.)

Siedentop, D., Mand, C., & Taggart, A. (1986). *Physical education: Curriculum and instruction strategies for grades 5-12*. Palo Alto, CA: Mayfield. (Devotes a chapter to each of six models.)

Chapter 5

Teaching Motor Skills

Two of the curriculum models described in chapter 4, the sports education model and the multiactivity model, especially if the units are lengthened, rely on the effective teaching of motor skills. Moreover, most of the other models include some motor skill instruction. However, the demonstration–drill–play process so typical of motor skill instruction in physical education has not held up very well under the scrutiny of recent research. That research (Siedentop, 1983) shows that physical education teachers tend to spend about a third of their time managing students, a third lecturing students, and a third observing students. Meanwhile, students spend a substantial portion of time (about 30%) waiting, with the rest roughly equally divided among receiving information, being managed, and actively engaging in motor skills. Further, the typical gymnasium environment is not very conducive to learning, because it is frequently punctuated with corrective comments (e.g., ''Change your stance'') and nags (e.g., ''Pay attention!'').

Recent research also suggests a number of specific instructional strategies for teaching motor skills. Therefore, if you plan to adopt for your 30 hypothetical students a model that includes any motor skill instruction, this chapter will be especially relevant for you.

The motor skill instructional framework depicted in the progression and teacher activities in Figure 5.1 is based on the major findings of recent research on effective teaching in physi-

cal education (Rink, 1985; Siedentop, 1983), which emphasize high percentages of on-task activity time, reliance on direct instruction (usually defined as teacher-prescribed goals and tasks with highly active monitoring and feedback that focuses on student progress), specific classroom management skills (see chapter 11), high student expectations, and a positive environment (see chapter 11). In addition, individualized instruction strategies are also shown in Figure 5.1. These strategies, which have theoretical strength (e.g., Mosston & Ashworth, 1986) but less support in the research literature, have been incorporated into the model in recognition of the variation in student skill levels and rates of progress.

SET

The set is intended to set the students for the specific lesson they are about to receive. The assumption is that students may not be ready to plunge into a demonstration and drill for a movement skill (e.g., a handstand or instep kick) without an appropriate introduction. We believe that, if possible, the set ought to involve playing the game or doing the activity, to ignite student interest and perhaps to demonstrate to them that they could learn to do it better (Pease, 1978). Management time can be a problem in carrying out this recommendation. However, if teams are required, it will help to simply split

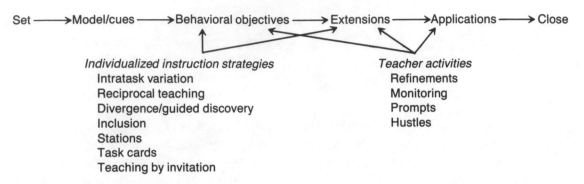

Figure 5.1. Motor skill instructional framework.

the group into two or four teams without regard for any criteria except reasonably equal numbers (perhaps with an investment in earplugs to block student objections) and simplify the rules. A teacher ought to be able to get the activity going within a couple of minutes, especially with a little practice. Five to 10 minutes of play is usually sufficient to set the activity the first time. After that, a reminder or brief activity can be devoted to setting the lesson. The whole operation should not take more than 15 minutes on the first day and much less after that.

MODELING AND VISUAL CUES

After the set, students are brought in for a demonstration of one of the motor skills involved in the activity they just participated in. The set can be extended into this second phase by talking briefly and in general terms about how this skill can improve performance in the activity. Then the skill is modeled or demonstrated, by either the teacher or a student or an audiovisual aid. Along with this demonstration, students

are given a few—very few—cues or tips that will help them perform the skill. For example, for the volleyball bump/forearm pass, "Keep your arms straight" is a cue. However, research suggests that cues that give a specific mental picture work better; therefore, "Keep your arms as straight *as boards*" is a better cue. Mental picture cues are limited only by the teacher's creativity. One teacher tells students that shooting a basketball is like reaching to the top shelf for a package of cookies. One of us has had a lot more success in teaching racquetball by giving only one cue for the forehand ("Hit the ball like you would throw it") and one for the backhand ("Flick your wrist like you are throwing a frisbee") and then adding more cues after students got the idea. Two or three cues at a time are probably all the kids can remember; beginning teachers tend to give too much information—often much too much.

SPECIFIC BEHAVIORAL OBJECTIVES OR CHALLENGES

Typically, as the next step in the learning process, teachers give students a drill to practice

Clues that convey a specific mental picture
work best.

the skill. As teachers will be the first to tell you, drills don't work very well (although teachers use them anyway). They are often boring, and the purpose, to practice the skill, seems remote or irrelevant to students. Instead, research suggests that the teacher should give students a specific behavioral (or performance) objective that challenges them to develop a specific motor skill. The behavioral objective should specify what has to be accomplished to meet the challenge—that is, the situation, the task, and the criteria for successful completion. For example, five volleyball forearm passes to yourself in a row (either specifying the height of the ball or allowing students to choose a height at which they can be successful); or 6 out of 10 free throws; or a 10-second headstand. You get the idea. And of course, the behavioral objective should be challenging but within the students' range. As soon as the stu-

dent has met the objective, she or he no longer needs to continue doing the task, unlike the typical drill.

Ideally, every student should have sufficient equipment to work on each behavioral objective. Taking turns reduces the amount of activity time each student gets. However, even when sufficient equipment is available, teachers often set up drills with only a few balls or other equipment so that students mostly stand around in lines waiting for a turn. Behavioral objectives can be done with partners or in small groups as long as everyone is involved. For example, in partners, students choose a comfortable distance apart from each other and set a volleyball back and forth to each other six times in a row.

The controversy surrounding behavioral objectives is exemplified in the treatment by Jewett and Bain (1985) versus that of Vogel and Seefeldt (1988). Vogel and Seefeldt are strong advocates of requiring behavioral objectives in curriculum planning, whereas Jewett and Bain see behavioral objectives as optional. Jewett and Bain (1985) are concerned about

becoming overwhelmed with a "scientific" or mechanistic approach to writing precise behavioral objectives. Some areas of great educational value do not lend themselves well to precise measurement. Teachers should never be satisfied to allow students' learning experiences to be limited to only those in which the intended outcomes can be precisely described and objectively tested. Neither should they allow themselves to become slaves to mechanistic series or instructional objectives that blind them to unanticipated teaching opportunities or restrict their creativity in enhancing the quality of the learning environment when ''teachable moments'' arise. (pp. 154-155)

Jewett and Bain are particularly concerned about attempting to develop behavioral objectives for personal–social development goals such as self-esteem development. Those of you who choose to emphasize personal–social development goals in your programs may find that some of your goals cannot be readily transformed into behavioral objectives. However, this chapter is concerned with motor skill development, and research suggests that behavioral objectives can be very useful in giving students specific motor skill challenges. Although some motor skills may be more difficult to transform into behavioral objectives—for example, fielding a softball or stopping shots on goal in soccer or floor hockey—we have found from personal experience that informally giving students challenges in the form of behavioral objectives (rather than the approach advocated by Vogel and Seefeldt, and others) is quite adaptable to a wide range of motor skills. Depending on how structured a person you are, they can be written very precisely based on a linear progression from one's curriculum model, or, if you are more like the two left-handers writing this book, they can be created in one's head and often on the spot, not only leaving considerable room for, but often creating them to respond to, teachable moments. From this perspective, the key is to challenge students in specific ways to improve their motor performance in the skill that is being taught. (You will have another brush with behavioral objectives in chapter 12 during our discussion of lesson planning.)

EXTENSIONS

Students who complete a specific behavioral objective are given more difficult challenges with the same motor skill. For example, students who have successfully completed five volleyball forearm passes to themselves could then be given the same behavioral objective but with a specified height to which the ball must travel; or they could be given the task of completing five forearm passes in a row off the wall; or they could be asked to complete 10 in a row with a partner who has also successfully completed the first behavioral objective. Having students report to the teacher (or go on to the next behavioral objective if more than one is presented to students) when they have completed the first behavioral objective automatically individualizes the process. Teachers who suspect that a particular student has not completed the behavioral objective can simply ask that student to perform the skill (although our work suggests, at least to us, that students generally respond well to being trusted).

APPLICATIONS

Demonstrate, drill, play the game. Sound familiar? The motor skill instruction model we are describing has already taken some serious potshots at this traditional approach to teaching motor skills and is about to take another. Research points out that very little skill learning is accomplished by playing a game. (See the next chapter for much more on teaching games.) Of course, games are fun for a lot of kids, and for most teachers they provide the purpose for teaching motor skills in the first place. However, this is a motor skill *instruction* progression, so whatever games are played need to be instructional in nature. To drive this point home, the term *applications* is used to connote the application of the motor skill being practiced.

Applications are really games that are modified so that the motor skill being practiced is the focus of attention. In this way, the skill gets additional practice time in a game-like situation, thereby placing students in situations in which (unlike the routines of behavioral objectives or traditional drills) they are required to demonstrate the skill under a bit of pressure and, often, in a changing environment. The game-like component also is fun for many (but not all) students. For example, if volleyball forearm passes are the focus of behavioral objectives and extensions, one application could be a competition among teams to see which team could bump the most balls in a row. Another application might be a modified volleyball game in which only forearm passes or only forearm passes and spikes could be used (or in which the first hit has to be a forearm pass). More on games in the next chapter.

CLOSE

Just as the set opens the class, the close is intended to leave students with something to think about at the end of class—for instance, a cue, a reminder of the role of this skill in the game, a brief discussion of an incident in class that exemplified the point of the lesson. It is also a time to give students some general reinforcement that they can take with them ("Way to go, gang!"). The close might also include what to look forward to in the next class period.

INTRATASK VARIATIONS

A major problem with this approach is that no one behavioral objective will appropriately challenge all students. Therefore, a number of individualized instruction strategies are suggested in Figure 5.1. Perhaps the most common modification, intratask variations (Graham et al., 1987), is to give all students one behavioral objective that is most likely to

truly challenge most of the students, and then individually adjust that behavioral objective for students who find the challenge too difficult or too easy. These adjustments can be made so that the objective is more difficult (e.g., make 6 free throws in a row rather than 6 of 10) or less difficult (e.g., make 4 out of 10 free throws). This modification solves one problem but causes others. For one thing, it gives the teacher one more job to do while students are practicing skills, and as we will see shortly, the teacher already has several jobs during that time. For another, it singles out students, especially those who are less skilled, who may not want the special attention. Other individualized methods are listed in Figure 5.1 and described below as alternatives to this approach.

REFINEMENTS, RECIPROCAL TEACHING, AND DIVERGENCE/GUIDED DISCOVERY

Something else is missing in this progression—the biomechanics (or form) of the motor skill involved in the behavioral objective. Specifying the task, the conditions under which the task is to be performed, and the criteria for success does not necessarily guarantee that the skill will be performed effectively from a biomechanical perspective. Students could achieve any of the goals listed above and many more like them without doing the skill correctly. For example, students could successfully execute five volleyball underarm passes (bumps) in a row against the wall above a line without keeping their arms straight and/or by striking the ball with their hands. Immediately the teacher is faced with three options:

- Refine the students' skills as students are working on the challenges by reminding them of the cues and giving them specific feedback concerning what they are doing right and what they are doing wrong.

- Build relevant biomechanical principles into the criteria for success.
- Tell students to accomplish the challenge in any way they can, thereby encouraging variations of common form (for example, Willy Mays's basket catch would be a permissible way to catch a fly ball).

The first option is the most common approach to this problem. During the teacher activity of refinement listed in Figure 5.1, motor skills are refined as they are being practiced—by the teacher giving individual feedback to as many students as possible, reminding them of the cues, and giving them feedback concerning their form. They will be getting plenty of intrinsic feedback (or knowledge of results) from their efforts to perform the behavioral objective but little or no extrinsic or augmented feedback on the process (knowledge of performance)—that is, proper biomechanics. This feedback needs to be specific—"Nice job" doesn't help students understand what they are doing right; "Your feet are aligned properly" works better. It is also important to have a balance of positive and corrective comments. Because physical education teachers (and coaches) tend to correct much more than they praise, most beginning teachers have experienced this approach as students and tend to repeat it as teachers. A ratio of one to one, positive to corrective, is generally considered acceptable (two to one, positive to corrective, is desirable), but it will take work to achieve this. A major problem is that beginning teachers, and old veterans for that matter, are unaware of their ratios in the first place. A teacher who has someone listen while she or he gives feedback and count the specific positives

and correctives given to individual students will have a better idea of what needs to be changed. The whole business of positive versus negative feedback has subtle implications (see Rink, 1985). For example, the teacher's correcting the student will more likely be perceived as negative than the teacher's correcting the performance. The teacher's emphasizing the errors of past performance will more likely be perceived as negative than the teacher's emphasizing future performance ("Next time try it this way").

If the teacher decides to choose the second or third option described earlier, rather than the first option, two of the individualized instruction strategies shown in Figure 5.1 will need to be employed to deal with the biomechanics (form) of the motor skill. In the second option, the biomechanical principles are built into the behavioral objectives criteria, but because these criteria often require external feedback (i.e., students cannot tell whether they are meeting the criteria, whether their form is correct), Mosston's (Mosston & Ashworth, 1986) reciprocal teaching style can be used to evaluate student performance. Reciprocal teaching requires that students learn the specific cues for the behavioral objective and, in partners, give each other feedback in relation to these cues. This approach shifts the burden of checking each student's form from the teacher to students and, in the process, emphasizes personal–social development (kids helping kids).

The third option draws on a different individualized instruction strategy, divergence, which allows students to select their own performance biomechanics and therefore involves the teacher giving a very different kind of feedback. Students are repeatedly asked whether what they are doing is helping them meet the behavioral objective and, if not, what adjustments they need to make. The teacher does not directly correct students' biomechanics, although suggestions might be made (e.g., ''You might try . . .''). Also, correct biomechanics are not modeled for students; students are encouraged to find out what works for them. In a variation of this method, called guided discovery, the teacher allows students to experiment but then points out the correct biomechanics (Mosston & Ashworth, 1986).

All three of these options address the biomechanics question. The teacher's choice depends on a number of factors including willingness to deviate from direct instruction and to what extent self-esteem and responsibility are valued.

INCLUSION, STATIONS, TASK CARDS, AND TEACHING BY INVITATION

We have already inserted three individualization strategies into the motor skill instruction progression: intratask variations, reciprocal teaching, and divergence/guided discovery. One of these, intratask variations, is designed to individualize the behavioral objective. As we mentioned above, this strategy is sometimes difficult to carry out; other individualized approaches may work better in certain situations. Inclusion (Mosston & Ashworth, 1986), for example, encourages students to adjust the behavioral objective themselves—for instance, make 6 out of 10 free throws but stand close enough to the basket to be able to meet this behavioral objective, or make as many volleyball forearm passes in a row to yourself as you can, then try to add one more. For inclusion to work, students have to understand how to do it and have to feel comfortable choosing easier challenges. This works better if there is no

standard; for example, the basketball free throw has a designated distance; students who shorten the distance sometimes feel as if they are not really shooting free throws. Adjusting in order to hit a target on a wall does not create this problem.

Inclusion encourages students to adjust behavioral objectives themselves.

Another individualized approach is to use stations with different behavioral objectives and allow students to choose from among these options. For example, different soccer challenges (behavioral objectives) could be posted in each corner of the room, all focusing on the instep kick but each at a different degree of difficulty (easily done by adjusting the size of the target, distance, or number of successive kicks).

Yet another approach is to create task cards that list all the behavioral-objectives extensions for a particular motor skill. Then students can start at the beginning and work through the list at their own paces, getting help from the teacher or other students if they get stuck at one of the behavioral objectives. Task cards can be put on individual pieces of paper to be tucked into shorts or socks (don't ask for them back!), or they can be posted on the wall. Several task cards for different motor skills, each with its own set of performance objectives, can be used at the same time, with students choosing which motor skills to work on. It is important to begin the task card with a behavioral objective that all students can perform and to include as the last behavioral objective a task that will be extremely difficult for the most skilled student in class.

Finally, teaching by invitation (Graham et al., 1987) can be used to adjust behavioral objectives. This approach calls for the teacher announcing to the entire group that anyone who wants to work on a more difficult, or less difficult, behavioral objective should come to a designated place. This enables students to choose whether they want to change the behavioral objective the teacher has selected for them rather than having the teacher make this decision for them. However, teachers need to be prepared to have no one show up! When students are allowed to choose, their feelings are better protected, but they do not always do what is best for themselves.

MONITORING

While students are doing their performance objectives and extensions of the performance objectives, the teacher must not only roam around refining skills (or using one of the other options that focus on biomechanics) and giving intra-task variations (or using other individualization strategies described earlier) but monitor the entire class for safety and off-task behavior. This

is best done by keeping as many students as possible within eyesight while working with an individual student (e.g., keeping one's back to the wall) and by frequently scanning the entire group left to right or right to left (Barrett, 1979).

Obviously, safety violations require immediate attention—if necessary, interrupting the progression, teacher activity, or individualization strategy; and off-task behavior also requires attention, although in many cases just looking or walking over to the problem area or a quick reminder is sufficient (see the principle of least intervention in chapter 11). There is a notable exception regarding off-task behavior: sometimes lots of kids are off task because they aren't sure what to do or because they have completed the assigned behavioral objective (or because it appears too easy to them). In these cases, stop the entire group and either describe the objective more carefully or assign a new one. It is very easy to get wrapped up in individual help and to ignore the rest of the class. Of course, during the application phase the teacher still needs to monitor for safety and off-task behavior.

PROMPTS AND HUSTLES

Another of the teacher's tasks during the behavioral objective–extension phase of the progression is to create a positive environment for learning by giving prompts and hustles to the group and to individuals. This point will be covered in chapter 11, but it bears noting here as an integral part of learning motor skills. Prompts remind students of what to do *before* they get off task and serve as a reinforcer for appropriate behaviors, whereas nags try to get students back on task ("C'mon folks, let's get back to work"). One PE major, in an effort not to get a nag recorded by an observer, told an off-task student, "This isn't a nag, but you'd better start paying attention!" Instead, a prompt might be "Remember to stay on task" or, before speaking to a group, "I'd like you to pay particular attention to these instructions."

Hustles create enthusiasm: "Let's go, everybody!" "Hustle up!" "Way to go!" They can also be nonverbal, as in handclapping.

SELECTING YOUR APPROACH TO TEACHING MOTOR SKILLS

Selecting your approach depends in part on your curriculum model, which defines the extent of emphasis on motor skill instruction and therefore how much time you will have to put any of these concepts into practice. In addition, you need to evaluate the effectiveness of the familiar demonstrate–drill–play approach versus the motor skill instruction progression we have described and the direct-instruction approach compared to the various forms of individualized instruction we have described. If your values reside more in organized recess or in exposure to a wide variety of activities, you will probably lean toward demonstrate–drill–play. If you value the personal–social development orientation, you will probably use more of the individualized instruction strategies. If, because of the model you have selected, you aren't able to allocate much time to motor skill development, it may be preferable to use direct instruction, which is more efficient.

At this point, you may experience a conflict between your values—what you believe in—and your preferred style of teaching. We have a little more to say about this in chapter 12, but there is no shortcut to confronting the conflict between values and comfort level. Rhetoric is easy—for instance, "I believe in self-esteem development for kids"; putting the rhetoric into practice is quite something else. That's because what you say you value may require substantial changes in what you are used to and familiar with. Drill–demonstration–play is familiar. Direct instruction, usually poorly executed, is familiar. Neither may give much support for what you value.

WRAP-UP

This chapter has described a motor skill instruction framework as an alternative to the demonstration–drill–play approach with which most of you have had considerable experience. The direct-instruction motor skill progression that begins with the set and ends with the close has the support of considerable research, as do the associated teacher activities. The individualized instruction strategies, perhaps because they are difficult to implement, do not have the same strength of research support. However, they do address an important weakness of the direct-instruction approach: the range of motor skills and rates of learning that teachers typically confront.

THE EXPERTS RESPOND

Lynn: I like it. It's data-based, and that's a real strength. My own understanding of the

literature, from reading and workshops, is that direct instruction is more effective, so I'm not so sure about the various individualized instructional approaches in which students make decisions about their goals and give themselves feedback. The rest sounds good.

Robin: (smiling): The thing I like best is the individualized approaches! It pays attention to the needs of individual kids rather than treating them like a herd of goats or something. I particularly like where kids get to make some choices. What I didn't like was the underlying tone of what's best for everybody. For example, I can't believe that all of us learn best with a one-to-one ratio of positives to correctives. Some kids need 20 positives for each corrective, or they fold like suitcases; others need a kick in the butt pretty regularly! Scientific approaches bother me, because they remove the humanness of teaching.

While I'm at it, I agree with this chapter's reluctance to endorse behavioral objectives as an essential component of effective teaching. They certainly wouldn't work with what I'm most interested in: personal–social development.

Pat: (frowning): My response to this chapter: yet another shot taken at traditional instruction! Research says this, research says that. What I am doing, and what many other teachers like me are doing, has withstood a more important test: the test of time. Do you think the demonstrate–drill–play approach would still be around if it didn't work? Give them the mental picture of the skill, practice it to get the feel, and do it in a game. It's simple, and it works. What this chapter advocates is anything but

simple, and who says it works? A bunch of college-professor researchers!

I'd even go farther than Robin and say that behavioral objectives aren't useful anywhere!

Lynn: I think the problem with drills, besides being boring, is that in most cases a lot of kids stand in lines waiting their turns. The idea of performance objectives is to give each kid a ball or whatever and get everyone active—to elevate the academic learning time, as those researchers you love so much say. If you'd pay just a little attention to research, Pat, you would understand why the traditional approach is weak: Kids spend very little of their time doing skills, and teachers spend little of their time teaching!

Pat: Why don't you come to my gym, Lynn, before you start making accusations? Who are these mythical PE teachers the researchers look at anyway?

I have another problem with this approach: the hassle of dragging out all that equipment and being accountable for it, not to mention convincing some administrator to spring for the stuff in the first place.

Lynn: I guess teaching well is a hassle.

Chris: (just back from his second job): Now, now, kiddos; let's not get nasty. I think Pat is right, but he doesn't go far enough. Students learn how to play games by playing games; it doesn't take research to see that, just plain observation. Look at how you learned motor skills. By doing performance objectives, extensions, and the rest of that garbage? No.

SELF-REFLECTION

Well, there you have it. A nice, neat, data-based (for the most part) progression torn to shreds by most of our experts. Let's take another look at this motor skill instruction framework.

1. On a sheet of paper mark down your evaluation of the various pieces of this framework, as indicated in the following chart. What does your experience tell you? Which of these ''pieces'' would you be willing to try with your 30 hypothetical students and stick with long enough to do it well and evaluate the results? (Look up those you don't remember.)

	Sounds good	Would try	Not for me
Set	_____	_____	_____
Model	_____	_____	_____
Mental picture cues	_____	_____	_____
Behavioral objectives	_____	_____	_____
Extensions	_____	_____	_____
Applications	_____	_____	_____
Close	_____	_____	_____
Refine skills	_____	_____	_____
Monitor for safety	_____	_____	_____
Monitor for off-task behavior	_____	_____	_____
Prompts	_____	_____	_____
Hustles	_____	_____	_____
Intratask variations	_____	_____	_____
Reciprocal teaching	_____	_____	_____
Divergence/guided discovery	_____	_____	_____
Stations	_____	_____	_____
Inclusion	_____	_____	_____
Teaching by invitation	_____	_____	_____
Task cards	_____	_____	_____

2. Think about physical education teachers you have had in elementary and secondary school. How many of these things did they do on a regular basis?

3. Interview a younger and an older physical education teacher in a nearby school. Have either ever heard of these concepts? Does either of them say that he or she does any of these things?

SUGGESTED READINGS

Graham, G., Holt/Hale, S., & Parker, M. (1987). *Children moving*. Palo Alto, CA: Mayfield. (This elementary physical education textbook not only breaks new ground by introducing the skill themes model but integrates data-based motor skills instruction as well, including several approaches to individualizing motor skills instruction.)

Mosston, M., & Ashworth, S. (1986). *Teaching physical education: From intent to action*. Columbus, OH: Merrill. (Mosston's spectrum of teaching styles is a unique approach to teaching physical education that emphasizes the gradual individualization of motor skills instruction.)

Rink, J.E. (1985). *Teaching physical education for learning*. St. Louis: Mosby. (Excellent and very complete description of how to teach motor skills based on teacher effectiveness research.)

Siedentop, D. (1983). *Developing teaching skills for physical education* (2nd ed.). Palo Alto, CA: Mayfield. (Another excellent and very complete description of how to teach motor skills based on teacher-effectiveness research. Despite their shared orientation, the Rink book and the Siedentop book each contributes uniquely to our understanding of effective teaching in physical education.)

Chapter 6

Teaching Games

One of our experts, Chris, has been arguing—ad nauseum some might say—for playing active games as the essence of physical education. Teaching games is central not only to the organized-recess model but to the sports education model, the multiactivity model, and to a lesser extent other models. In this chapter, we analyze game playing in physical education: its benefits, its problems, and how to best teach games. Your job, as usual, is to determine to what extent and in what ways game playing fits into your curriculum model (or models) with the 30 hypothetical students we assigned you and, if you decide to include game playing, how best to teach it.

We've all had a lot of experience in game playing—on playgrounds and sandlots, in PE classes, in organized sport. On the surface it's pretty simple: Learn the rules and a few strategies and start to play. Pick up the skills as you go, or practice the skills before playing or in between games. However, if one begins to dig a little deeper, it gets more complicated, as we shall see.

THE PURPOSE OF GAMES

Let's start our analysis with the question we opened this book with: What's the purpose of, in this case, game playing in physical education? According to the motor skill instruction progression described in the last chapter, the purpose of games is to help develop specific

motor skills. The implied ultimate purpose of this motor skill instruction progression is to play games skillfully (although some would argue that learning the skills for their own value is sufficient purpose). This skillful game-playing purpose is also central to the sports education model, which argues that, because sport is integral to the culture, learning to become skilled sport participants and good sportspersons will help to enhance the health and vitality of the culture.

Games can also be used to promote competitive achievement by emphasizing the end product, winning, over the competitive process. When someone asks, "How'd ya do?" after you just finished playing a competitive game, do they want to know how you felt, whether you had fun, whether you played up to your potential, and so on? Or do they want to know whether you won or not? Your answer to this question suggests the extent to which competitive achievement is bound up in game playing. Teachers who believe in competitive achievement emphasize the importance of winning not only in their relationships with students (e.g., in preferential treatment of the motor elite) and in their speeches to the class but also in their use of elimination games, mandatory tournaments, prizes, winners' names posted, students choosing teams, and related activities.

A different purpose for playing games was offered by the organized-recess model. Although this perspective is not taken seriously by university teacher educators, secondary school physical educators often argue for it. As we mentioned in our discussion of organized recess, teachers at a workshop in New York argued for games and "felt strongly that a major purpose of secondary physical education, particularly at the high school level, ought to be stress reduction and relaxation rather than the continuation of an academic day filled with pressure to achieve" (Veal, 1988).

The multiactivity model also makes extensive use of games, in part to teach skills in a wide variety of physical activities, in part to promote physical activity in general, and in part, although this purpose is implicit rather than explicit, to help reduce the boredom of drill after drill in unit after unit. The moral education BIDD model also uses games to help students examine issues of right and wrong, and the responsibility model empowers students to make decisions about self-development and sensitivity to others, in part by using game playing. Morris and Stiehl's (1989) six purposes of games show linkage to several models: skill development (sport education and multiactivity, especially with longer units), fitness development (fitness model), enjoyment and satisfaction (organized recess and, depending upon interpretation, other models), cognitive skill development (concepts model), self-esteem (self-esteem model), and sense of community (cooperation and responsibility models). Finally, from the perspective of the Eastern approach, game playing is an opportunity to achieve a sense of mind–body oneness.

So the teaching of games has considerable support from a variety of perspectives. As we have already suggested in the last chapter, the purpose to which game playing is put will determine how games are taught. If games are to be used for fun, they must be structured so that the vast majority of participants, not just the

skilled kids, have fun. If they are to be used for skill development, they must contribute to the skill development of most of the students. If they are to be used for moral development, the planning must include attention to moral education. If they are to promote mind–body oneness or responsibility or any other model goals, they must focus on those specific purposes.

SOCIAL GOALS IN GAME PLAYING

We will save a description of the role of game playing in the personal–social development models for chapter 9. Suffice it to say that these kinds of outcomes do not occur automatically by playing games—that is, the associated learning theory has been discredited by researchers. To achieve progress toward, say, moral reasoning or respect for others, specific instructional strategies such as postgame discussions or an awareness–empowerment–reflection process need to be employed. In a similar way, cooperation requires more than the presence of teams; it requires a conscious effort to emphasize cooperation.

SPORTS EDUCATION

Games are central to the sports education model. In this model (see Siedentop, 1980a; and Siedentop et al., 1986), the curriculum is organized around seasons rather than units (or themes), with one sport occupying each season. For each seasonal sport, the class is divided into teams that practice together and play together in a formal schedule of competition with a culminating event such as a tournament. As in organized sport, teams practice more at the beginning of the season and less as the formal schedule of competition gets into full swing. The teacher acts as the coach of all teams, although team captains may provide considerable leadership. This model replicates organized sport in physical education, with two or three exceptions. For one thing, team records are kept, but individual statistics are not emphasized. For another, modified games may be part of the formal schedule. For example, the first games of the soccer season may be three-aside games so that everyone can get involved in the game. In this example, several three-aside teams from each team represent their team (rather than choosing three students to represent the whole team). A third possible exception is student involvement or empowerment in decision making. Team captains can act as coaches, and student boards can schedule games, deal with disputes, and so on.

SKILL DEVELOPMENT IN GAME PLAYING

We have suggested that several models have some interest in motor skill acquisition, particularly multiactivity and sports education. And in chapter 5 we questioned the relation of games to skill development. Let's take another look at this issue in more depth, because skill development is often claimed as an outcome of game playing. The last chapter made the point that very little skill learning is accomplished by playing a game. There are several reasons for this. For one thing, most kids don't get very many turns during a game; a few players dominate. Graham and his associates (1987, p. 618) cite an analysis of the game of kickball by Nettie Wilson (1976), who found that the players averaged two attempted catches and, other than the pitcher and catcher, one throw per game, and that a third to half of the kids never caught or threw the ball, most of these being girls.

Check this out for yourself; watch kids playing a game, and focus on one kid at a time, keeping track of his or her participation in the game.

Another reason why game playing produces little skill learning is that usually the games are not at some students' skill levels, causing these kids to just attempt to survive the experience. For many students, and not just the few who really struggle, the pressure of the game is so great that they resort to safe skills (skills they know they can do) instead of using the game to practice or refine their skills. Finally, students receive no individual feedback on their performance during a game except knowledge of results—that is, whether they achieve performance-based goals such as scoring a goal or making a pass in traffic. They receive jeers and criticism from their peers if they "screw up"; but their skills are never refined (see chapter 5), except perhaps after the game.

The applications described in the last chapter attempt to deal with these criticisms by focusing on specific skills in modified games. Morris and Stiehl (1989) expand the notion of applications by suggesting both a process for modifying games so that skill development is a focus and a number of specific games that have been modified to not only help skill development but include everyone as well. (Some of their suggestions are discussed later in this chapter.) Why bother? So students can practice the skills in realistic situations *and* to add some fun to learning. Games are fun—that is, they are fun *if* one is able to participate and have at least some perceived success. They aren't fun for the student who is just trying to survive or who is jeered and criticized.

Refinements of skills by the teacher are more difficult to integrate into game playing. Teachers can sometimes give brief refinements, depending on the game. In tennis, for example, a cue can be reinforced between points, or a brief

Game playing produces little participation or skill learning.

refinement such as ''Good stiff wrist!'' can be shouted during a point. The teacher can also stop play to give feedback to the entire group, amid grumbles by the players, of course. Between games or after the game is a more popular time to talk to the players, although the timing (i.e., the time between the behavior and the refinement) is often lost.

PROMOTING FUN IN GAME PLAYING

Fun is certainly a purpose of the organized-recess model and other models as well. But how can games be taught so that they are fun for everyone? According to what we have just said, kids need to get beyond a feeling of survival, to find some success, to get into the flow of the game. That means they need to get their share of turns and have some success when they take these turns, at least enough so that they feel part of the game and can turn their attention away from the discrepancies in their performance and toward the process and even the product of the game itself. But how can this be accomplished with, say, 30 students of a wide variety of abilities and interests? Not easily!

One way, of course, is to use some form of ability grouping. That way, there would be fewer instances of domination and less pressure. This approach is problematic (see chapter 3 and Pat Griffin's model on p. 51), but two approaches to grouping may have merit. Temporarily grouping students, say for half a period from time to time, gives all students a chance to experience both ability and heterogeneous groupings. Another approach, suggested in the responsibility model, is to give students the choice of playing in the competitive (blood 'n' guts) group, the recreational (hit 'n' giggle) group, or the practice (not-ready-for-a-game-yet or would-rather-work-on-skills) group. Both of these approaches reduce the criticism that ability grouping labels students. Another way, taken from the personal–social development models, would be to allow students to modify the game so that it is fairer for all students. If this approach is used, care needs to be taken that the less skilled have a strong voice in this process. That, of course, is difficult, because they will be intimidated by the skilled kids.

Teachers can also modify the games themselves, as we have already suggested. Modifications can be made in a number of components of any game (see Morris & Stiehl, 1989). The number of players can be changed so that, for example, several games of 5-aside soccer are played instead of one 11-aside game with substitutions. Equipment can be changed so that, for example, two balls are used in a soccer game instead of one. (Try this one, and observe the changes in the action.) Dimensions of the game can be changed—for example, using lower baskets or lower nets. Gary Barette of Adelphi University recommends lowering the volleyball net when the shorter students are on the front line, then changing the lines and raising the net. He also recommends changing the rules of the game so that, for example, in one-pitch softball players get one pitch to hit (pitched by the teacher), players who swing and miss have to be thrown out, and fielders must change positions after each pitch. For younger kids, the elimination game Skunk can be changed by, for example, having the student who got eliminated go to a designated space, take a fake shower to wash off the skunk smell,

and then return to the game. As director of a summer sport camp, one of us organized volleyball and softball games on the side of a mountain. The kids complained at first; it wasn't much like the organized sport they had been experiencing in their communities. They had to find the ball in the tall outfield grass, hit around trees, chase the volleyball down hill, and so on; but they adjusted and became so competitive at these "new games" that we wound up fiddling with the scores ("What's the score? 5-2? I thought it was 6-6?") just to make sure that fun rather than competitive achievement was the major criterion for a successful game. You get the idea. If teachers can loosen up their thinking and focus on how to make the game fun for everyone, they will come up with their own ideas.

Modifications promote fun in games.

GAMES FOR UNDERSTANDING

Werner (1989) argues that games instruction has undergone a number of innovations in the last 10 years, among them New Games and Playfair, which lost momentum after the novelty wore off; cooperative games that deemphasized competition; and game modifications by kids, which requires a talented teacher and underplays the role of games that are popular in the culture. He suggests yet another approach, games for understanding (Almond, 1983; Bunker & Thorpe, 1986). In this approach, students are taught the basic game forms so that they understand the nature of the game, and then game modifications are introduced to teach them the simple tactics and strategies of the game. Motor skill instruction is integrated at appropriate times *after* students have played the game and are motivated to learn more. Game modifications are gradually changed so that the game becomes more and more complex. Three game forms are used as the basis for this approach: wall and net games (e.g., tennis, volleyball), invasion games (e.g., basketball, soccer), and striking and fielding games (e.g., softball, kickball). This approach could augment the concepts model or provide an alternative for sport education or a reorganization of the multiactivity model.

The rationale behind this approach is based on the link between cognition and action, where knowing facilitates doing, and vice versa. Practice conditions in the lesson are structured so that students are taught the minimum rules and procedures and immediately start to play the game. For example, a child's early exposure to tennis may involve a simple throw-and-catch game on a small court in the initial stages, or the use of a higher net, slower ball, and lighter racket to alter the speed of the game. An underarm serve from behind a baseline may be enough to allow a game in which students can experience hitting into space and moving around the court. The exploration of angles will eventually lead to students' making decisions regarding the type of shots to use. Progress is child-paced rather than class-paced, and techniques are taught when they become essential to a child's performance of basic skills. Such an approach makes adaptation to the recognized adult game a small step rather than the huge leap that it often is under traditional methods. It may also lead to better transfer, as students see more readily the relationships among different skill requirements of different games. For example, badminton, tennis, and volleyball have common principles regarding placement of the projectile: length, height over the net, angles, and so forth. Once students understand the principle of placement, it is likely that they will participate in net games more effectively than without such understanding.

A good introduction to an invasion-games course is the game of Keep-Away, because the two-against-one situation is fundamental in the playing of invasion games. The game becomes the focus of the lesson when the players are required to keep possession of the ball for 30 seconds. Immediately students have to think about their roles. For example, the child with the ball may decide to do very little except hold onto it. But the defender, in deciding to attack the ball, may not allow this to happen. Then, because the defender has been drawn toward the ball, space has been created and the pass can be made. This now requires the receiver to take up a good position and so establishes the need to move off the ball, to change direction, and to provide the best possible passing angle.

Now the rule could be changed so that the aim is to pass the ball as many times as possible in 30 seconds. Each pass made counts one point, but each time the ball is touched or intercepted by the defender, the passing team loses three points. Tactical awareness in the form of making and denying space and keeping and preventing possession comes into play. In considering whether it might be better to hold onto the ball rather than release it immediately, students are encouraged to make decisions about what to do and when and how to do it. Such decisions will be based on principles common to invasion games such as soccer, basketball, or hockey. Note that there has been no reference to skills and techniques in this example. However, although skills are not the central aim of the lesson, students are helped to develop new skills (e.g., in passing and controlling) only when they see the need. The emphasis in the games-for-understanding approach is on the need for tactical awareness rather than physical ability in order to understand and appreciate the nature of games.

Further development of the course can include playing small games, such as skittle ball or bench ball, or small-sided games with a reduced goal size. The idea is to develop a passing game in which players are involved in making decisions. For example, when defending, students will decide whether to use a zone defense or mark each opposing player individually, and when attacking, when to create space, support the player in possession, or attack the target. Decisions such as these can be explored through principles of play common to invasion games in general, rather than specific strategies in a particular game (e.g., floor hockey). Timely teacher intervention in the game situation will aid skill selection and promote overall enjoyment of the game.

MIND–BODY ONENESS

The Eastern approach discussed in chapter 4 involves more than game playing. Yoga and Eastern forms of the martial arts, for example, are central to this approach. However, the achievement of mind–body oneness, an avowed purpose of the Eastern approach, is associated with game play in the work of Gallwey (1976), Leonard (1974), and others.

Mind–body unity is an elusive goal, especially when it is perceived as a goal to be achieved. Peak-experience research (Ravizza, 1973) suggests that game players have no control over the occurrence of a peak experience. However, Gallwey (1976) describes a number of instructional strategies designed to promote mind–body oneness by focusing the mind on the moment-by-moment action during game play. Perhaps the most popular of these is the bounce–hit drill, in which players say ''bounce'' every time the tennis ball bounces on the court and ''hit'' every time either player hits the ball. By occupying one's mind in this way, both the mind and the body focus on the moment (rather than one's mind thinking about the last shot or the score or keeping the wrist stiff or . . .). Baseball coach Dan Thompson draws colored stripes on the baseballs he uses in practice and requires hitters to tell him the color and spin of the stripe, thereby causing them to focus on the ball. He believes that this strategy has had a dramatic impact on his players, and he attributes their improvement to an integration of mind and body.

WRAP-UP

Games play a role in most of the models described in chapter 4. Even the fitness model could use games to achieve its objectives (Graham et al., 1987). However, to achieve a specific purpose (depending on the model), games must be taught in a specific way or slanted in a particular direction.

Some models use games to enhance motor skill development, others to add fun to a student's life in school. However, games as they are traditionally played often accomplish neither of these goals. Games need to be changed in accordance with the intended purpose. Fortunately options are available, including applications from the motor skill instruction progression, game modifications, and games for understanding.

THE EXPERTS RESPOND

Chris: You're getting closer (finally), but you still make too big a deal of whatever you are dealing with. Most kids enjoy most games; of those who don't, most of them aren't trying and get what they deserve. If a kid really is having trouble, I take him or her aside and give some specific help. Then back into the game they go. It works!

Robin: This chapter shows a lot of sensitivity to differences among kids and the impact of PE experiences on their feelings. I appreciate the perspective shared here. However, it's not so easy to make a game accessible to all kids, nor is it easy to do cooperative games or to have kids create their own games. I've been trying for several years; modifications sometimes help, and some games work better than others. But it sure isn't foolproof. Yet they expect games as part of the program. It's a problem.

Lynn: Physical education is for skill development. It isn't recreation. Therefore, the only purpose for games is to aid in skill development. Therefore, the only way to teach games is to use the applications idea in the last chapter. Period.

Pat: I tend to agree with Chris. Of course I think kids need demonstrations and drills, but a game is a game. They don't want to play some modified game; they want the real thing. I've tried ability groups; sometimes that has worked, but if we're playing 11-aside soccer, it isn't really possible. And I do want to play the real game. Another thing: Giving an out, such as practicing instead of playing, to kids who don't want to play the game makes no sense to me. They need to learn some discipline; life isn't always a piece of cake; people have to do things they don't want to do sometimes . . . more than sometimes.

SELF-REFLECTION

We're back to you and your 30 students. How much game playing should you do? For what purpose?

1. If you want games to be a part of your curriculum, which of the following purposes makes the most sense to you? Take out a sheet of paper and rank them.

_____ Social goals

_____ Sport education

_____ Skill development

_____ Fun

_____ Competitive achievement

_____ Games for understanding

_____ Mind–body oneness

_____ Other _____

How do these rankings compare to your model rankings at the end of chapter 4? If they don't match up very well, you need to rethink your values and rework your lists (one or the other or both).

2. Is Chris right? Are games the essence of physical education? Is fun the major purpose of physical education? Is Pat right when he says that kids ought to play the real game, not some modification? He also said that everyone ought to play, whether they enjoy the experience or not, in order to learn some discipline and experience what life is really like. Is he right about that? Is Lynn right when she says that motor skill instruction is the only reason for games and therefore that applications make the most sense?

3. Conduct two experiments. Observe kids playing an adult-organized game and look for two things: (a) Count the number of turns each player gets; (b) notice whether the game has been modified in any way. Then observe a kid-organized game and observe the same two things. Any differences? Do kids have any more insight into game playing than adults? You might want to take a look at Coakley's (1986, p. 231-238) research on what happens when kids run their own games versus when adults are in charge.

4. Visit a local school. What kind of game playing typically goes on in physical education? Are cooperative games ever used? Are kids ever asked to modify the games? Are games ever modified to include more kids? Is the games-for-understanding approach ever used? In your opinion, does the game playing you observe help in skill development?

SUGGESTED READINGS

Bunker, D., & Thorpe, R. (1986). *Rethinking games teaching*. Loughborough, England: University of Technology. (A complete description of the games-for-understanding approach.)

Gallwey, W.T. (1976). *Inner tennis*. New York: Random House. (Specific instructional strategies for promoting mind–body oneness in game playing.)

Graham, G., Holt/Hale, S.A., & Parker, M. (1987). *Children moving* (2nd ed.) Palo Alto, CA: Mayfield. (Includes a good chapter on teaching games.)

Morris, D., & Stiehl, J. (1989). *Changing kids' games*. Champaign, IL: Human Kinetics. (The most systematic approach available for modifying games; includes a process for game modification and a number of specific games.)

Orlick, T. (1978). *The cooperative book of games and sports*. New York: Pantheon Books. (Describes a wide variety of cooperative games.)

Siedentop, D., Mand, C., & Taggart, A. (1986). *Physical education: Curriculum and instruction strategies for grades 5-12*. Palo Alto, CA: Mayfield. (Overview of sport education; includes strategies for putting sport education into practice.)

Chapter 7

Teaching Fitness

Perhaps the most popular curriculum model in recent years has been fitness. The fitness/wellness boom in the United States is by all appearances alive and well, at least for individuals who are white, middle class, upwardly mobile, and in the 20-to-40 age range. Advocates have forcefully argued, sometimes in prestigious publications such as *Sports Illustrated*, that school physical education ought to abandon its play/sport focus and substitute strong fitness-based wellness programs, thereby (finally, from their point of view) legitimizing the teaching of physical education in public schools. "If anything," *Sports Illustrated* writer Robert Sullivan (1989) recently wrote, "phys-ed classes need to be made more . . . rigorous . . . [with] activities that improve cardiorespiratory endurance." No less a spokesperson for the nation's health than the surgeon general of the federal government joined the fitness campaign by setting fitness goals for the nation's youth to be achieved by 1990, among them 70% fitness testing and 90% participation in cardiovascular fitness activities (U.S. Department of Health and Human Services, 1980).

Of course, this recommendation has not been without its share of problems. From the physical education teacher's point of view, kids ordinarily don't share the 20- to 40-year-old, white, upwardly mobile middle class's enthusiasm for fitness; many of them just don't find aerobic exercise and strength training all that enticing. (Some do, of course, and some teachers have

been known to develop a motivation for fitness among their students.) In addition, the litany of complaints described in chapter 2 has created a backlash to the trendy wellness movement.

All the same, fitness awareness is at an all-time high in the United States, and more physical education teachers are trying to plug fitness activities into their curricula than ever before. We still hear the associated-learning argument—that fitness is a natural by-product of learning motor skills and playing games—but as people, including physical educators, become more knowledgeable about fitness, they increasingly understand that fitness development requires specified intensities and intervals and, in some cases, specific activities.

A distinction is sometimes made between health-related fitness and performance-related fitness (or motor fitness, or some similar label). Health-related fitness usually refers to flexibility, muscular strength and endurance, aerobic capacity, and weight control (or body composition). The health–fitness connection has received considerable qualified support. For example, Dotson (1988, p. 26) argues that the development and maintenance of these components "provides a buffer to the natural degeneration that comes with middle age," and Casperson (1987) reports that physical inactivity has been identified as one of four primary risk factors in the development of coronary heart disease. Further, health problems that can be ameliorated by fitness have been found in children and youth. For example, coronary heart disease often begins in childhood, not middle age, and some evidence suggests that many children are affected by one or more coronary heart disease risk factors (Heitmann, 1988). Lower back pain has also been found in 25% of youth studied (Liemohn, 1988).

Performance-based fitness, on the other hand, refers to those components necessary to perform well in organized sport and other physical activities, such as strength, power, anaerobic capacity, and agility (if there is such a component). Sports education proponents (such as Siedentop, 1980) argue that performance-based fitness is the only kind of fitness legitimately done in physical education, that health-related fitness belongs in health education. For all the talk about these two different conceptions of fitness, especially regarding choosing an appropriate fitness test (discussed on pp. 84-87), health-related fitness, especially when strength is included (as it almost always is), not only has been shown to be related to physical health but provides a basis for most cultural physical activities as well. For this reason we focus on the health-related fitness components in this chapter.

We have encouraged you to sort through the various curriculum models presented in chapter 4 with the goal of deciding your instructional focus for your 30 hypothetical students. Even if the fitness model is not your first choice, you may want to include some fitness activities for your 30 students—for example, as one or more units in the multiactivity model or blended with the concepts model or as part of your curriculum for teaching responsibility to students. The following instructional concepts will help you determine how much time you will need and what activities are supported and contraindicated in the fitness literature.

TEACHING FLEXIBILITY

Traditionally, flexibility exercises were used to "warm up" young (and old) bodies to prevent injuries. When you were a student in physical education classes or a member of an organized sport team, you may have begun class or practice with a few "cals" (calisthenics), at least some of them involving bouncing this way and that in order to "loosen up" your muscles. Research now suggests that the proper way to warm up is to raise one's body temperature a bit, perhaps by breaking a sweat, and *then* to do flexibility exercises. The easiest way to accomplish this in class is to have students engage in some low-intensity rhythmic activity, such as jogging, low-impact aerobic dance, modified jumping jacks, or a low-intensity game. The point of flexibility is to get the joints to move through their full ranges of motion, and this is best accomplished after the body is warm. There is little evidence to suggest that flexibility exercises prevent injuries; however, doing flexibility exercises without first warming up may *cause* injuries!

Though we just referred to the traditional method of "loosening up," bouncing, this too has been abandoned as the result of research. Injuries can be caused not only by failing to warm up properly but also by vigorously bouncing and jerking the muscles and their attachments. All flexibility exercises need to be executed gently, either by going through the full range of motion at the joint slowly or by going to the point of pain in the range of motion and holding at that point for a count of 10 to 20. Unlike strength and aerobic capacity, too much flexibility can be detrimental, because the stability of the joint is sometimes jeopardized if it becomes too loose. On the other hand, basic orthopedic health is enhanced by a gentle stretching program that maintains range of motion around the joints.

Range of motion exercises can be applied to the neck, shoulder, elbow, wrist, hip, knee, and ankle. To prevent injury at these sites, a few other precautions are necessary. For the neck, the spinal column can be protected by not extending backward. The head should be gently circled forward and to each side; it can also be turned from side to side without extending backward. For the hip and knee, it is safer to do all exercises lying down, thereby stabilizing the lower back and reducing the weight-bearing problem as the range of motion is executed. For example, stretching the hamstrings can best be accomplished by lying on one's back and raising one leg, with knee kept straight, to the perpendicular position or further. Adductors can be stretched by lying on one's side and raising the leg. Knees can be fully flexed while lying on one's back.

Before doing flexibility exercises, raise the body's temperature, perhaps by jogging.

TEACHING STRENGTH

Muscular strength and endurance are somewhat different fitness components, but unless the teacher has access to weight training equipment, they can be treated identically. Without equipment, push-ups, sit-ups, and perhaps a shoulder retractor exercise will work the major upper body muscle groups, which ordinarily are not worked often enough or intensely enough. Of course, such equipment as a pull-up bar, a pegboard, rubber tubing, and a climbing rope offers variety as well as exercise for different upper body muscle groups.

Push-ups work most of the upper body major muscle groups including the triceps, pectorals, deltoids, and, in the flexion phase, biceps. They are easily modified by doing them from the knees instead of the toes or, if necessary, pushing off of a wall with feet placed 3 or 4 feet from the wall. (These modifiers are designed, of course, for those who need them—not for girls, as in "girls' push-ups"). They can also be made more difficult by elevating the feet or, if someone really wants a challenge, by repeatedly pushing up from a headstand position against a wall.

Sit-ups, if executed by curling up 30 to 45 degrees from the floor (90 degrees would be a full sit-up) with knees bent and feet *not* held down, will work the four abdominal muscles rather than just the hip flexors, which are already quite strong in almost all students. The abdominal muscles do not get much work and soon become weak and atrophied unless overloaded. Keeping the feet free helps to force the abdominal muscles to work, and keeping the knees bent while curling up places less stress on the lower back. The abdominal muscles are most active during the first few degrees of the sit-up; therefore, a full sit-up is not necessary.

The hands should not be interlaced behind the head because of the tendency to jerk the head forward at the neck; instead, the hands can be placed on the chest or, to shift gravity toward the head making the sit-ups more difficult, students can hold their ears. Sit-ups can also be modified by doing sit-downs: Start in the sit-up position and slowly let the head and shoulders down until they touch the floor, then scramble back up the easiest way and repeat. Leg lifts to work the abdominal muscles are contraindicated, because when the legs are lifted, considerable strain on the lower back occurs *unless* abdominal muscles are sufficiently strong to hold the back against the floor.

We suggest a third exercise to work another area that receives little attention: the shoulder retractors (the rhomboid and trapezius muscles that restrain the shoulders from slumping forward) and neck extensors. Without equipment, two exercises will work the shoulder retractors: (a) isometric contractions with one's head, shoulders, back, buttocks, and heels against a wall—pushing backward with the upper arms stretched out against the wall but staying against the wall; and (b) lying on one's back and doing a slight reverse push-up by pushing with elbows. Pressing the scapula together is contraindicated according to some sources.

All of these exercises also activate other muscle groups that serve to stabilize the body. However, if a student gets tired and begins to do an exercise differently, inappropriate muscle groups may be recruited.

In order for these and other similar exercises to be effective (that is, to develop strength), students need to overload the targeted muscle groups. This simply means that they need to do more repetitions than they are comfortable doing. However, this is not a simple matter. What is overload for one student is underload for another and over-overload for yet another.

The old "Do 20 push-ups!" is not very effective if one's goal is to overload the major upper body muscle groups. Students must be taught to do as many repetitions as they can. Those who choose not to overload themselves voluntarily either need to be told "It's your body" or else grouped together and given more specific instructions (e.g., "Do 20 push-ups [if possible]"). One of us has told students that they can either overload themselves and get better or go through the motions and by so doing choose not to develop themselves.

Of course, the not-very-hidden message here is that direct instruction (see chapter 5) is ineffective if the teacher's goal is strength overload. The counterargument, which you need to seriously consider if you plan to include strength training in your program, is that a specific number of push-ups for the entire class is more easily monitored and is more likely to ensure some strength development for more students than an individualized approach that allows students to choose their number of repetitions.

In addition to overload, students need to do the same exercises at regular intervals in order to achieve the developmental benefits. This means that bouts of push-ups and sit-ups, for example, need to be repeated at least twice weekly every week. Three times a week is usually recommended as optimal, but the number of class meetings or other model priorities may require a reduction to twice a week or less (although less than that is problematic if the goal is development). Detraining begins to occur when training stops (although detraining occurs gradually in someone who is generally active—i.e., not bedridden), so regularity is important if fitness development and maintenance rather than exposure or conceptual knowledge is the goal. Another option is to use the concepts model to teach students the concept of exercising regularly and then encourage students to exercise outside of class.

The other side of this coin is that the target muscle groups also need to rest and recover between bouts. This is an important consideration in organized sport, especially in these days of multiple seasons and daily doubles and even triples; but physical education classes usually have the opposite problem: getting kids to overload with some regularity.

If weight training equipment is available, a few guidelines will help your program planning. Free weights are more dangerous but work more muscle groups (however, we're sure that legal liability will be more influential than student development in such decision making). Fewer repetitions will build strength (maximal effort in one repetition) a bit more, whereas more repetitions will build more muscular endurance (repeated repetitions). Two or three sets of 4 to 10 repetitions are usually recommended, although some evidence shows development from one set and even one or two reps. Again, at least 2 days a week are recommended, although once a week has sometimes shown slight gains. Record-keeping helps many students stay motivated, not only by showing their improvements but through the reinforcement provided by following the activity with a recording of the activity.

TEACHING AEROBIC ACTIVITIES

Because aerobic activities have been linked to coronary heart disease prevention and to caloric expenditure (and thus to the reduction of body fat), they have received a great deal of attention in both research and practice. Research suggests that aerobic development requires 20 to 60 minutes (with some individual variation) of rhythmic exercises—such as jogging, biking, or swimming—at 60% to 80% of maximum heart rate (approximately 150 to 170 beats per minute for adolescents) 3 to 5 days a week. Again, the concepts of overload, here defined in length of time and percent of maximum heart rate, and interval are essential. The associated learning argument is severely tested here: Any activity that claims aerobic benefits must meet the above criteria. This doesn't mean that aerobic exercise has to be drudgery. However, most games are not made up of medium-intensity rhythmic activities, and most don't elevate and hold the heart rate at the specified level. One caveat in applying these research findings is that most of the studies that provide the basis for these guidelines were relatively short in duration and used subjects unrepresentative of the whole population. We will return to this point shortly.

To the extent that these guidelines are valid, any activity can be used if the intensity and duration can be controlled. Full-court basketball often qualifies, but many team sports such as soccer are more anaerobic (short bursts of exertion followed by rest) than aerobic. However, games can be modified so that they meet aerobic guidelines (Graham et al., 1987; Morris & Stiehl, 1989). Doing aerobic exercise to music has been a popular way to meet these guidelines, but as we will discuss in a moment, it is not without problems. Of course, submaximal continuous activities such as jogging, swimming, cycling, and jumping rope are most likely to meet the aerobic guidelines, but these activities are not always popular with kids, nor are all of them available in all school settings.

Aerobic exercise to music (aerobic dance, aerobics, slimnastics, jazzercize, etc.) has helped to make aerobic exercise fun, but not without some problems. Because orthopedic injuries rose dramatically when aerobic exercise became popular, due to the impact on the joints from bouncing to music, low-impact aerobics were developed. The use of rhythmic music also encouraged bouncing flexibility exercises, some of which are contraindicated, so slow music for slow stretching was introduced to remedy this problem. Individualized exercise was initially ignored, forcing everyone to exercise to the same beat. Creating two sets of exercises, one more strenuous and one less so, helped to the extent that students can now be given at least two choices (assuming that they feel free to choose the less strenuous option).

Aerobic exercise that meets the above guidelines is boring for many kids who are not motivated by extrinsic benefits such as heart health and weight control. One alternative, first suggested by Kenneth Cooper in his 30-points-a-week program (Cooper, 1968), is to focus on the accumulation of exercise time per week rather than on the required guidelines for aerobic development. The most recent research-based recommendation along these lines has been to do activity sufficient to burn 2,000 calories per week above the caloric requirements for basic life activities (Paffenbarger & Hyde, 1980). Calculating caloric expenditure simply requires a chart, which can be found in almost any fitness book. The advantage, of course, is that everything counts, from washing one's car to playing a game of Horse. In addition, this approach circumvents the criticism that the guidelines for aerobic development are based on studies of short duration and a limited population sample. This line of research has helped to spawn the latest fitness craze: walking! Walking possesses the important advantage of producing only low impact on joints, thereby greatly avoiding the orthopedic injuries caused by jogging. For some, fast walking can also approach the aerobic development criteria described above, which have been repeatedly implicated in coronary heart disease prevention.

TEACHING WEIGHT CONTROL

Skinny is in, these days. Ultra-thin models reflect this image, and statistics of beauty pageant winners and centerfolds also show a definite trend toward the fit male body as the ideal female figure according to men. Moreover, the rapid acceleration of incidences of bulimia and anorexia nervosa among young women attests to the impact of this new ideal on some women. Fatness among males is fading fast as a symbol of success. The haranguing of pop fitness experts notwithstanding, percent body fat, the newest significant statistic, is as much a matter of aesthetics as of health. Although much lower figures are often given (based on norms for young, athletic people), for health purposes less than 20% body fat for males and less than 30% for females are reasonable guidelines, although the optimum level of body fat varies from person to person (Katch & McArdle, 1988).

For both aesthetic and health-related goals, the three most important teaching tips are these:

- Spot reducing doesn't work (e.g., sit-ups will not cause a loss of stomach fat); fat accumulates in gender-specific sites and is reduced in these sites in no predictable pattern.
- To lose body fat, exercise or exercise plus diet is required; diet alone tends to atrophy muscle mass.
- A steady pulse rate of 120 to 140 bpm is most efficient for burning fat.

IMPLEMENTATION

What does all of this mean for teaching fitness? First of all, it means that the teacher must pay close attention to what research says about how to do various exercises, in order to prevent injury (e.g., flexibility stretches should be done slowly). Second, it means that students must be overloaded regularly if improvement is to be expected—for example, if upper body strength is the goal, students must do the maximum number of push-ups (for them) at least twice a week. Third, it says that fitness is specific; if aerobic fitness is desired, specific guidelines must be followed to achieve aerobic fitness. Fourth, especially for adolescents, appropriate weight control practices need to be addressed.

A simple fitness program would involve a short warm-up period followed by flexibility exercises, sit-ups, push-ups, and a shoulder retractor exercise. Overload needs to be stressed, and this routine needs to be followed at least twice a week. For aerobic development, at least 20 minutes of medium-intensity rhythmic exercise is required, preferably three times a week, followed by a cool-down period to prevent blood pooling and give the body a period of adjustment. This level of activity will contribute to weight control, and students need to make this connection. In working with kids who resist the idea of 20 minutes of continuous exercise, one of us has used a white lie: "Just jog for a little while and make sure your pulse rate is around 150 when you finish." Then, after they have done this routine for a while, the kids were told, "I told you a white lie a while ago. If you want to improve your aerobic capacity (which we've already talked about), you need to jog longer than you have been, probably about 20 minutes."

Implementation requires more than adherence to fitness concepts. It may be important to review the four sets of alternative strategies for implementing these concepts that have been woven into this chapter. First of all, the teacher is faced with the choice of direct versus individualized instruction throughout this process (as in the motor skill instruction progression in chapter 5). If direct instruction is chosen, students are given the exact task to do (e.g., the number of repetitions). Direct instruction gives the teacher control of the instructional process and is more easily monitored (the teacher knows what to look for). However, the range of student fitness levels reduces the effectiveness of this approach. The alternative is to individualize the tasks, either by shifting the decision of how much to do (e.g., repetitions, time, pulse rate) to the students—"Overload yourselves" or "Try to keep your pulse rate at 150" and so on—or by individually adjusting each student's task after giving the group a task most likely to challenge most of them. (This should sound familiar; it is the intratask variations approach borrowed from the motor skill instruction progression.)

Second, the number of exercise bouts per week and per year will depend on a number of factors, despite the recommendation of 3 days a week for the entire year. The teacher may be interested not in development but in illustrating a particular concept or in exposure to fitness activities or in something else; it all depends on the teacher's model—in the responsibility model, some of these decisions would be turned over to students. And some programs may not have three class meetings per week. Third, the teacher may choose aerobic exercise to music with choices of intensity left to the students or, again, use direct instruction to control everyone's workout intensity. Fourth, the 2,000-calories-per-week approach to aerobic development could be substituted for the more popular aerobic development intensity and frequency guidelines. Or, if the responsibility model is used, students could choose the approach that best motivates them.

Teachers have various options for scheduling these implementation ideas. Leslie Lambert suggests (a) 2 days a week of fitness in a 5-days-per-week program, (b) about half of each period devoted to fitness, or (c) skill-related fitness activities based on the activity focus of the unit (not associated learnings but planned fitness activities that build in skill development—for example, during a soccer warm-up, students may be required to continue moving while they kick and trap).

The fitness program at Forest City Elementary School (K-5) in Garner, Iowa, exemplifies implementation of the fitness model (Kopperud, 1986). The components of the program are (a) an individualized, progressive-overload fitness program planned by the physical education teacher but carried out by the classroom teacher outside of physical education for 15 minutes twice a week; (b) a take-home exercise program; (c) seven fitness concepts that are taught during the physical education class (see chapter 8); and (d) fitness testing twice a year (see the next section).

FITNESS TESTING

Traditionally, fitness tests are administered near the beginning and end of the school year, often without much attention to what goes on in between. (Again, the associated-learning argument has sometimes been used to defend this practice.) Besides the obvious need to help students become fit if they are going to be tested for fitness development, several other matters require attention in testing students for fitness,

among them whether to test, what tests to use, how to administer the tests, and how to handle test results.

Assuming valid tests that are administered properly (which is a large assumption), some test scores can give students an indication of how they compare to other students of the same gender and age (these are called "norm-referenced" tests). Test scores can also give students an indication of their improvement or whether they have reached a specific goal or have met a standard set by the teacher or other authority (e.g., to bench-press one's own body weight as a strength standard). Thus test scores can give students different kinds of information: how they stack up in relation to others, whether they have improved, whether they have achieved their goal or met a standard. Which of these, if any, to emphasize in teaching fitness is open to question. Teachers who emphasize improvement or goal setting argue that this individualizes the testing process, that all students can be successful this way. Teachers who emphasize standards believe that all students must achieve at certain levels that represent minimum competencies to be expected of everyone. Teachers who emphasize norm-referenced tests contend that students need to see where they stand, that such information is motivational, and (sometimes) that students who stand out in such comparisons deserve recognition. If fitness tests are used, how the scores are presented to students will depend on the teacher's purpose for testing. That decision should not be made lightly.

Dotson (1988) argues that norm-referenced tests give the mistaken impression that a particular percentile is a standard, when percentiles are often chosen quite arbitrarily. Scoring at the 85th percentile means that 85% of all students of the same sex and age scored lower and 15% scored higher. Dotson presents standards

Which type of fitness-test result will you emphasize?

for the mile as an indicator of aerobic fitness based on "current protection from the manifestation of risk factors and early onset of degenerative conditions" (p. 30). The actual percentile varies by sex and age, so that, for example, a 13-year-old girl must run the mile in 10 minutes, which is the 57th percentile, whereas a 13-year-old boy must run the mile in 8 minutes, which is the 52nd percentile. These standards are presented in Table 7.1.

Fox and Biddle (1988) have suggested some guidelines for fitness testing that are unusually sensitive to the effects of testing on kids and, as a result, blend the fitness and self-esteem models. They argue that the goal of teaching fitness ought to be lifelong involvement because health-related benefits are not the result of achieving a high fitness score. Fitness then becomes a lifetime "choice behavior," and because kids who don't do well on tests may discount the importance of fitness to protect their self-esteem (as we all tend to do with things that we aren't good at), those who fall below the average on fitness tests require "extra consideration." As further support for emphasizing the fitness process rather than fitness test scores per se, Fox and Biddle cite the influence of genetic ability and stage of maturation on test scores and the need for long-term involvement in order to modify risk factors. These observations led Fox and Biddle (1988) to recommend the following:

- Elimination of skill tests as part of fitness (e.g., shuttle run, softball throw)

Table 7.1   Aerobic Health Fitness Standards for the 1-Mile Run/Walk

| Age | Health fitness standard | | Percentile (norms) | |
	Boys	Girls	Boys	Girls
10	9:30	11:00	58	56
11	9:00	11:00	51	54
12	9:00	11:00	46	49
13	8:00	10:00	52	57
14	7:45	10:00	54	51
15	7:30	10:30	50	56
16	7:30	10:30	49	52
17	7:30	10:30	50	52
18	7:30	10:30	53	55

Note. From "Health fitness standards: Aerobic endurance" by C. Dotson, 1988, *Journal of Physical Education, Recreation, & Dance, 59*, p. 27. Reprinted by permission.

- Emphasis on goal setting and improvement rather than on comparisons to others through norm-referenced tests
- Self-monitoring of improvement
- Confidentiality of test results
- Deemphasis on reward schemes, such as the President's Council's badges for those who score over the 85th percentile ("overcompensates the already gifted [and] may lull the genetically gifted into false sense of security about their health status" [p. 52])
- Treating fitness as a "manageable lifestyle concern" (p. 52)

Several award schemes are available besides the President's Council's performance award. The AAHPERD Physical Best (American Alliance for Health, Physical Education, Recreation and Dance, 1988) offers three awards: a fitness activity badge for participation, a health fitness badge for youth who meet minimum criterion-referenced standards (i.e., specific levels of proficiency based on predetermined criteria, for example, the percent body fat determined to be beneficial to health), and a fitness goals badge for individual improvement. Another award program, Fitnessgram (Institute for Aerobics Research, 1987), offers a similar set of awards. Corbin, Whitehead, and Lovejoy (1988) reviewed the theoretical and empirical evidence related to these reward schemes and concluded that awards for engagement in the process rather than for achievement are preferable:

> In the absence of research to document various reward schemes designed to motivate fitness and regular exercise among youth, we would be wise to apply the best theoretical evidence available. If awards are to be used, we recommend process awards. If performance awards are to be used, we recommend criterion referenced

awards based on good health standards. For special populations, improvement awards can be effective. We do not recommend the use of exclusive normative performance awards. (pp. 213-214)

This research on award schemes supports and clarifies the Fox-Biddle argument concerning the detrimental effects of fitness testing. Fitness tests can be useful indicators and motivators if they are chosen carefully and thoughtfully.

AAHPERD's Physical Best is a specific example of a health-related fitness test battery. Physical Best consists of five tests: a mile run, the sit-and-reach, sit-ups in 1 minute, pull-ups, and a skinfold-caliper body fat test (at two sites).

These tests have reasonable levels of validity and reliability (for field tests) if they are administered properly. Administration time is always a factor, but if the tests are not administered with care, the results will not approach the validity and reliability levels reported for them. With computers, fitness scores can be stored and analyzed much more easily, once they are recorded. However, computers will not improve the validity and reliability of the scores; that depends on test administration.

Should students be allowed to administer fitness tests? Validity and reliability will certainly suffer unless the students are carefully trained, which of course takes up much of the time saved by having students administer the tests. However, if the teacher adopts the responsibility model, shifting responsibility to students is an important consideration. One of us has tried a version of this approach. All students were instructed in the administration of a particular test and then allowed to test themselves, with a partner if necessary. Scores were recorded, but students were told that the scores were for their own information and so they could see their improvement; if they did not take the test process seriously or needed to cheat in reporting their results, that was their choice. Students appeared to work hard, appeared to report true scores, and, after administering posttests in the spring, seemed very interested in whether they had improved. Of course, even if some of them did not work hard or report true scores, that was truly their choice (and, in the social development model, worthy of self-reflection).

As we have said, several fitness test batteries are available for use in physical education classes. The decision about which (if any) to use is important, because it will determine what fitness components are to be tested and, by implication, what fitness components are being promoted as the most important.

WRAP-UP

Developing student fitness—when it is defined as flexibility, strength, weight control, and aerobic development—requires a considerable commitment on the part of the physical education teacher, certainly more than a few cals at the beginning of the period. Although there is still some controversy in the literature, the scientific basis for a sound fitness program has been established. The questions that remain include the role of fitness in American society, the role of fitness in a physical education program, the role of individualization in fitness instruction, and the role of fitness testing.

THE EXPERTS RESPOND

Pat: This is getting tiresome: another attack on traditional physical education. Research tells us this, research tells us that. I don't trust research, and I'll tell you why. I've been doing 5 minutes or so of cals at the beginning of my classes for years now, with—horrors—some bouncing and—more horrors—without what research now says is the proper warm-up, and guess what? My students have reported no injuries! And don't tell me they don't get an aerobic workout from playing basketball or soccer; you can tell they are from how hard they are breathing. I know, not all the kids breathe hard—but nothing reaches all the kids, and certainly not what has been suggested in this chapter.

Also, I'm getting sick and tired of the strong bias in this book toward individualizing everything. It's clear that these authors have never taught real kids! You need to shoot the middle (for example, give them a specific number of push-ups to do that fits the average kid) just to survive (I'm beginning to sound like Chris!), but it works pretty well, anyway. Besides, life is a matter of meeting other people's standards, not setting your own.

Lynn: I couldn't disagree more with your comments on research. Research provides us with some answers based on evidence, so we don't have to fly by the collective seats of our pants. Don't tell me you still have your kids do straight-legged sit-ups, Pat? I'll bet not. I also bet you don't teach them that sit-ups reduce stomach fat or that water deprivation is good for you during exercise. Of course not. You pay attention to research and don't even know it!

Because research supports direct instruction, so do I. However, I'm not sure about its relevance for fitness.

My concern with this chapter is not its research basis but the time it takes to properly teach and test for fitness. I'm not sure I want to take time away from motor skill development—based on research of course—to teach fitness.

Robin: That's very interesting, Lynn. You've just made a decision, to teach motor skills rather than fitness, based not on research but on your own values! (Pat smiles.) Research has its place, but our beliefs and values often fall outside the boundaries of science. For example, I use a lot of fitness activities, not because they promote health but because they are easily individualized, are not necessarily competitive (especially if norm-referenced tests are avoided), and for a lot of kids are easier to get better at than motor skills (if you keep doing push-ups you'll get better at them, but you can shoot jump shots forever and not get better without feedback, and so on). And I like the idea of kids testing themselves. My decision to use fitness is not based on science; it's based on my goals for my kids, my purpose for physical education. I guess I couldn't be farther apart from you, Pat, on this direct instruction business; it is just the opposite of my program's purpose.

Of course—and this is another place where Pat and I part company—I try to follow the guidelines of science in teaching fitness so that no one gets hurt and they get the most benefit from the exercises.

One more point: If norm-referenced fitness tests are used, we are setting up one more tournament for kids to navigate through. Those kids who are successful at competitive games will like the challenge, but the others, who could have found something different in fitness, will be turned off to fitness just as they are to other forms of competition. If, on the other hand, they are allowed to set their own goals and/or are judged on their improvement, they will be reinforced (note that research word) and will be motivated to continue . . . and will feel good about themselves!

Chris: This whole discussion is pretty irrelevant from my point of view, because I don't teach fitness. Playing games is my focus. Kids like games; they don't like fitness. That doesn't mean they aren't getting fit; despite what these chapters keep saying about associated learning being hooey, kids get fit by playing. More importantly, playing games makes my job easier, and, despite all this altruistic talk about what's best for kids, let's face it: We teachers have got to survive. And that goes double for administering fitness tests. They are a pain! I do them when my principal tells me to, which is when he wants to show the PTA or school board some statistics!

SELF-REFLECTION

Our experts' discussion highlights the importance of clarifying what contribution you want your physical education program to make to your students. It also emphasizes the importance of knowing the science of fitness, if teaching fitness is to be part of your program. We agree with Lynn that even Pat probably pays more attention to science than he cares to admit.

Here is a little true–false fitness concepts quiz you can use to check your own fitness science base. (This quiz will also prepare you for the next chapter.) On a sheet of paper, write the number for each question, and next to it a *T* or *F*. Then check your answers against the answer key at the end of the quiz.

1. Flexibility exercises are known to help prevent injuries.

2. Slow stretching is better than bouncing.

3. Shoulder retractor muscles are sufficiently strong without being exercised.

4. Sit-ups should be done with the feet held down.

5. Sit-ups should be done with hands interlaced behind head.

6. Leg lifts are good abdominal exercises.

7. Females should do push-ups off their knees.

8. Burning 2,000 calories a week in some form of exercise will offer some coronary heart disease protection.

9. For most of us, sustaining a heart rate of 150 beats per minute for 20 minutes three days a week is sufficient to give us some coronary heart disease protection.

10. To be healthy, males should have no more than 15% body fat and females no more than 22%.

   (Answers: 1-F, 2-T, 3-F, 4-F, 5-F, 6-F, 7-F, 8-T, 9-T, 10-F. If you missed any, look up the answers and explanations in this chapter, so that in the future you will know not only what but why.)

Observe two or three school physical education classes. What is the role of fitness in each? To what extent are the scientific principles described in this chapter followed in the fitness instruction you observe? Are the fitness exercises individualized, or is direct instruction

used? Does the approach you observe seem to work?

If you do decide to teach fitness to your 30 hypothetical students, a number of questions need to be addressed.

1. What fitness components will you teach? Flexibility? Strength? Aerobic development? Weight control? Others?

2. Can you devote sufficient time to whatever fitness components you choose to teach and still reach your other goals?

3. Will you individualize so each student overloads appropriately? Or are you persuaded that direct instruction is more likely to achieve more fitness for more students?

4. Will you test your students? If so, for what purpose? If so, what test will you use? Will you use an award scheme? If so, which one?

5. Will you teach fitness concepts to your students? This last question is the focus of the next chapter.

SUGGESTED READINGS

American Alliance for Health, Physical Education, Recreation and Dance. (1988). *Physical best: The American Alliance physical fitness education and assessment program*. Reston, VA: Author. (A fitness test battery and awards scheme recently developed by recognized fitness experts; offers an alternative to the President's Council tests and awards.)

Dotson, C. (1988). Health fitness standards: Aerobic endurance. *Journal of Physical Education, Recreation, & Dance*, **59**, 26-31. (Excellent discussion of standards, rather than norms, for aerobic endurance.)

Fox, K.R., & Biddle, S.J.H. (1988). The use of fitness tests: Educational and psychological considerations. *Journal of Physical Education, Recreation, & Dance*, **59**, 47-53. (Excellent discussion of fitness testing from the perspective of the self-esteem model.)

Institute for Aerobics Research. (1987). *Fitnessgram*. Dallas: Author. (Another fitness test battery and awards scheme devised by recognized fitness experts; offers an alternative to the President's Council tests and awards.)

Katch, F.I., & McArdle, W.D. (1988). *Nutrition, weight control, and exercise*. Philadelphia: Lea & Febiger. (Research-based fitness book; contains valuable tables.)

Kopperud, K. (1986). An emphasis on physical fitness. *Journal of Physical Education, Recreation, and Dance*, **57**, 18-22. (A fitness model exemplar for elementary physical education; described in sufficient detail for replication.)

Liemohn, W. (1988). Flexibility and muscular strength. *Journal of Physical Education, Recreation, & Dance*, **59**, 37-40. (Good description of flexibility and sit-up principles.)

President's Council for Physical Fitness and Sports. (1985). *The presidential physical fitness award program*. Washington, DC: Author. (Norm-referenced approach to fitness awards.)

Siedentop, D., Mand, C., & Taggart, A. (1986). *Physical education: Curriculum and instruction strategies for grades 5-12*. Palo Alto, CA: Mayfield. (A chapter on fitness that describes in some detail several school fitness programs.)

Chapter 8

Teaching Concepts

An important consideration in teaching fitness and motor skills is whether to teach students the underlying concepts. Of course, teachers must know the concepts in order to teach—students won't become more fit unless they are taught to overload, and they won't improve in motor skills without practice and feedback. However, do students need to learn these concepts or just to follow the teacher's instructions?

The concepts model introduced in chapter 4 emphasizes learning the why and how of movement throughout the physical education curriculum. In this model, students often engage in problem-solving experiments to discover the underlying concepts. Take a wrestling class, for example. From the down wrestling position, the student on top is told to try to take down his or her partner, and the student on the bottom is told to resist. Afterward, students are asked what principles they used in the takedown and in resisting the takedown (e.g., breaking down the base of support, lowering the center of gravity). Classes sometimes resemble university exercise physiology, kinesiology (biomechanics), or even sport psychology or sociology courses. Diagnostic testing is common, and evaluation is often based at least in part on written assignments and written tests.

In general, this model has received more attention at the college level as a general education course. However, noted scholars such as

Chuck Corbin and Hal Lawson have argued for its inclusion in school programs, and the conceptually based *Basic Stuff* series has been promoted vigorously by the National Association of Sport and Physical Education since its inception in 1981.

Why has the conceptual approach received all this recent attention? Two reasons stand out. First, the notion of physical education as a lifetime pursuit has led some physical educators to advocate teaching kids the concepts so that they possess a sound basis for teaching themselves in their future activities. For example, if students understand concepts such as overload, they will be able to build their own fitness programs. Otherwise, they will only be able to duplicate, insofar as they can remember, what they did in their physical education classes without knowing why or, importantly, whether what they are doing will achieve the results they desire. Corbin (1987), probably the most articulate and prolific spokesperson for this model, argues that teaching concepts requires teachers to employ higher order objectives such as problem solving. An old saying has been quoted often in this regard: ''Give me a fish, and I'll eat for a day; teach me to fish, and I'll eat for a lifetime.''

A second reason for the recent popularity of this approach (in the literature, if not among practicing teachers) involves the reconceptualization of physical education as an academic discipline in higher education. In the 1960s,

Will you give your students a fish, or *teach* them to fish?

following the lead of exercise physiology, several subdisciplines emerged—including biomechanics, sport sociology, sport psychology, and sport philosophy—each with the avowed purpose of expanding the body of knowledge in its specialized area and each with its own parent discipline (e.g., physics, sociology, psychology, philosophy). Even the area of curriculum and instruction succumbed, renaming itself (at least in many universities) ''sport pedagogy'' and aligning itself with the popular lines of research in education. All of this activity was aimed at demonstrating that physical education is an academic discipline with a distinct body of knowledge rather than ''just'' a profession, thereby (although there is some disagreement concerning the intention of this trend) tending to legitimize physical education in higher education. Of course, the field paid a price for attempting to gain academic respectability. For example, the relationship between the academic discipline and the profession became a heated issue as the expansion of the body of knowledge clashed with the need for addressing applied problems. Moreover, how all these subdisciplines with different parent disciplines fit into a coherent whole has been the subject of seemingly endless position papers. The implication of this recent history for teaching concepts is just this: For whatever reasons, physical education has now developed a substantial body of knowledge (some would say bodies of knowledge) that can be taught not only to university physical education majors but to students at all levels.

THE INTEGRATED APPROACH

Three approaches to teaching concepts have been implemented in school physical education classes. The integrated approach is perhaps the most popular and is often advocated by those whose primary physical education purpose is other than the conceptual model. However, it is the most often abused as well. The integrated approach simply involves teaching concepts in the course of whatever lesson is being taught. For example, while students are doing push-ups, overload can be explained. The relation of pulse rate to aerobic exercise can be explained while students are taking their pulse rates after jogging. The importance of practice can be explained in an introduction to a drill or challenge. The reason for feedback can be explained as part of the instructions for doing reciprocal teaching. The historical-cultural context of sport can be slipped into an introduction to soccer (e.g., "Not using the hands in sport used to be considered unAmerican!").

This approach is often given lip service. Many physical education teachers say that they use it, but when they are observed, very little concept teaching goes on. In other words, it is very easy to intend to integrate concepts into one's lesson, but quite another matter to actually do it.

Technically, such integration is not very difficult if one knows the concepts. It simply requires developing one-liners ("To get better, you need to do more than you are comfortable doing; that's called *overload*") for each concept and then working these one-liners into the lesson. Perhaps the most organized way to deal with this approach is to list the concepts to be taught in a particular lesson, then to transform each concept into a one-liner, and finally to figure out when each of these one-liners will be introduced. To be certain that this plan is carried out, a note (mental or otherwise) can be made after class of how many one-liners were actually used in class, or an evaluation of what students are learning can be conducted by using brief paper-and-pencil quizzes. Teachers who engage in this process for a while will find that it will become an integral part of their teaching, and they won't need to prepare in such a detailed way.

As an example of this approach, consider a lesson focused on the volleyball forearm pass. These concepts might be identified for the lesson: warm-up, mental image of the skill, rebound, and practice. For each of these concepts a one-liner is needed, accompanied by its place in the lesson. For example:

Warm-Up: "Get your body temperature up a little, so that you'll be less likely to injure yourself." Use: When students are told to jog around the gym a few times to open class.

Mental Image of the Skill: "You need a picture in your head of what this skill looks like, in order to do it correctly." Use: Just before the skill is modeled and cues are given.

Rebound: "The ball will rebound high enough that you won't have to swing your arms much, based on the speed of the incoming ball." Use: When the cue about how to strike ball is given.

Practice: "You won't improve if you don't do the skill correctly a number of times." Use: When giving students the behavioral objective of bumping 10 in a row.

LAB DAYS

A second approach, more or less segregated from (rather than integrated with) the rest of the physical education program but perhaps easier to pull off, involves conducting laboratory days, sometimes referred to as lecture-lab sessions, on a regular basis (e.g., once every week or 2 weeks or month). Once lab days are scheduled, the teacher is forced to identify concepts and related experiences that will serve as lessons for each lab day. As a result, lab days pressure teachers to comply with their own intentions to a greater extent than the integrated approach.

Lab days can be organized around any number of concepts. Usually lab days are used as part of a unit. For example, the lab day for a weight training unit could encompass overload exercises, differences between strength and muscular endurance, experiencing both full range and limited range of motion, principles of angles and levers, and so on. The lab day for a wrestling unit could entail concepts of stability, balance, and joint action. An aerobic dance lab day could involve concepts of aerobic development through discussion of pulse rates and the advantages of slow stretching. Of course, all of these concepts could be integrated into the unit rather than treated as separate lab days, depending on one's rate of compliance in the integrated approach, organizational preference, and other factors.

Lab days force teachers to comply with their concept-oriented intentions to a greater extent than the integrated approach.

Some teachers prefer to reserve a classroom (if available) for the lab day or for the lecture part of the lab day, reasoning that the gym connotes movement to the students or that the classroom encourages a more serious attitude toward studying concepts. Bill White brought his inner-city physical education classes to the classroom about once every 2 weeks (sometimes more often), based on his belief in the concepts model, and when one of us interviewed these students at the end of the school year, he learned that almost all of Bill's students felt that these sessions were not only beneficial but essential for a PE class, even though they weren't much fun. Other teachers who use lab days shun the classroom, because they believe that the association of the classroom with physical education makes teaching concepts more difficult or that concepts ought to be taught along with, rather than separated from, movement.

SPECIAL UNITS

The special unit approach is the most full-blown application of the concepts model and most closely parallels the subdisciplines in higher education. It is fully explicated in Lawson and Placek (1981). Rather than have units of soccer, gymnastics, basketball, and so on, or in addition to these kinds of units, units are based on the subdisciplines. For example, Lawson and Placek suggest units of exercise and fitness; nutrition, exercise, and cardiovascular disease; biomechanics; play, games, and sport; mind–body unity and aesthetics; and motor learning. In each of these units, students both learn and experience the concepts, so that physical education is still a movement experience, albeit a heavily cognitive one. Here are some examples adapted from Lawson and Placek:

Exercise and Fitness: Design a training program based upon scientific fitness principles.

Nutrition, Exercise, and Cardiovascular Disease: Keep caloric expenditure data based on the amounts and kinds of exercise being done.

Biomechanics: Analyze the effect of spin in a basketball shot.

Play, Games, and Sport: Analyze the ethics of fair play after playing a game. (Note that this may be similar to the moral education model, depending on the extent to which a specific concept is being investigated.)

Mind–Body Unity and Aesthetics: Identify factors that determine aesthetic satisfaction in a particular activity.

Motor Learning: Identify a learning problem being experienced and a solution for this problem.

WRAP-UP

Concepts form the basis for effective instruction. If the teacher is not aware of, or does not implement, the latest conceptual developments, his or her physical education program will not be very effective. However, whether to teach these concepts to students is another matter. The concepts model is founded on the notion that students need to understand not only what they are doing and how they are supposed to do it but also why it is important and why it works that way. If they learn the concepts underlying what they are asked to do, they may better understand the importance of the activity and be able to apply the concepts in their postschool lives.

Three approaches are used to promote the conceptual basis for physical education activities. The integrated approach is most common but requires some diligence to apply. Lab days, if scheduled, force the teacher to teach concepts but may disrupt the flow of the activity. Special units are a modified replication of the recent development of subdisciplines in higher education physical education programs.

THE EXPERTS RESPOND

Pat: It seems to me that three fourths of this chapter is pure hooey and one fourth is good old common sense. Why in the world would any teachers worth their salt want to drag students through lab days or special units? These gimmicks are watered-down versions of PE-major classes, which all of us know were mostly irrelevant to what it takes to be a good physical education teacher, let alone what it takes to be good at motor skills and fitness. Sure, I learned a few things about fitness and a few things about teaching motor skills. But the Krebs Cycle? The socialization process? Short-term memory? Newton's laws? They were worthless in teacher training, and they're worthless now! I'm surprised I remember some of these irrelevancies; as a matter of fact, they're taking up space in my brain that could be used for much better purposes!

As for the integrated approach, any good teacher does some of this. That's where the few good things I did learn in college and elsewhere—mostly elsewhere—come in. It helps kids to understand why, especially in today's world when they're always asking why—that is, as long as it doesn't take away from doing the activities.

Robin: I like the concepts approach, to a point. I think Pat is right—although I can't believe we are agreeing on something—that the subdisciplinary business is pretty irrelevant for teachers, at least as I experienced it. However, if I want my students to exercise some responsibility for their own physical education programs, and I do, then they will need to know some concepts. How can I expect a student who wants to lose weight to develop a program for this if he or she has no knowledge of how to lose weight? My students who want to get better at, say, basketball, almost always say the best way is by playing; they need to know the concepts of having a mental picture, practice, and feedback—and maybe even closed and open skills—before making their own plans.

Chris: Concepts have no place in my model of teaching, which is what you call organized recess, unless you count strategies in team

sports. I give them a little of that sometimes, but it wasn't mentioned in this chapter. Pretty typical of this book so far from what I can see: Ignore the stuff that would really help PE teachers, and emphasize a bunch of loony-tunes ideas that no one takes seriously.

Lynn: My argument all along, in case you missed it, is that we need to pay more attention to science. The concepts approach does just that. Students who experience this approach will be much better informed than most of the rest of society. My only hesitation is that it takes away from motor skill development. As Robin has painfully pointed out in another chapter, that is what I value. Perhaps by using the integrated approach, I could do both.

SELF-REFLECTION

We are on the verge of calling in another expert, because none of these four advocated either lab days or special units. Perhaps it is sufficient to say, if you haven't figured it out yet, that these experts do not have the final word. Nor do we. You do.

Whether you choose to teach concepts to your 30 hypothetical students depends, as we have emphasized again and again, on your own sense of purpose and your interpretation of what your students need. Unlike Chris and to some extent Pat, we don't believe that good teaching can proceed without a sound conceptual foundation—that is, teachers need to know things like overload, skill analysis, the relationship of practice and feedback to learning, and so on. But do students need to be taught these things?

1. Interview a physical education teacher who you think has a good grasp of the concepts

necessary to teach motor skills and fitness. Does she or he teach concepts to students? Why or why not? Would you teach concepts to your 30 hypothetical students? Why or why not?

2. Suppose for a minute that you were required to teach concepts to your students. Let's say that you were required to teach three concepts during a physical activity unit (we're not implying that units are the best way to organize a program) of your choice. What would they be? How would you teach them? The integrated approach? Lab days? Or would you rather develop a special unit—say, exercise physiology (or whatever)—to teach your concepts?

3. If, like our experts, you prefer the integrated approach, how would you make certain that you did indeed teach the three concepts, especially if your job were at stake in this little scenario?

SUGGESTED READINGS

Corbin, C.B., & Lindsay, R. (1985). *Fitness for life* (2nd ed.). Glenview, IL: Scott Foresman. (A very popular conceptual approach to teaching physical education, with specific lessons and activities.)

Kneer, M. (Ed.) (1981). *The basic stuff series*. Reston, VA: AAHPERD. (Six booklets designed to give conceptual answers to questions that kids might ask in different subdisciplinary areas, and three booklets that show how to teach concepts to students of different ages.)

Lawson, H.A., & Placek, J.H. (1981). *Physical education in the secondary schools: Curricular alternatives*. Boston: Allyn & Bacon. (A detailed description of the subdisciplinary unit approach to teaching concepts; includes sample lessons.)

Chapter 9

Personal and Social Development Models

In chapter 4 we described personal–social development as one of many possible curriculum perspectives currently available to physical educators and pointed out that personal–social development claims have been an integral part of physical education's history. Personal–social development refers to a wide range of affective-domain attributes such as self-esteem, courage, cooperation, and fair play. In a review of the publications of past physical education leaders, Miller and Jarman (1988) provide considerable evidence not only of the central role of "moral and ethical character development" in the exhortations of past leaders but of their awareness that physical education teachers must consciously teach toward these outcomes if they are to occur. For example, in 1947 Oberteuffer stated

> that the teaching of values of the ethical-moral plane must assuredly be as definite and planned for as those of skill. . . . We need to isolate them, see them, teach them, and evaluate their development as surely as we measure speed in swimming. (Miller & Jarman, 1988, p. 75)

Personal–social development has occupied such a central role in physical education because the gym, as a place of high emotion and interaction, holds the potential for educating not only the body but the whole person as well.

The attraction of physical activity for some young people also provides a "door-opener" to dealing with broader life issues. This notion of "life in the gym," with its potential for personal and social as well as physical development, is seen by personal–social development advocates as a way of helping students navigate through, or rise above, the escalating social problems in American society. Despite the claims and exhortations of physical education leaders, research has for the most part shown little evidence of personal and social development in physical education programs. Two factors account for this dismal showing. First, conceptualization of the affective domain is beset with confusion, so it is necessary to clearly specify and limit the number of goals in any personal–social development model. Second, personal–social development claims have not been accompanied by specific instructional strategies despite the exhortations of some physical education leaders, so it is also necessary to develop instructional strategies specific to these goals. Until recently, neither of these conditions has been met.

Recently, several personal–social development models containing both goals and instructional strategies have been developed and are now available for implementation. This chapter describes the work that has been done in self-esteem and moral education, introduces outdoor pursuits and adventure education as a different kind of subject matter for this purpose, and closes with an extended discussion of a self- and social responsibility model that has been under development for 20 years and that encompasses many of the concepts and strategies of the other personal–social development models.

SELF-ESTEEM

Self-esteem, one of the personal–social development models described in chapter 4, is often viewed as a primary indicator of a person's emotional adjustment and mental health and therefore often appears as a curriculum objective in school programs. Hales (1985) argues that one of the most basic human needs is the management of one's self-esteem, a time-consuming activity necessary in order to feel good about oneself. The nature of self-esteem is still under investigation, but it appears that everyone possesses a global self-esteem—a general feeling that "I am OK" or "I am not OK"—which is composed of a number of more specific feelings about various aspects of the self (e.g., myself as student, myself as friend, myself as athlete). Just how a person computes her or his global self-esteem from these various more specific self-esteems is not clear, but the physical self is part of this process. Harter's (1986) research shows that children over 8 identify physical appearance and athletic ability as two of five distinct dimensions of self-esteem, the others being scholastic ability, social acceptance, and behavioral conduct. Fox (1988) suggests that four components—sport competence, physical strength, physical condition, and attractive body—contribute to physical self-esteem (or body image), which in turn contributes to global self-esteem.

The determination of a person's self-esteem is further complicated by the value a person places on each of the factors contributing to global self-esteem, so that self-esteem becomes the discrepancy between a person's evaluation of each self-esteem component (e.g., physical appearance) and how much that person values success in that component (Harter, 1986). A person's values are to a great extent determined by social influences, although "there is also scope for individuals to customize their self-esteem structure" (Fox, 1988). This means that, unless powerful social forces intervene, students can discount those activities in which they don't perform well, thereby protecting (or managing) their self-esteem. Powerful social forces related to physical activity are at work here, of course. The value of physical appearance is particularly strong, and the active play world is very important to most children, although its importance diminishes with age for many individuals. Competitive achievement in sport is also a value in our culture, more so than in almost any other culture (Coakley, 1986).

To further complicate this issue, everyone possesses both an inside (or phenomenal) and outside (or social) self (Thomas, 1983). The outside self consists of everything others can see—behaviors, appearance, "stats" (e.g., batting average), and so on. The inside self is less visible. Here resides a person's aspirations and hopes, personal victories and defeats, personal struggles, hidden feelings. To the extent that one's self-esteem is the product of comparing oneself to others directly and indirectly and of feedback from significant others, one's inside self is minimized.

What strategies should a physical educator interested in developing self-esteem in students employ? The recommendation made in chapter 5 to improve the ratio of positive to corrective feedback statements would help, but this is only a beginning. Based on research (Weiss, 1987) that suggests that perceived competence rather than competence itself is crucial to self-esteem development, two of Fox's (1988) recommendations make sense:

- Teachers need to redefine success for students, so that the focus becomes improvement and effort rather than peer comparisons and norms, at least for those students for whom achievement seeking does not lead to perceived competence.
- Remedial support needs to be given to those who perceive themselves to be fat, weak, clumsy, or afraid.

If self-esteem is the goal, teachers need to pay more attention to students' inside selves. This means listening to students (see chapter 13); building in one-on-one conferences, during class if necessary (remembering that if self-esteem is the program's goal, such activities are warranted); and giving students choices including the use of verbal and written contracts. Many of the decision-making processes described below as part of the responsibility model would be helpful here. Furthermore, research (Weiss, 1987) suggests that self-esteem is enhanced less by skill and fitness improvement than by perceptions that such improvement is attributable to the performer rather than the teacher. If this is true, teaching students to be responsible for their own learning and development would contribute to positive self-esteem. Again, the responsibility model described below would be helpful from this perspective.

Another way to promote self-esteem is to use coping models rather than ideal models in demonstrations and play (Schunk, 1987). A coping model communicates to students that the instructor is not perfect, that the instructor has to struggle to master skills, too.

Listening to students helps build students' self-esteem.

As we have already pointed out, personal and social development as a model for physical education does not define the subject matter to be taught. However, fitness activities—because they are easier to individualize, less competitive, and easier to improve—may offer more potential for developing self-esteem than team sports.

MORAL EDUCATION

A recent line of research (Weiss & Bredemeier, 1986) suggests a different model of personal–social development: moral education. The goals of moral education are to promote moral reasoning, put moral reasoning into action, and deepen affective commitment to moral reasoning. Several strategies can be used to reach these goals. The first, and perhaps most carefully studied, is the Built-In Dilemmas/Dialogue (BIDD) (Romance et al., 1986), which is based on the structural-developmental work of psychologists Norma Haan and Lawrence Kohlberg. In this approach, students are routinely confronted with moral dilemmas related to fairness and student welfare in games. One way to do this is to ask students whether the game they have just played was fair for everyone—did everybody get turns, did everybody have fun, and so on. Another BIDD approach is to create moral dilemmas in game situations. For example, students are told to shoot baskets in teams of two, with the first team to get 10 baskets to be declared the winner. They are then asked how they decided who was to shoot first and whether their approach was fair. In another basketball example, students are told to play two-on-one basketball with the same person always playing defense, except that they can change the game if this approach proves unsatisfactory. After the game, students are asked whether the two students on offense voted to change the game so that the defender could play offense and whether they should have changed the game. In other examples, students play games with and without officials and with competitive and cooperative rules, followed by discussions of the advantages and disadvantages of these approaches.

A related approach is to process problems as they arise in class. Fair play, cooperation, competition, and other issues are certain to be part of the typical physical education experience.

Another BIDD approach is to have students create their own games by following fair-play rules such as everyone participates and everyone has fun. Morris and Stiehl (1989) suggest a seven-step process to help kids create their own games:

1. Introduce the idea that any game can be played several ways.
2. Show how to analyze the components of a game.

3. Allow students to generate alternatives to a specific game, preferably in small groups.
4. Try out some of the alternatives.
5. Encourage students to continue to generate and try out alternative ideas.
6. Consolidate student ideas, and show students what they have accomplished.
7. Use this model with different games *and* encourage the creation of entirely new games.

Almond (1983) suggests a slightly different set of criteria for creating new games that emphasizes developing rationales for rules of the game and teaching others how to play the newly created game. In one of Torbert's and Schneider's (1989, p. 19) efforts to modify floor hockey to make it safer, a second grader, in response to the "bunching and mob-like battles over the puck . . . came up with the idea that once you have possession of the puck and are not moving, no one else can touch the puck until it has been played."

Still another moral education approach is to link specific sport-related moral issues to general life situations whenever possible. For example, how much cooperation is needed to play a competitive game? How much cooperation is needed to drive a car in traffic? Is cheating in sport any different than cheating in life?

Finally, principles underlying discipline procedures ought to be stated and discussed according to this moral education model so that students learn to conceptualize right and wrong—to question and understand why rules are needed.

Personal–social development models tend to dictate subject matter less than most other models; however, implementing these approaches to moral education often requires team sports and games. Also, moral education requires an allotment of time, which limits emphasis on other program goals, although one study (Romance et al., 1986) demonstrated that, at least in one activity, skill development was not impeded by introduction of the moral development model.

Weiss and Bredemeier (1986) also discuss the relevance of social learning theory for moral education. Although they believe it is not as powerful a construct, such strategies as modeling good sportsmanship by teachers, developing a sportsmanship code with appropriate rewards and punishments, and providing explanations for sportsmanship are helpful in promoting moral education.

Another moral education model is advocated by Orlick (1978a), who argues that "all of the major problems confronting man, including violence, destructiveness, war, poverty, pollution, crime, corruption, human exploitation, even rampant strikes and inflation, can be solved by a new ethic—a cooperative ethic" (p. 238). Several scholars outside physical education have contributed to a growing body of research that supports a curriculum based on cooperation (Kohn, 1986). Based on Orlick's (1978b) work, on games borrowed from cultures that value cooperation, and on the creativity of many physical educators, a repertoire of cooperative games is now available to practitioners. Most of these games are either totally cooperative in purpose (e.g., how long two volleyball teams can keep the ball in the air) or cooperative within a competitive framework (e.g., all players on a basketball team must touch the ball before a shot can be taken). Cooperative games can be adapted from traditional cultural games, as in the two examples just given, or they can be games created specifically to promote cooperation.

OUTDOOR PURSUITS AND ADVENTURE EDUCATION

Unlike the other approaches, the third approach to personal–social development is centered on subject matter. Personal and social development claims are central to the arguments that outdoor pursuits and adventure education leaders make for their programs (Siedentop et al., 1986). Among their most prominent claims are that these activities develop self-awareness, risk taking, problem solving, and cooperation. Some evidence (Segrave & Hastad, 1984) suggests that delinquency-prone youth who become involved in outdoor pursuits such as whitewater rafting, rock climbing, and backpacking change their attitudes toward self and others and that these changes often last. Adventure education, which creates ropes and obstacle courses in or near the school and promotes cooperative "survival" games, may have similar effects. Whether all of these claims can be substantiated or not, it is clear that outdoor pursuits and adventure education offer students experiences different in kind from sport, fitness, and dance.

These kinds of programs are not without their problems. For one thing, physical educators are not often trained in these areas. For another, time and travel are problems for outdoor pursuits activities, and funding is necessary to build adventure education facilities on campus. In addition, legal liability is an important consideration in these high-risk activities. For extended descriptions of this model, see Darst and Armstrong (1980) or Siedentop et al. (1986).

A RESPONSIBILITY MODEL

A fourth approach contains elements from the theories of self-esteem, moral education, and cooperation, and some teachers who use the responsibility model have integrated adventure education into their curricula as well. The responsibility model has been repeatedly cited as an exemplary curriculum for personal and social development (Bain, 1988; Jewett & Bain, 1985), especially for at-risk youth (Siedentop et al., 1986; Winnick, 1990); it is described in detail by Hellison (1985). Its specific focus is on teaching self- and social responsibility by empowering students to take more responsibility for their own bodies and lives in the face of a variety of barriers and limitations, and by teaching students that they have a social responsibility to be sensitive to the rights, feelings, and needs of others. This educational process is intended to cause students to *feel* empowered and purposeful, to experience making responsible commitments to themselves and others, to strive to develop themselves despite external forces, to be willing to risk popularity to live by a set of principles, to understand their essential relatedness to others, and to distinguish between their own personal preferences and activities that impinge on the rights and welfare of others.

Goals and Subgoals

These high-sounding purposes are transformed into practice by a specific set of goals (with subgoals) and strategies as shown in Figure 9.1. The four goals provide a specific framework for teaching self- and social responsibility (and the related concepts described earlier), thereby giving some direction and structure to the empowerment process and resolving the tension between commitment to self and com-

Goals or levels

1. Self-control and respect for the rights and feelings of others
   A. Self-control
   B. Inclusion
   C. Negotiating conflicts
   D. Internalizing respect
2. Participation and effort
   A. Going through the motions
   B. Exploring effort
   C. Redefining success
3. Self-direction
   A. Independence
   B. Goal-setting
   C. Knowledge base
   D. Plan and evaluate
4. Caring and helping
   A. Supporting others
   B. Helping others
   C. Group welfare

Strategies

Awareness
Experience
Choice
Problem-solving/student sharing
Self-reflection
Counseling time
Teaching qualities

Figure 9.1. The responsibility model.

mitment to others. The four goals and the subgoals are arranged in a loose progression to help both teachers and students prioritize their efforts, and they are often presented as developmental levels (e.g., in general, Level I needs to be established first, Level IV is most difficult for most students, and so on). They can be taught cumulatively (each builds on the prior levels); this presents students a clear, if sometimes unrealistic, sequence of values and behaviors. However, they can also be taught as goals, which still gives teachers and students a common vocabulary (e.g., Level or goal I) or as concepts (e.g., self-control) with less emphasis on the progression.

However they are taught, they are intended to represent values as well as behaviors and are *not* meant to be used to categorize or label students (e.g., ''You Level IIs go over there''). The intention is to help students become aware of, experience, make decisions about, and reflect upon what they think and believe as well as how they act.

Level I

Level (or goal) I, self-control and respect for the rights and feelings of others, is a nonnegotiable social responsibility aimed at protecting the rights and feelings of everyone in class. Empowerment is limited to negotiations over definitions of Level I (e.g., what is disrespect?), how to get oneself under control, and situations involving a conflict of rights. The emphasis of Level I is on doing no harm. Therefore, this level does not necessarily include participation in program activities and is not intended to encompass social conventions such as a required uniform, no swearing in class, and no gum chewing. (Social conventions are generally agreed-upon standards of dress, manners, and the like; they do not deal with moral issues such as doing no harm.)

The first step (or subgoal) in the Level I process is to behaviorally control one's impulses to physically or verbally harm (abuse, intimidate, manipulate) others. Students who are successful at self-control manage to control their behavior without being supervised, even though they may not have internalized self-control as a value. The alternative is a police state (i.e., martial law) to ensure that all students have a physically and psychologically safe place to work and play.

The second step in the Level I process is to

introduce activities that require the inclusion of all students—both sexes, all skill levels, and all racial and ethnic groups. For example, Ultimate Frisbee has a built-in cooperative component, and basketball can be modified so that all team members must touch the ball before it is shot. Cooperative adventure activities can also be used, and students can be asked to set group goals in any activity (e.g., goals scored in a floor hockey drill by all teammates or number of consecutive racquetball hits against the wall by the class). The point is to require students to include others, that it is their right to participate fully. In the process, students have numerous opportunities to practice self-control when teammates make errors. The moral education BIDD approach, which confronts students with questions of what is fair for everyone in class, can also be used at this step.

The third step in the Level I process is to teach students how to peacefully negotiate conflicts of rights and opinions. Horrocks's talking bench (1978) as a place to go to solve these conflicts and Rudy Benton's emergency plan (cited in Hellison, 1985) in which students decide ahead of time how to solve conflicts that might arise during a game are aspects of this process. Drew (1987) suggests this progression: cool off first, state each other's side and feelings, take responsibility for the process, and figure out a solution where both sides win.

The fourth and most difficult step in the Level I process is to teach students to internalize the value of Level I. This internalization is based insofar as possible on students' taking responsibility for and understanding both the motives and the consequences of their behaviors, taking the other's perspective (empathizing) in matters of rights and feelings, and being able to evaluate their behaviors from the perspective of ''What if everyone did this?''

Level II

Level (or goal) II, participation and effort, emphasizes participation as opposed to "cruisin' in neutral," alienation, and learned helplessness; the exploration of effort as a strategy for self-improvement; and trying new things in order to open up new opportunities.

The first step (or subgoal) in the Level II process is to encourage uninterested students to at least "go through the motions," to let them know that they don't have to exert a lot of energy but just give the task a minimal effort. However, if the activity requires cooperation (as do most team sports), they must either agree to cooperate or be given an alternative activity in which their low level of motivation does not interfere with the rights of others (i.e., Level I).

The second step of Level II is to explore different degrees of effort to determine for oneself whether effort leads to improvement or whether it matters one way or the other.

The third step of Level II (which will be the only step needed with some kids) is to help students redefine success for themselves in a way that best challenges them or suits their purposes: for instance, success can be defined as effort, improvement, goal setting, achievement of a norm or standard, or being socially responsible (being a fair player or a leader).

Level III

Level (or goal) III, self-direction, emphasizes self-improvement in areas of personal preference identified by the student—aspirations (e.g., to be a competent gymnast) and problems (e.g., to lose weight). This level offers an alternative to being externally controlled (e.g., by socialization or peer pressure) but presents self-improvement as a choice rather than a requirement. Although age is a factor in the capacity for self-direction, at least the introduction of self-direction as a concept can begin early.

The first step (or subgoal) in the Level III process is development of the ability to work independently, without supervision, on specific tasks.

The second step of the Level III process is the development of some kind of personal vision, some kind of goal or intention. The specifics of goal setting need to be negotiated with each student, although students can be presented with a choice of predetermined goals as an early substep in this process. These goals can be different tasks such as push-ups, basketball free throws, and racquetball kill shots, whereby students choose two or three tasks. Tasks can be linked to purposes such as health, appearance, safety, achievement, stress management, and play. In this approach, students select their purpose and the tasks they think will help them accomplish their purpose (see Hellison, 1978 for specific examples). Gradually, students need to be confronted with such questions as "Who do I want to be?" and "Who can I be?" as well as the external forces–related "Who am I supposed to be?" (Hellison, 1978). Some students will focus on one specific goal, some can work with several at one time, and some work better with a general intention (Sternberg, 1990). In all cases, students must possess the courage to disregard peer and other pressures.

The third step in the Level III process requires students to have or develop a knowledge base in order to achieve their goals or intentions. For example, students cannot embark on a weight-loss program unless they know what exercises burn calories and that spot reducing doesn't work. Students who want to improve a motor skill need to know the cues, need to practice, and need to get feedback (e.g., refinement input) on their progress.

The fourth step in the Level III process requires that students make plans to carry out their purposes and then be able to carry them out, especially in the face of boredom and the difficulty of reaching goals (e.g., plateaus). (Being able to work independently helps here.) This step can be modified by offering a choice of plans based on different goals.

The fifth step in the Level III process is that students develop and carry out an evaluation plan: Was it worth doing? To what extent did it work? Again, teachers may need to help with this step by giving some structure (e.g., pre- and post-test ideas, keeping a journal) at first.

Level IV

Level (or goal) IV, caring and helping, is usually the most difficult for students unless they have been socialized into these kinds of roles, because it requires going beyond oneself ("me first" egocentrism), beyond one's friends ("us first" ethnocentrism), and beyond prejudices and stereotypes (such as those of sexism, racism, motor elitism). It is based on the notion of the essential relatedness of all people (Raywid, Tesconi, & Warren, 1984), that people need each other, and is an extension of the Level I concept of respect for others. Unlike Level I, Level IV is treated as a choice. Students are invited to experience it, but it is not a requirement as is Level I.

The first step (or subgoal) in the Level IV process is to support others by positive gestures such as saying "Nice job" or giving high fives as a form of congratulations. These gestures must be genuine to qualify as Level IV, not phony or contrived.

Genuine, positive gestures are the first step of Level 4.

The second step of the Level IV process is helping others, sharing one's knowledge or skill with another person. Such sharing must be done without acting superior and only if help is desired by the other person. Examples are teaching assistants chosen for their sensitivity and not just for their motor skill abilities, cross-age teaching, and reciprocal teaching (see chapter 5).

The third step in the Level IV process is working toward the entire group's welfare (Trotter, 1985). This is the end of the process that begins with concern for self, moves to concern for others, and ends with concern for all. It may be done by individuals, small groups, or the entire class. One way is to agree upon a welfare-related group goal such as to teach fourth graders what they have learned about fitness. Another way is to discuss how the class could work better for everyone (including changes in the levels). A third possibility is to introduce games that require cooperation, followed by group discussion of the concept of group welfare.

Level Zero

Sometimes, another level is used as a teaching device: Level Zero. Level Zero is the level below Level I and refers to abusive attitudes and behaviors.

Strategies

In the responsibility model, strategies are processes for helping students to become aware of, experience, make decisions about, and reflect on the model's goals. The gym is viewed as a microsociety perhaps quite different from the students' experiences on the street, at home, and in the rest of school. Students are encouraged to become temporary members of this microsociety and in the process to determine for themselves the extent to which the goals and processes have application in their lives outside the gym. The tension between empowerment and social responsibility is particularly acute at this point in the model. The teacher's role is to emphasize student responsibility to make these decisions while at the same time doing his or her best to make the goals and strategies come alive in the gym, including teaching by personal example.

This model requires a conceptualization of the teaching act that is different from more traditional models. If students are to become responsible, they must experience some responsibility. This does not mean that anything goes; the goals and strategies are intended to give some structure to the process. But the old notion of "I say, you do" or, more accurately, "I say, you try to get out of doing" must give way to invitation, negotiation, and joint decision-making.

There are six instructional strategies designed to implement the model's goals we have described.

Awareness

Students are taught the levels (or goals), not as indoctrination but so that they know the purpose of the program. Several approaches can be used: a brief teacher talk at the beginning of class to remind students of the levels or to use examples of the levels from the previous class, posting the levels for quick reference, pointing out level-related attitudes and behaviors as they occur, and conducting student sharing sessions to discuss or negotiate what constitutes each level and why they are important (or why they aren't).

Gradually, teacher talks can focus on some of the nuances of the levels—for instance, what it feels like to be the victim of abusive behavior, how effort leads to improvement, the courage that is necessary to operate at Level III.

Experience

Students are invited to try out the levels. For example, at Level I a student can be asked "Can you say that a different way?" or students can be invited to play a cooperative game that includes everyone. At Level II, students can be told that going through the motions is okay during fitness, but if they want to get better they will have to overload themselves. At Level III, everyone can be invited to try working independently for 10 minutes. At Level IV, students who know an activity can be invited to help those who don't.

Experiences can also be built into the instructional strategies of the lesson. For example, a Level III choice of tasks can be given to all students, or, to emphasize Level IV, reciprocal teaching can be used as part of a skill development lesson. Also at Level IV, each student can be assigned another student at the beginning of class with the task of reporting something good that student does during class.

If invitations don't work, contingencies can be created to encourage students to experience the levels. For example, at Level I, name-calling (e.g., "You're a jerk") and other put-downs ("You're no good") are often problems. To deal with these problems, game length can be altered according to the amount of name-calling (followed by a discussion of whether a game without name calling is better or worse than a game with name calling). At Level II, a new activity that is greeted with a lack of interest can be made a prerequisite for participating in a popular activity during the last part of the period. Level III can be a reward for doing Levels I and II for a specified period of time.

Choice

At each level (goal), students are faced with choices. For example, at Level I, abusive students can be given the choice of sitting out or changing their behaviors, followed, if necessary, by being asked to sit out with the stipulation that they can choose to come back when they are under control. Teacher and student can also negotiate a plan to reduce the abusive behavior. Abusive students for whom these strategies don't work can be given the choice of membership in a direct-instruction Level Zero group (not as punishment but as recognition of the need for tighter controls). Level I choices also are involved in negotiating conflicts of rights and creating emergency plans for future disputes.

At Level II, students can be allowed to choose level of effort (as long as lack of effort does not affect others), choose level of game intensity (e.g., three stations are offered: a competitive game, a recreational game, and a practice station, all in the same activity), redefine success (see above), or negotiate an alternative to the planned activity.

Level III choices include whether to participate in Level III activities (or be teacher-directed as with the Level Zero group), a choice of preplanned programs, and the opportunity to carry out and evaluate a plan based on personal goals. Students can also be confronted with any disparity between goals and plans, with the choice of changing one or the other—for instance, if a student wants to lose weight but chooses to do tumbling with her friends, she needs to be confronted with deciding what is more important: losing weight or being with her friends?

Level IV choices include whether to do Level IV activities, optional participation in a number of helping roles (e.g., teaching assistant, cross-age teaching, or coach certification program [discussed later]), participation in group welfare discussions and plans, and selecting a jury to adjudicate Level I violations.

Problem Solving

Student sharing sessions are used to solve problems that arise at each level. For example, at Level I, discussion topics could include widespread name-calling, defining Level I, what motives are valid for violations of Level I, and whether a particular behavior would be acceptable if everyone did it. At other levels, discussion topics could include generally low motivation (Level II), general difficulty in being self-directed (Level III), and whether Level IV is only "for girls" (Level IV). Student sharing also provides opportunities for students to evaluate the program—what they like and dislike, and how it might work better.

Self-Reflection

At the end of every class, students are asked to reflect on what they intended, did, and felt during class in relation to the levels (goals).

This can be done in writing (e.g., in journals), on a checklist, by discussion, by students reporting on their way out of the gym or touching their level on the wall on the way out, by a show of hands, and so on. Key questions include: What level or levels were you at? (If cumulative levels are used, what counts at each level needs to be clarified—e.g., is 2 minutes of Level Zero equal to a Level Zero for the day?) Why do you think you were at these levels? How do you feel about it? How do others feel? Did you learn anything about yourself that you want to use in other aspects of your life?

Like teachers, students can benefit from self-reflection.

Counseling Time

Time needs to be set aside, for instance during preclass activities or games or Level III time, to talk with individuals about specific problems, about the teacher's observations (positive and not so positive) in relation to the levels (goals), and about how things are going in general. These talks need to be based on questions rather than answers (i.e., dialogue rather than mono-logue); students need to feel that their views matter. The teacher can (and often should) give her or his opinion, but the student should be able to do so also.

This kind of counseling is appropriate at each level. For Level I, discussions can include patterns of abusive behavior, possible underlying motives (e.g., retaliation, attention getting, power, street survival), how it would feel to be a victim of this behavior, and so on. It is also appropriate at Level I for the teacher to admit that he or she might be part of the cause of a particular problem and to discuss this as openly as possible.

Level II counseling can include discussions of the role of effort and new experiences in a student's life, whether she or he is trying, how it feels, and so on. Level III counseling is the time to discuss student short-range and long-range goals, plans, and visions as well as the role of peer pressure, courage, and persistence. Level IV counseling can involve discussions of appropriate ways of helping—by being genuine, by not being arrogant, by being sensitive to whether someone wants the help.

Teacher Qualities

Chapter 13 deals at some length with teacher qualities. However, because the teacher is central to the responsibility model's successful implementation, a few comments concerning relevant teacher qualities are in order. The teacher must be able to relate to most kids, must be able to size up kids and situations, must value the levels (goals), must be able to teach by personal example as well as by structuring experiences according to the strategies (including giving kids some responsibility), and must be vulnerable (i.e., human, genuine, willing to admit mistakes). The ideal teacher for this model is holistic in perspective, reflective, and sensitive, and possesses both personal and social goals.

Implementation

Implementation of this model can take a variety of forms (see Hellison, 1985), from posting the levels and discussing them during teachable moments to a very structured program of contingencies (e.g., when students show they can do Levels I and II, they will get the opportunity to try Level III). A daily format often includes some reference to the levels or sublevel concepts (often by using examples from class), some Level III time (or Level III lead-up activities), some team sport or cooperative activities (to practice Levels I and IV), and a few minutes of reflection time at the end of the period.

Recently, a basketball coaching certification program based on the responsibility model was developed for inner-city youth in Chicago. The levels were reconceptualized as coach (Level IV), self-coach (Level III), player (Level II), bench (Level I), and cut from the team (Level Zero), and students were given coaching and self-coaching tasks if they wanted them. Final levels for the program were determined primarily by self-reflection, and students who earned Level IV were invited to become assistant coaches in the program.

Because this model continues to be field-tested with at-risk youth, questions have been raised concerning its applicability to other populations. It is currently being used in suburban as well as urban elementary and secondary schools, rural and small-town settings, and alternative programs. However, these teachers have adopted and adapted this model because they perceived it to meet their needs and the needs of their students and setting. Whether it meets yours is a question only you can answer.

The goals and strategies of this model are only effective in moderation (like most things, we suspect). For example, reflection can be taken to the point where a person becomes obsessive. Or self-direction could be interpreted as a pop-psychology message that says, "Take charge of yourself and your problems will disappear." Instead, the message of this model is that our best hope is to take charge of ourselves to whatever extent we can and to be sensitive to others along the way. And that we shouldn't forget to laugh at ourselves. Striving against external forces (deCharms, 1976) is essential if we are to gain any ground in these endeavors, but the striving may be as important as (or more important than) whatever success results. As Kopp (1972) states:

> The world is not necessarily just, being good does not often pay off, and there is no compensation for misfortune. . . . All solutions breed new problems. Yet it is necessary to keep struggling toward solution. . . . We have only ourselves and one another. That may not be much, but that's all there is. . . . We must live within the ambiguity of partial freedom, partial power, and partial knowledge. All decisions are made on the basis of insufficient data. (p. 166)

It may be, as Becker (1973, p. 259) suggests, that the "most one can hope to achieve is [to become] . . . less of a driven burden on others." If so, at least that is something.

WRAP-UP

This chapter has given considerable space to one personal–social development model, the responsibility model. It is your senior author's favorite curriculum model, but there are other reasons for the extended discussion. This model is perhaps the most well-developed and field-tested of all personal–social development models (although all of these models are very recent). In addition, it incorporates elements of self-esteem, moral education, cooperation, and adventure education models.

However, the other models described in this chapter also have their place. For example, the moral education BIDD and cooperative games strategies are specific strategies that can be integrated into a multiactivity model. The self-esteem model clarifies both self-esteem's relation to physical education and the kinds of strategies that must accompany self-esteem claims. If nothing else, perhaps physical education teachers will make fewer personal and social development claims after reading this chapter!

THE EXPERTS RESPOND

Chris: I've got to get out of here for a while to go to my second job, so I'll make it short and sweet: All of this stuff sounds nice, but it isn't PE.

Pat: I sort of agree. It's PE, but this stuff happens automatically if you teach well. It's what good sport and exercise is all about: building character, cooperation, the competitive spirit, and all that. But you don't have to do all these strategies to get it.

Lynn: I can't believe it; I agree with Chris: It isn't PE!

Robin: I can't believe you three! Of course it isn't PE; it's life! It's about what kids need to survive in today's world, whether dealing with their health, their leisure time, or their friends. It's about basic principles of self-esteem, fair play, self-development, and sensitivity toward others; and, Pat, how to put them into practice. It's a framework for PE or anything else for that matter, a way to approach our subject matter so as to teach more than just how to grip a tennis racquet or how to get an aerobic effect.

Pat: What's wrong with teaching the proper tennis-racquet grip?

Robin: That stuff's okay; it's our subject matter. But the point is that there is more to life than tennis and jogging. There's how we feel about ourselves, how we deal with our aspirations and our problems, and how we treat others. Pretty important stuff, I'd say.

Lynn: But not our job. We've got enough problems just trying to get kids to learn to set a volleyball. Let health education and social studies teachers—and counselors or social workers if necessary—do the things this chapter describes. I don't think all of this stuff happens automatically, but we don't have the time or the expertise to do it—after all, we're not psychologists.

Robin: You missed an important point early in this chapter: PE is a great place to do these things. It's highly interactive and highly emotional; kids can experience and reflect upon these concepts rather than just learn about them or discuss how they might behave or how they behaved last week.

Pat: Maybe we could add a 3-week unit of this stuff—call it "Social Interaction" or something.

Robin: A little dab of social development to add to little dabs of a bunch of other things, huh?

Pat: I see you're not into compromising!

Lynn: Nor am I. I agree that kids today bring a lot of problems into the gym. That's why we need good discipline and motivation strategies to first of all minimize the number of problems that occur and then to deal effectively with the ones that do occur. That will clear the way for us to do our real job: teach physical activities. I'm still waiting for this book to give us those data-based discipline strategies!

SELF-REFLECTION

While these three (Chris left) continue to bicker in the background, we just want to remind you, the reader, that you still have to face the 30 hypothetical students we assigned you.

1. Do you dare try some of what has been described in this chapter? Or is Chris right (roll out the ball, and your troubles will be minimal)? Or Pat (assert your authority from the outset)? Or Chris, Pat, and Lynn (personal–social development has no place in physical education)? Of course, the kids you have will dictate your choice to some extent. But—and this is a theme you may be getting tired of hearing—so will your values: what kind of a contribution you want to make to these 30 kids.

2. Whether you try any of this stuff may depend in part on whether you have experienced any personal–social development goals and strategies in your own sport and physical education background. If you did, what was the nature of your experience? Did it help you, or was it a waste of time? Did the teacher or coach do it very effectively? What, if anything, could have been done in the areas of self-esteem, moral education, and social development in the physical education classes you had?

3. Many PE teachers claim to teach self-esteem, cooperation, and so on. Interview a teacher and ask him or her whether personal–social development is among the program goals. If so, try to find out whether this teacher uses any specific strategies to achieve this goal.

Lynn does make an important point. We haven't discussed discipline and motivation strategies that you could use if the personal–social development models don't appeal to you. We will remedy this by devoting the next part of the book to discipline and motivation. (Who says we don't listen to our experts?) First, though, chapter 10 will describe how you can create your own model.

SUGGESTED READINGS

Bredemeier, B.J., & Weiss, M.R. (1986). Moral development. In V. Seefeldt (Ed.), *Physical activity and well-being* (pp. 373-390). Reston, VA: AAHPERD. (An excellent summary of moral education theory and models for physical education.)

Darst, P.W., & Armstrong, G.P. (1980). *Outdoor adventure activities for school and recreation programs*. Minneapolis: Burgess. (A detailed description of the outdoor pursuits/adventure education model.)

deCharms, R. (1976). *Enhancing motivation: Change in the classroom*. New York: Irvington. (Both deCharms's theory of personal causation and the application of this theory to the education of inner-city kids provide support for the responsibility model; the first and last chapters summarize his research and argument.)

Fox, K.R. (1988). The self-esteem complex and youth fitness. *Quest*, **40**, 230-246. (Probably the best explanation of the relevance of self-esteem theory for physical education, although Fox limits his discussion to fitness.)

Harter, S. (1986). Processes underlying the construction, maintenance, and enhancement of the self-concept in children. In J. Suls & A.G. Greenwald (Eds.), *Psychological perspectives on the self* (Vol. 3, pp. 137-181). (A good review of the self-concept literature and its relation to physical activity.)

Hellison, D. (1978). *Beyond balls and bats: Alienated (and other) youth in the gym*. Washington, DC: AAHPERD. (An experiential account of one teacher's effort to put the responsibility model into practice. The appendix contains specific contracts and other materials.)

Hellison, D. (1985). *Goals and strategies for teaching physical education*. Champaign, IL: Human Kinetics. (The most complete description of the responsibility model to date; instructional strategies are described in separate chapters for each developmental level.)

Morris, G.S.D., & Stiehl, J. (1989). *Changing kids' games*. Champaign, IL: Human Kinetics. (This book is devoted to helping teachers modify games for children; contains a detailed process for helping kids create their own games.)

Orlick, T. (1987). *Winning through cooperation*. Washington, DC: Hawkins. (Theory and some practical applications of a moral education model based on cooperation.)

Romance, T.G., Weiss, M.R., & Bockoven, J. (1986). A program to promote moral development through elementary physical education. *Journal of Teaching in Physical Education*, **5**, 726-736. (An exemplar of the moral education model.)

Wigginton, Eliot. (1985). *Sometimes a shining moment: The Foxfire experience*. Garden City, NY: Anchor Books. (An extraordinary personal account of teaching that captures in often-eloquent prose what personal–social development is really all about.)

Chapter 10

Creating Your Own Model

Some, perhaps many, teacher educators in physical education believe that preservice teachers (those of you who are now preparing to teach) need to be taught a single way to teach rather than to be introduced to a bewildering array of models and instructional strategies. Then at least you will know how to teach one way well, hopefully well enough to survive. Eventually, the argument goes, new teachers can learn to reflect and to adjust to individual circumstances.

As you know by now, we reject that argument on a number of grounds. For one thing, the range of available models and strategies strongly suggests that physical educators have not been able to agree on which approach to adopt. Recently, yet another national task force was appointed to determine what being physically educated means, attesting to this confusion. Choosing a particular model for preservice teachers also ignores the values and beliefs of these future teachers. If it is true that commitment stems from one's values and beliefs, such commitment is jeopardized if value decisions are made for teachers. How will preservice teachers learn to create their own models of teaching if they are only taught one? Finally, although some experts argue that most of the curriculum models and instructional strategies we have discussed aren't a part of typical public school physical education programs and therefore are irrelevant to the "real world," such a world is not one we must accept as unchangeable. From our perspective, that is an issue each teacher needs to confront.

The alternative to learning "one way to teach" is for each of you to develop your own model of teaching (or, as critical theorists call it, your own theory-in-action) and continue to modify it throughout your career. How to get started is the message of this chapter. Of course, you can start anywhere, but we have argued in previous chapters that you will be best served if you start with your own values and build from there. That way the core of your teaching model has some intrinsic strength, bolstered by thoughtful rationale. Or you could start the other way, with some activities or strategies, and eventually infuse your values

Which will work for you?

into your model of teaching. Let's try it both ways to see what works best for you. Perhaps by focusing on the 30 hypothetical students we have assigned you, you will get some idea of which approach makes the most sense.

FROM ACTIVITIES TO A MODEL

Although we have argued for beginning with your values, we have been around long enough to realize that most teachers and preservice teachers prefer to begin with activities. That is, when asked to plan a program, they most often begin by deciding what activities they want their students to do and then, if asked, they search for values that support their decisions. This approach has the advantage of being very concrete; the basic question is what is to be taught. It is also familiar territory; the activities selected come out of one's own experiences or from tradition. On the other hand, beginning with one's values assumes that teachers are conversant with their own values, can discuss and defend them, and are comfortable doing so.

Teachers who prefer to start by planning activities are more likely to draw on their own experiences or tradition for their planning, so they tend to shy away from asking what is worth doing from a perspective of human values. Instead these teachers ask, ''What have I experienced in PE?'' or ''What is usually taught to this age group in PE?'' Thus a teacher's source of knowledge (Schubert, 1986)—whether tradition, experience, values, or some combination—is very influential in program planning.

Tradition, experience, and values are three common sources of teacher knowledge, but there is a fourth source of knowledge: science. Teachers who utilize science as their primary source of knowledge would be persuaded by the low fitness scores of American youth, for example, to build a strong fitness program. Such teachers also tend to be persuaded by the research on teaching (see chapters 5 and 11) and the precision of behavioral objectives (see chapter 12).

In our view, you may start planning for your 30 hypothetical students by lining up activities for them to do, if that is most comfortable for you. However, we believe that your job is not over until you ask what values these activities represent and whether these values are defensible from both a rational and a scientific perspective. For example, you may plan a series of 3-week units in a variety of popular, seasonal sports, planning within each unit to demonstrate, drill, and play the game. Let's look at the values underlying these activities. Your program purpose is to expose kids to a variety of popular activities using a traditional method of instruction. You will need to argue not only that your goal of exposure is a valid one, but also that your method of instruction is preferable to more recent scientific findings about teaching motor skills (see chapter 5). In other words, traditional planning requires two additional steps: (a) Identify the values represented by the activities and instructional strategies of the program, and (b) explore the defensibility of these values.

FROM VALUES TO STRATEGIES

Let's go back to the values underlying the various curriculum models we have been discussing. If you were to define physical education—to describe what it means to be physically educated—how would you rank these qualities?

- Fun
- Exposure to many activities
- Motor skill development
- Competitiveness
- Fitness development
- Knowledge
- Body–mind unity
- Self-esteem
- Fair play
- Cooperation
- Responsibility

These qualities are, of course, values. Each of them can be associated with one of the curriculum models described in chapter 4. Do you have strong feelings about any of them? Which of them best represent a physically educated person? Which of these values do you most want to stand for as a professional physical educator? Which are you most comfortable teaching? Which do kids need most? If you were planning a program for your 30 hypothetical students, and you had them three times a week for 12 weeks (and that was it), which of these values would you emphasize, which would you want as outcomes of your program?

You may find yourself wanting to include all or most of these values. If so, given the time limitations of most physical education programs, you are probably opting for exposure to these values rather than a truly developmental experience for kids. That's okay as long as you can defend this approach; lots of PE programs are exposure oriented. Choosing to include everything or almost everything means you should use the multiactivity model. As a result, the selection of a specific model emerges out of the seeming chaos of trying to do everything.

On the other hand, none of these values may move you very much. That probably means one of two things: (a) You're not ready to teach; it's not a priority in your life (you're too preoccupied with other things); or (b) you are more comfortable starting with activities and working back to values. As we have said, this is perfectly okay (as long as you do, eventually, work back to values).

If two or three of these values or two or three of the curriculum models make more sense to you than the rest (either way, you will achieve the same thing), you can then choose one of three ways of building your own model of teaching:

- Building a framework first
- Using the 51% rule
- Selecting key components

Building a Framework

One model can provide a framework for your teaching, within which aspects of other models can be fit, followed by relevant instructional ideas and strategies. For example, fitness could become your framework. That would mean that nearly everything you do would relate back to fitness. Let's say you wanted to teach motor skills but to place more emphasis on fitness. Using fitness as the framework for your curriculum, you could do fitness preparation specific to the motor skills you want to teach, and during games (or applications), pulse rate could be taken to show students the extent to which the particular activity contributes to aerobic development. Fitness concepts could also be taught, and discipline and motivation could be dealt with by using the strategies in the next chapter rather than relying on any of the personal–social development models.

As another example, the responsibility model could provide a framework for teaching fitness, motor skills, or concepts (depending on the teacher's values). Program content would be planned, presented, and evaluated using the four developmental levels as guidelines. No matter what content was being taught, respect for others would be emphasized, students would be confronted with decisions regarding effort, time would be set aside for independent skill or fitness improvement, and helping roles and activities would be available. The teacher would keep the levels "in front" of students in every lesson, and at the end of every period students would reflect on their self-control, participation, self-direction, and caring about others.

Using the 51% Rule

Another way to put one's values into practice is to build a program around one primary curriculum model, filling in the gaps with pieces of other models. We call this using the 51% rule, because a significant portion of the program—perhaps half of it—will be based on one model. For example, if fitness is the primary model, a complete yearly fitness program is designed first. Then, with the remaining time, a modified multiactivity model or modified sports education model (or other model) could be developed to fill out the rest of the curriculum. As another example, one five week sport unit in each season could serve as the sports education model; pieces of other models could be implemented between the seasonal sport units. The 51% rule is especially relevant when your values are not congruent with those of your students' parents, students, administrators, or colleagues. In this case, you can build your program partly on what they want and partly on your own values. You may not have

the authority to devote 51% of your program to your values, but by using this rule, a portion of your program could be based on your values and beliefs.

Selecting Key Components

A third way is to select desired components from a variety of models and put those components together into one program. This eclectic approach sounds easy, but it requires considerable thought to get the various pieces to fit together. One teacher used this approach with her upper-elementary and middle-school students. She was well aware of her own physical education values—development in fitness concepts, motor skills, and responsibility. Her assessment of her students indicated that they had low motor skills, low fitness, and low levels of self- and social responsibility; their needs corresponded to her own physical education values, so she decided to select key components that would enable her students to experience development rather than exposure and would also best meet her values and their needs. She instituted the developmental levels from the responsibility model, skill themes (Graham et al., 1987) for fundamental motor skill development (which then could be used informally or in sport education programs), and selected fitness concepts and experiences from the concepts model. To keep both herself and her students focused on the key components, she put together a student workbook that contained checklists of the levels, fitness concepts, and skill themes that were central to her program.

UNITS VERSUS THEMES

Whether one starts with activities or values, our contention is that both values and activities are essential to program development, that they ought to match up, and that a defensible case needs to be made for the resulting program. Then the activities and experiences need to be organized into some kind of coherent program. Although this is the subject of chapter 12, one misconception needs to be cleared up here: the assumption of lesson plans (see chapter 12) that are intended to help teachers plan the daily lesson, and unit plans that are intended to help teachers plan their units. These planning procedures are based on the assumption that teachers have not only lessons but also units to plan. Of course they have lessons; every physical education period is a lesson. But do they necessarily have units? The traditional unit represents a particular sport or activity—a few weeks of this followed by a few weeks of that. Some of the curriculum models we have been describing lend themselves to units—for instance, the multiactivity model, the sports education model, the special-unit approach in the concepts model. However, some models would benefit more from a themes approach.

Just what is a themes approach? Themes are identified based on value and model selection, and these themes are repeated throughout the year. Skill themes are sometimes taught this way, so that, for example, throwing is experienced for a few days, then experienced again a week or two later, and again later in the year, and so on. Activities could also be taught this way; after an introductory experience, activities could be revisited briefly, or a mixed curriculum could be offered in which students have some choice of activities they have already experienced. Fitness could be—should be, if development is the goal—taught this way, instead of as a unit, so that part of every period or designated periods every week are devoted to fitness activities.

Concepts such as overload or personal-social development values, such as fair play, can become themes as well, and probably ought to if the teacher wants students to learn them. A unit in concepts is no doubt less effective than lab days sprinkled throughout the year or a limited number of concepts introduced into lessons each week.

Unit planning can easily be replaced by monthly or yearly planning in which themes are built into the plan. The point is that units ought not be assumed to be part of the planning process. As you will learn, they may be part of the real world (see chapter 14), but even then teachers have some choices. They can ''sneak'' themes into scheduled units, especially concepts, fair-play discussions, or the responsibility levels. Even lab days or a different activity can be integrated into an existing unit in many cases. Whether units or themes or some combination makes the most sense depends once again on you—what your goals are and how you want to accomplish them.

WRAP-UP

We strongly believe that you need to be the chief decision maker of your own physical education program. That may stand to reason if it is your program, but you will find that there is no shortage of administrators, state guidelines, and even teacher educators like us ready to tell you what to do and how to do it. Instead, we hope you will develop your own model of teaching and continually modify it throughout your career. If you do a good job of identifying and justifying your own values, your teaching model will have intrinsic strength.

Traditionally, physical education programs are based on a selection of activities and instructional strategies drawn from tradition and personal experiences. Sometimes, teachers will also draw on science for information. In our view, your values are the key to model building, and whether you identify and justify your values after you have selected activities and instructional strategies or as a first step, the value basis of your program is central to everything you do.

We suggest three ways to build a model: Start with a framework, utilize the 51% rule, or select key components from a variety of models. However you do it, it ought to be you who does it, reflecting as completely as you can on your own and alternative values. Truly the question is: What's worth doing?

THE EXPERTS RESPOND

Robin: I think I'm pretty reflective and have a good sense of my own values, but I often plan activities first—by units, of course—and only work my values in by trying to be a caring teacher. This part of the book has given me some insight into the planning process. I need to get better at it.

Lynn: You've called me on this already, Robin, but I'm just beginning to see your point. I value motor skills, and I value science; that's why I like the motor skill instructional progression so much. Up until now I didn't see that point. Also, I always think in terms of units, so lengthening the multiactivity model units seemed to be my best bet. Now I see that some version of themes instead of units would better serve my purpose . . . and yes, I do see that it is MY purpose.

Pat: I don't want to be a wet blanket on all this hooray-for-the-authors-of-this-book stuff, but I didn't learn much from this chapter or those that preceded it. Maybe it's just that I know where I'm going and how to get there. My source of knowledge, as Schubert calls it, is tradition. I don't apologize for that.

Chris: Do I need to say it again? What's the big deal? My source of knowledge is my experience, which tells me that if I survive and the kids have fun, all is well. Roll out the ball folks, either now or, after you get burned out, later.

SELF-REFLECTION

1. Plan a 12-week, 3-days-per-week program for your 30 hypothetical students. Where will you start: with activities for students to do, or with the values you want to promote? Start either way, but don't quit until you have justified your selection of activities and instructional strategies.

2. Go back to the plan you have just made. Did you use units or themes or both? Justify whatever you used. Is there a better way to structure the experiences you want your students to have?

Part IV

How Can You Solve Discipline and Motivation Problems and Implement the Ideas Suggested in This Book?

Whew! Despite Chris's refrain that we make teaching too complicated, it is apparent to us (and we hope to you) that good teaching in-

volves both knowing a lot and making a lot of decisions. Your teaching needs to be informed by reflection on the larger social issues of our society and by reflection on the range of available purposes and processes. We hope that in the process of raising these questions we have not only fattened your bag of tricks for teaching but have also provided you with the basis for developing your own model of teaching.

We now turn to our last question: How do we implement these ideas in the real world? Of course, everything in this book is intended to have real-world applications; we assigned you 30 hypothetical students and reminded you of this assignment throughout the book just to make this point. But the first 3 parts of the book have focused on the reflective development of a curriculum and instruction model. To put your ideas into practice, you will need more; you will need to confront discipline and motivation problems, the daily lesson (''What am I going to do on Monday morning?''), your artistry in putting your ideas into practice, and the real world itself. Chapter 11 discusses strategies for dealing with motivation and discipline in addition to those contained in the personal–social developmental models. Chapter 12 addresses the nuts and bolts of planning and evaluation. Chapter 13 describes the artistic components of teaching—those qualities that go beyond the grasp of science but fall (slightly) short of magic. Chapter 14 describes the real world out there, into which you will take your first teaching ideas.

Chapter 11

Discipline and Motivation Strategies

We hope you haven't forgotten your 30 hypothetical students; we haven't. It is likely that they will possess at least some of the characteristics described in chapter 2 (e.g., less adult guidance, more choices, feelings of powerlessness and alienation). If so, you will not be able to teach them very effectively unless you are able to deal with the personal and social problems they bring into the gym. Fortunately, recent research has given teachers a number of strategies for both preventing and handling discipline and motivation problems. You may remember that one of our experts, Lynn, has already pointed this out to us. In addition, as you learned in chapters 4 and 9, personal–social development can be a major curriculum purpose for physical education, thereby emphasizing the development of specific personal and social qualities rather than simply treating discipline and motivation problems as barriers to the development of motor skills, fitness, or other physical education goals. Another of our experts, Robin, seems to be headed in this direction.

These are two very different solutions to student discipline and motivation problems. The personal–social development models attempt to help students develop qualities they can use to better their lives, such as self-esteem, cooperation, and self-responsibility. On the other hand, the discipline and motivation strategies in this chapter are aimed primarily at creating a better environment for the development of goals more germane to physical education, such as motor skill development, sport education, fitness, and fitness concepts. Your choice will depend on the values you want to promote in your program. If you want your 30 hypothetical students to experience personal and social development as a primary outcome of physical education, one of the personal–social development models would be better suited to your purpose. However, if you are primarily concerned with motor skill, fitness development, game playing, knowing concepts, or some similar outcome, the discipline and motivation strategies that follow would provide a more useful framework for dealing with student attitude and behavior problems.

There are some other approaches to dealing with motivation and discipline problems. One is to be a caring teacher (see chapter 13). Another is to use teachable moments to stop the activity, point out the problem, and correct it. Both of these have some merit, but they are usually more useful in combination with one of the approaches we have just described. It is rare that the personal qualities of the teacher are sufficient to prevent or curb all discipline and motivation problems, and to effectively use the teachable moment, one must be quick (able to "seize the moment"), skillful enough to make the point dramatically, and be clear about the point that needs to be made. And even if a teacher is able to do all these things, there is no guarantee that the problem won't occur again (and again).

Another approach is to combine the personal–social development model with the strategies presented in this chapter, but this requires careful planning. For example, some of the guidelines in this chapter, such as using a few very clear rules and the principle of least intervention, could be used with any of the personal–social development models *to a point*, but they do potentially conflict with the responsibility model, for example, insofar as the responsibility for rules and for controlling oneself are not gradually shifted to students. Other guidelines found in this chapter, such as a high percentage of activity time and behavior modification strategies, conflict more directly with some of the premises of the personal–social development models.

PREVENTION

Recent research has tended to replace well-worn admonitions for new teachers, such as "Don't smile until Christmas" (Ryan, 1970), with data-based guidelines. This shift has been spurred by recent social changes (see chapter 2); by the recognition that kids don't readily respond to threats these days (e.g., "I'll send you to detention"); and by recent research in physical education that shows students spend a lot of time waiting and not much time performing motor skills, that both teachers and students spend a lot of time involved in class management, and that the typical gymnasium environment is mildly negative (Siedentop, 1983).

Research conducted recently in this area (Brophy, 1988; Siedentop, 1983) has also fo-

cused on what more successful classroom (and gymnasium) managers do in comparison to less successful managers. (The term *manager* refers to the teacher's role in managing the class—dealing with problems, taking roll, handing out equipment, and so on). In general, this line of research concludes that teachers who establish and maintain effective learning environments, especially by keeping students involved in appropriate learning tasks, have fewer problems than teachers whose major goal is to establish and maintain their roles as authority figures or disciplinarians. What this means is that many, although not all, problems can be prevented by creating an environment conducive to learning. The following are the key preventive strategies that have come out of this line of research:

Rules

Have a few very clear rules and routines, to facilitate management of the class. These rules should include how class will start and stop (including a specific time at which class will begin), what students are to do when they first come in the gym, the signal for attention and their expected response, roll-taking procedures, how to select partners, and so on. Post these rules, and take extra time to practice them the first couple of weeks of class, until students know them and can do them. Then stick to them! Students will know what to do and what to expect as a result.

The Motor Skill Instructional Framework

Concentrate on having a high percentage of activity time and low percentages of teacher talk time and management time each class period. Physical education teachers typically spend about a third of their time talking and a third

Classroom rules should include a specific time at which class will begin.

managing, while students typically spend nearly 80% of their time waiting, listening, and being managed. It is obvious from these data that physical education teachers give their students excellent opportunities to get into trouble! One researcher (Pangrazi, 1987) advocates no more than 30 seconds of teacher talk at any one time! One of the problems common to many teachers is overdwelling—saying more than is necessary for students to understand. This approach strongly advocates that teachers have someone time their talks and the time they spend taking roll, handing out equipment, getting groups organized, and so on. These times, especially management time, ought to be minimal. This means that all management tasks must be carefully planned until this kind of time-saving becomes a habit.

A Supportive Environment

The gymnasium learning environment is supposed to be supportive, yet PE teachers tend to monitor their students without much one-to-one interaction, to correct much more than they positively reinforce, and to nag (e.g., telling students to pay attention) a lot. In general, research argues for increased one-to-one interaction, more specific positive-feedback statements than corrective statements, more prompts (reminding kids what to do before they do it wrong), more hustles ("a verbal or non-verbal behavior that is used to energize student behavior") (Siedentop, 1983, p. 76), and fewer nags.

Positive Expectations and Images

There is also some sketchy evidence that teachers ought to promote positive expectations and images:

> Students who are consistently treated as if they are well-intentioned individuals who respect themselves and others and desire to act responsibly, morally and prosocially are more likely to live up to these expectations and acquire these qualities than students who are treated as if they had the opposite qualities. (Brophy, 1988, p. 11)

This means that teachers need to model, teach, instruct, cue (give brief tips), prompt, and reinforce these expectations and images.

Variety of Teaching Methods

Finally, teachers who vary their methods tend to prevent more misbehavior than those who don't. This means that teachers need to change what they say (not always "Nice job") and the ways in which they interact with students (how, when, where, size of group).

INTERVENTION

The classroom management literature contends that in the early grades students are more likely to want to cooperate with adults and simply need to know the rules and routines. However, by the fifth or sixth grade, that terror known as adolescence begins, marked by increased interest in peers and resistance to adult authority.

Accountability systems are advocated for the junior high years, and intervention strategies become increasingly necessary to deal with students who become abusive, disruptive, or just uninterested.

How would you prevent a fight? How would you intervene if a fight started?

The principle of least intervention (Wolfgang & Glickman, 1980) is ordinarily invoked when students are off task but not seriously interrupting or harming others. The very least intervention is to ignore minor off-task behaviors. If necessary, a brief response that does not interrupt the flow of instruction or signify overreaction can be used. For example, a look may be enough. If that doesn't work, walking over and standing by the student(s) may be the next step, followed, if necessary, by a question or other nondirective statement. Younger kids respond well to pointing out those students who are acting appropriately. If necessary, a directive statement can be made, such as "I'd appreciate it if you wouldn't talk while I'm giving instructions." The point is to react at the level

of the problem and especially not to become part of the problem or to disrupt class more than the original problem is doing.

Teachers also need to learn how to use verbal desists effectively. An effective desist "contains specific information telling the student exactly what was wrong" (Siedentop, 1983, p. 100), is delivered with firmness but not harshness, and is well timed. For example, a student who comes to class late can be told that she is tardy, that excuses don't matter, that it counts against her grade, and that this rule is posted.

More serious intervention strategies may be required in some situations. Rather than resort to invoking fear, threats of calling parents, corporal punishment, and other "time-tested" strategies, research has supported the use of behavior modification (which is also called contingency management and other names, some of which are a bit derogatory) and progressive separation from the group, coupled with appropriate counseling if necessary.

Books have been written on behavior modification as an intervention strategy. However, the major principles can be briefly stated:

1. Identify the behavior in which change is desired.
2. Get a "baseline" reading of the behavior (i.e., the number of times the student does or does not do the target behavior during a specific period of time).
3. Select a contingency (reward) for doing the desired behavior. (It is also possible to use a contingency, such as a specific punishment, for a behavior you want the student to stop, but research suggests using the positive approach whenever possible.)
4. Apply the contingency as consistently as possible.
5. Monitor changes from the baseline reading.

6. Gradually eliminate the contingency so that the student will do the behavior without a reward.

Of course, this sounds a lot like bribery to some teachers (one PE major called it blackmail), but it works! Here are some examples: A class of inner-city high school students would not take a yoga lesson seriously. The teacher (one of us) told them that the first half of the period they would do yoga, and if they stay on task, the second half they could play basketball (the city game). Disruptions in the yoga lesson were reduced to a negligible level! Another inner-city class was being very disruptive, to the point that perhaps only 3 or 4 boys (out of 35) were not causing problems. The teacher (again, one of us) told the students that those who show up on time, listen, stay on task, and don't interfere with anyone's rights for 5 days in a row will receive a free-play day (which meant basketball, for most of them). Within 2 weeks, over half the class conformed to these rules! Within a month, most did.

If one student is being disruptive, a behavior contract can be drawn up and signed by both the teacher and student. The contract should specify what behaviors need to be performed under what conditions and, importantly, what reward will result from fulfilling the contract.

We mentioned accountability systems for junior high students a bit earlier. These encourage compliance from less willing students by holding all students accountable for what the teacher wants them to do. That in turn simply means creating contingencies (if necessary) to ensure compliance, either by withholding something valued from those who don't comply or bestowing something valued on those who comply. For example, students who commit high sticking (a safety problem) in floor

hockey can be required to go to the "penalty box" (bench) for 5 minutes. Those who don't can get first choice of positions in the next game.

Progressive separation from the group (Glasser, 1977) simply means to have some sort of progression based on the policies of the school for separating from the group those students who fail to comply and don't respond to other strategies. One of us has used the following progression in one school situation: (a) sit out, (b) sit out down in the locker room under the supervision of a locker-room guard, (c) call parents, (d) refer student to the vice-principal, (e) suspension, and (f) expulsion. Each school setting requires a different progression, at least to some extent, depending upon numerous factors including extent of administrative and parental support.

WRAP-UP

Discipline and motivation continues to head the list of teacher concerns, largely due to the social problems described in chapter 2. Although physical education teachers used to set the tone for discipline in the school, this task is becoming more difficult to do. One reason is the social problems discussed earlier. Another is that invoking fear doesn't work very well any more as a discipline technique.

However, several approaches are available to physical education teachers. The personal-social development models in chapter 9 help students to feel better about themselves, deal with fairness, cooperate, and take responsibility for their actions—all of which can reduce discipline and motivation problems while promoting positive human qualities. The prevention and intervention strategies described in this chapter more straightforwardly deal with discipline and motivation problems, thereby providing an appropriate environment for teaching physical education subject matter, but they do not contribute to personal and social development. Other strategies, such as positive teacher qualities (see chapter 13) and using the teachable moment, can also provide some assistance but will not, standing alone, effectively treat discipline and motivation problems.

THE EXPERTS RESPOND

Lynn can't wait to say something about these discipline and motivation strategies.

Lynn: You bet I can't. It's about time—this is only the third chapter in which you've said something that has a basis in research. Why we continue to philosophize and rely on experience when we have systematic, objective data upon which to base our programs is beyond me. The only problem is that you haven't said enough; you've given a cursory overview of this area. I'd recommend Daryl Siedentop's *Developing Teaching Skills in Physical Education* as the best treatment of this topic; he devotes two chapters, both longer than this one, to it.

Chris: You want more on this subject, Lynn? Good grief! If you would just listen to me for a minute, you'd stop recommending more reading and start recommending that people interested in teaching read less, including this book (despite the royalties I get for each copy sold). A good substitution for reading would be to observe kids. If you let them play, they don't cause problems, believe me. No, don't believe me; go watch some kids in a PE class where the teacher lets them have fun. I rest my case (until the next chapter).

Pat: I've already said my piece—in chapter 2. Not that anybody listened. This whole chapter, from the very beginning, gets under my skin. Like it or not, we are authorities; we are—we've got to be—disciplinarians. A certain amount of fear is important; kids respond to it, no matter what the research says. You can't misuse it, of course, but the kids need to know who's boss. I tell them, "It's my way or the highway," and they know I'm not kidding. A benevolent dictatorship—that's the answer.

Robin: I love it: We've got advocates of threats and authority, fun as a panacea to all our problems, and the great god science. Good grief is right! What about the kids? What about their feelings, their aspirations, their struggles? Do we scare them out of their problems? Do we substitute escape and let someone else deal with the problems? Do we invoke science and turn the kids into little pieces of clay? That's the scariest to me, because in our society science is so persuasive. And it misses the point. These aren't bodies we're dealing with (do I sound like a broken record?); they are human beings trying to get through a difficult period of their lives in what some would argue is a difficult period of history. This whole chapter is high-level manipulation thinly disguised and blessed by research.

Authors: Good grief is right! We have just summarized what we believe to be a fairly benign, inoffensive summary of the literature on discipline and motivation, and no one is happy. Just what have we said that is incorrect?

Lynn: Nothing from my point of view. We just need more of it and less of everything else.

Chris: The focus is incorrect. A positive environment isn't created by running around shouting compliments to everyone; it's created by letting kids have fun. My talk time and management time are kept to a minimum: I tell students what game we're playing, I hand out the equipment, and away we go. Once in awhile some kid gets out of hand, and I might use some behavior modification (sit out for a while) or progressive separation from the group if the problem continues. Otherwise, this stuff just isn't relevant.

Pat: What's wrong is the very first statement, upon which most of the rest of the chapter is based. I'm not saying that being positive is wrong or that keeping kids active isn't a good thing; I'm saying that the key is knowing who is boss and what won't be tolerated. Tell them and mean it. I suppose you could interpret some of what I do as behavior modification: Do it my way, or else!

Robin: I just think this approach only deals with the tip of the iceberg. I guess it's okay as far as it goes, but it doesn't go far enough. We need personal and social development goals, not just some management strategies. Also, it seems too mechanical, too inhuman, for me. Positives, prompts, hustles, contingencies—we're dealing with unique human beings here, not robots. Also, what if I need to talk to my kids about a problem that has come up—say, sexism or exclusion of somebody? Do I get downgraded for talking too much and not having enough activity?

SELF-REFLECTION

Again our experts disagree (somewhat vehemently). Chris and Pat seem to feel that this is the wrong approach, and Robin's opinion is that it doesn't go far enough, doesn't get at the human side of the problem, doesn't address the issues raised in chapter 2. Only Lynn is supportive of this approach, and she wants more of it!

1. Did you find yourself siding with one of our experts? If so, why? What in this expert's argument appealed to you? Did you like this expert's argument in the last chapter as well?

2. Get into groups of four, with one person in each group taking the position of one of our experts. Argue it out. Who can put together the best argument? This exercise works best if each person believes in the position he or she is arguing, but it can work even if people play roles.

3. Here is a list of the strategies described in this chapter. On a piece of paper, mark down which of these strategies you think you would be most likely to use with the 30 hypothetical students we've assigned you and which ones you would be least likely to use.

   - Few rules and routines, which are practiced and reinforced

   - Low percentages of teacher talk and management time

   - Lots of one-to-one teacher–student interaction

   - More specific positive-feedback statements than corrective statements

- More prompts and hustles
- The promotion of positive expectations and images
- Variation in teaching methods
- The principle of least intervention
- Use of verbal desists
- Use of behavior modification (contingency management)

4. On a sheet of paper, write out what you would do as the teacher in the following situations.

- A student who seems to get into trouble every day just spit on another student.
- Two students are arguing over whether the ball went out of bounds or not.
- A student is talking while you are trying to explain and demonstrate a skill.
- Your lesson plan calls for handing out three different sets of equipment in a 40-minute period.
- At least half of your class is off task on almost every task you give them.
- You are observing, and your class appears to be on task. You would then . . .

5. Compare your answers to the strategies suggested in this chapter. Did you tend to follow the management strategies we have described, or did you draw on your own experiences (what was done to you, what you have used in your own coaching or teaching)? Or did you create some "new" strategies?

SUGGESTED READINGS

Brophy, J. (1988). Educating teachers about managing classrooms and students. *Teaching and Teacher Education*, **4**, 1-18. (An excellent summary of classroom management research.)

Siedentop, D. (1983). *Developing teaching skills in physical education* (3rd ed.). Palo Alto, CA: Mayfield. (The best description of classroom management strategies in the physical education literature.)

Wolfgang, C.H., & Glickman, C.D. (1980). *Solving discipline problems*. Boston: Allyn & Bacon. (An excellent source for discipline strategies based on a continuum of least to most intervention.)

Chapter 12

Planning, Organizing, and Evaluating: The Nuts and Bolts

Imagine it's time for class and that heterogeneous group of 30 kids we've assigned you comes bursting into the gym. The question is, are you ready? It's Monday morning, and it's time to put the many ideas of this text into action. It's time for you to implement a lesson that will result in a positive experience for your students—it's time for your students to learn something. This is the key to any lesson—having a plan for learning. The purpose of this chapter is not so much to help you to learn the elements of lesson planning, but to reflect on

- your preparation for a lesson,
- the implementation of a lesson, and
- the evaluation of a lesson.

We think it would be best to first point out some recent findings related to lesson planning. The classic approach to lesson planning involves determining objectives, implementing learning experiences to promote objectives, assuring class organization to promote lesson smoothness and momentum, and evaluation of the lesson to maintain or adjust the plan (Tyler, 1949). Research shows little support for this four-stage model and indicates that teachers have varying concerns when initiating lesson plans. Some focus on lesson content, others on the time available for tasks, and some on pupil

characteristics and needs. Some teachers have no lesson plans whatsoever—they "wing" it.

The small amount of research on lesson planning within physical education seems to suggest that PE teachers do very little planning at all (Placek, 1983, 1984). Furthermore, there seems to be little concern with learning. That is, a successful lesson is one in which the children are "busy, happy, and good" (right, Chris?); whether the lesson accounts for learning is not a major consideration. We wonder why. There does seem to be enough corresponding data related to teaching effectiveness that suggest that a lesson should not only keep children "busy, happy, and good" but also incorporate the following strategies adapted from Siedentop et al. (1986, p. 375):

- The lesson should devote a large percentage of time to curriculum and goals.
- The lesson should minimize management, wait, and transition time.
- The lesson should keep student on task.
- The lesson should assign tasks that are meaningful and match student abilities.
- The lesson should maintain smoothness and momentum.

The teacher must be accountable for reflecting, planning, implementing, and reflecting again on the lessons that are intended to facilitate student learning. This is the challenge in preparing for your lesson on Monday morning.

OBJECTIVES AND TASKS: WHICH COME FIRST?

As with the proverbial chicken and egg, one may wonder what should be the initial concern of the teacher, determining objectives or the tasks the students are to be involved in? Observation leads us to believe that most teachers select activities first ("What should we do today?") and possibly then think about what objectives might be achieved through involvement in a given activity. For whatever reason, it appears that the key for most teachers is activity selection for selection's sake alone, rather than a means–ends concern. Do you think this is an appropriate approach to lesson planning?

We don't think so. We believe that developing your own curriculum model (see chapters 4 and 10) and selecting appropriate instructional strategies (see chapters 5 through 10) are

Which should come first?

crucial decisions the reflective teacher must make. Your curriculum model describes the purpose of your program—your program goals. Your instructional strategies facilitate delivery of your program purpose or goals, and your instructional strategies are your objectives—learning outcomes that are specific enough to provide direction for a given lesson or phases of a lesson. It is a mistake to determine or be concerned about program goals and objectives only as an afterthought. The most important criterion for selecting tasks is their potential for bringing about various learning outcomes—movement toward the goals we have been addressing throughout the book and those that you should consider for your lesson on Monday. Hence, the process of selecting tasks and objectives are not independent processes, but closely linked acts, both of which are part of your curriculum model. What seems most important is to not lose sight of the fact that your lesson must be reflected upon. What is your Monday morning lesson trying to accomplish? How does the lesson relate to your overall curriculum model (i.e., program goals)? What should your students be able to do at the end of a class period? Should they be able to throw a ball a certain distance? Should they be able to describe an offensive strategy in a basketball game? Should they be able to run so far in a given time period? Should they be expected to interact with their classmates in a certain way? Should they feel good about themselves as they leave your gym?

These questions bring up another question. Namely, should your objectives be behaviorally stated? For example, consider the following:

- The student will be able to run 100 yards in 9.4 seconds.
- The student will be able to make three of four foul shots.

- The student will be able to define aerobic capacity.

These objectives are characterized by having observable behavior and criteria, and certain conditions for performance. For some, a lesson is incomplete without the identification of the specific observable behaviors desired of students by the teacher. For others, the objective need only be specific enough to assure that appropriate instructional strategies are employed. For example, if moral education is a program goal, and the objective is to involve students in determining fair play in a basketball game, then the instructional strategy that helps students confront fair-play issues in basketball (see chapter 9) might be sufficient.

Of course, the behavioral-objectives advocates would want to define a learning outcome in terms of observable behavior at a certain level under certain conditions. The objective that "during a volleyball game the student will not engage in name calling" may or may not bring about the desired behavior. The teacher may simply discuss this goal with her or his students before class and not necessarily state it in behavioral terms. The teacher may describe what she or he is hoping for and engage students in a brief discussion about name calling with the expectation that the discussion will translate into the behavior desired. Again, this doesn't necessarily mean that the teacher has to write a behavioral objective in order to move toward this goal. Whether they are stated behaviorally or not, again the key principle for the teacher is to have a realistic objective or two in mind for each lesson.

Behavioral objectives assume behavior, specific behavior, as learning outcomes. This means that goals that focus on thoughts or feelings, such as some goals in the personal–social development models, need to be transformed into behaviors. Some teachers believe that this transformation changes the intention of the goal or at least reduces it to less than is intended.

Finally, goals emerge and change according to the characteristics and progress of students. As a consequence, one has to be flexible and open to changing goals. One must also recognize the importance of allowing students to establish their own goals for a lesson. Why not? Aren't secondary students capable of thinking about what they might like to achieve? This brings up the issue of empowering students to develop goals and pathways to achieve those goals on their own (see the social development model in chapter 4). We think this should be considered as an alternative to teacher-centered approaches that fail to recognize the importance of involving students in the decision-making process.

Thus, the time has come to start thinking about what you and your students might try to achieve on Monday morning. Have you thought about it?

THE IMPACT STAGE

Once you have an idea of the activity you are going to teach and the goals or objectives you wish to promote, your lesson must take into account the ways these may be achieved. In other words, how are students going to get there? What tasks will they be involved in, and how will you oversee their participation? Again, the teacher must reflect on a strategic plan for instruction. If we think back to Chris, Lynn, Pat, and Robin, they would seem to have very different strategies for implementing lessons. Their strategies could be plotted on a continuum (see Figure 12.1) that ranges from a very loosely structured lesson (organized recess) to one that is highly structured and teacher-centered, wherein lesson goals and activities are accounted for in each phase of a lesson.

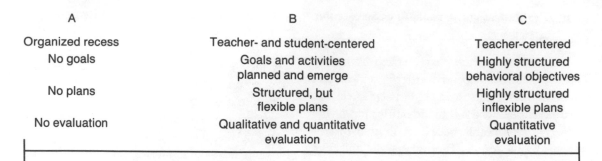

A	B	C
Organized recess	Teacher- and student-centered	Teacher-centered
No goals	Goals and activities planned and emerge	Highly structured behavioral objectives
No plans	Structured, but flexible plans	Highly structured inflexible plans
No evaluation	Qualitative and quantitative evaluation	Quantitative evaluation

Figure 12.1. A continuum of teaching methods and lesson planning.

As you reflect on the way you plan and implement a lesson, think about where you might fall on this continuum. Will you walk into the gym and just wing it? Will you have a flexible plan or one that is rigid and not open to change? Will your plan allow room for students to provide suggestions? Will plans emerge as you assess lesson sequencing? Will you have a plan for assessing your lesson, or won't you care about its effectiveness? How will you assess student performance and your lesson? Will you measure student performance both quantitatively (assigning numbers and weights to student performances) and qualitatively (assigning descriptions to performances) before making judgments about your students? These questions represent the essence of the continuum of teaching methods and lesson planning—a continuum one must continually reflect upon.

A more structured approach may be associated with many lesson-planning models (see Tables 12.1 and 12.2) offered in the literature (Hunter, 1984; Mosston & Ashworth, 1986; Posner, 1989). These models present a progressive structure for organizing a lesson, in which decisions may be made relative to planning for the beginning, middle, and end of a lesson. The beginning of your lesson will enable your students to settle down and will let you take attendance, outline the lesson's goals and activities, give explanations or demonstrations of a skill or concept, review previous lessons, or spell out your expectations for student performance and conduct.

The middle of the lesson is the heart of the lesson in terms of students' actually engaging in activity. The movement phase of your lesson must assure that students are engaged in meaningful pursuits and that wasting time is at a minimum. This is the time when students pursue lesson goals and the time when you as the teacher can be most helpful by interacting with your students, providing direction and feedback. It is not a time to retreat to the bleachers or to your office to make a phone call or to plan for basketball practice. During this phase of the lesson, it is the teacher's responsibility to promote the characteristics we have outlined of an effective lesson.

The end of the lesson is a great opportunity to review the day's activities and to ask students to reflect on their progress toward learning. It's a time to make sure equipment is returned and the gym or playing field is readied for your next class. Most important, the students should leave the class with a positive feeling—one that engenders an eagerness to return to physical education because your class is meaningful and enjoyable.

Table 12.1 Preliminary Planning Sheet

Planning element	Planning question	Planning answer (plans)
I. Direction		
1. Activity	What activity do you plan to initiate or lead?	
2. Objectives	What are the students supposed to learn from the activity?	
3. Entry characteristics	What prior skills and understandings do you expect the learners to bring into the lesson?	
II. Specifics		
4. Content	What specific content will you cover?	
5. Procedures	What specifically will you and the learners do during the lesson?	
6. Results	What results do you expect?	
III. Provisions		
7. Resources	What facilities and materials will you and the learners need in order to carry out the lesson activity?	
8. Feedback	How will you and the learners be provided with feedback regarding their progress?	
9. Time	How long will the activity take?	
10. Follow-up	What activities will you assign as a means of extending or reinforcing the lesson?	

Note: From *Field Experience: Methods of Reflective Teaching* (p. 134) by George J. Posner. Copyright © 1989 by Longman. Reprinted with permission.

The Lesson Blueprint: Keeping an Open Mind

The advantage of having a set structure to planning a lesson is that it gives the teacher an idea as to what to do and what to look for as a lesson progresses. The disadvantage is that this blueprint may not be the best plan for every lesson. You may find that your plans for Monday morning are incomplete or just not what you anticipated, and adjustments may be necessary.

Hence, planning is a continuous process as one assesses a lesson and one's mode of interaction with students. It's important to keep an open mind relative to adjusting your plans—this is a sign not of failure but of good and sensitive teaching.

Let's take a look at a few of the lesson elements we feel are particularly important for you to be sensitive to as you examine, develop, and implement your blueprint. By no means are these topics discussed comprehensively. But it

Table 12.2 Mosston and Ashworth's Anatomy of Any Teaching Style: Lesson Decisions

Sets of decisions	Decisions that must be made

Pre-impact
(content: preparation)
	1. Objective of an episode
	2. Selection of a teaching style
	3. Anticipated learning style
	4. Whom to teach
	5. Subject matter
	6. Where to teach (location)
	7. When to teach
	  a. Starting time
	  b. Rhythm and pace
	  c. Duration
	  d. Stopping time
	  e. Interval
	  f. Termination
	8. Posture
	9. Attire and appearance
	10. Communication
	11. Treatment of questions
	12. Organizational arrangements
	13. Parameters
	14. Class climate
	15. Evaluative procedures and materials
	16. Other

Impact (content: execution and performance)	1. Implementing and adhering to the Pre-impact decisions (3-13) 2. Adjustment decisions 3. Other
Post-impact (content: evaluation)	1. Gathering information about the performance in the impact set (by observing, listening, touching, smelling, etc.) 2. Assessing information against criteria (instrumentation, procedures, materials, norms, values, etc.) 3. Feedback: corrective, value, neutral, and ambiguous statements 4. Assessing the selected teaching style 5. Assessing the anticipated learning style 6. Other

Note. From *Teaching Physical Education* (p. 6) by M. Mosston and S. Ashworth, 1986, Columbus, OH: Merrill. Copyright 1986 by Bell and Howell Company.

is hoped that each element will provide some food for thought in the preparation of your lesson.

Content

The question here is what and how much you should cover in your lesson. Don't be overambitious; that can result in your students trying to learn a lot of things but mastering none. Too many tasks, too many concepts to learn, too many laps to run or sit-ups to perform or balls to hit may be counterproductive to learning. Have realistic expectations about what is achievable for your lesson on Monday.

Teaching Styles

There are countless ways to present your lesson content and have your students engage in it. Mosston and Ashworth's (1986) spectrum of teaching styles (see Table 12.3 and chapter 5) illustrate this. This spectrum presents seven teaching styles that represent a range of methodologies from teacher-centered to student-centered. Examine the description of each style closely and refer to Mosston and Ashworth's text (1986) to further understand each style. The style you select and operationalize will depend on a host of factors, such as the characteristics of your students, the type of teaching style you feel most comfortable with, the resources available to you, and the nature of the activities the students will engage in. Whether you teach ''by command'' or allow your students to work independently or with partners or in groups is a matter not of right or wrong but of appropriateness and depends on your ability to select one style, varying styles, or a combination of styles best suited for any given lesson. It is equally dependent on your ability to make midstream adjustment during a lesson if another style seems to better fit the particular group of students (see chapter 13 for more on adjusting the lesson).

Questioning

The process of asking questions plays a major role in the development of a lesson. It seems ironic that such a process might not be continued during the lesson itself; that is, isn't the process of questioning an effective strategy for getting students to think about lesson content or their success in achieving their goals? Would it be appropriate for a teacher to ask a series of questions at the beginning, middle, and end of a lesson, to get students to reflect upon and key into lesson goals and content?

Time

It is our impression that some teachers have a hang-up with time. Specifically, if a lesson calls for the students to do something at a given point in time, come hell or high water that's what they are going to do regardless of the appropriateness of such a transition. This seems very odd. If a student is task involved and working diligently toward a goal, why in the world interrupt that progress?

An appropriate strategy might be to build in alternative goals and activities for those who have progressed according to the teacher's schedule and to allow those having difficulty or those who are a bit slower in their progress to keep plugging along. The point is to allow for individual differences. Admittedly, one has to establish some maximum transition point, for students to vary their tasks, but it is unsound pedagogy not to recognize differences in learning rates.

Behavioral objectives are often assigned specific periods of time (see Vogel and Seefeldt [1988] for a formula), and a specific percent of students (e.g., 70%) achieving a specific

Table 12.3   Mosston and Ashworth's Styles of Teaching

Style	Description
Command	A teacher-centered style in which uniformity, conformity, immediate response, and maintenance of standards are central.
Practice	Primarily a teacher-centered style in which the student initiates some decision making as the student engages in tasks in varying organizational patterns. Typically thought of as station teaching.
Reciprocal	Greater responsibility is assumed by the student in giving feedback to a partner or partners as students work in dyads or small groups. The students learn the skill of observation and how to provide feedback. Criteria sheets assist students in the feedback process.
Self-check	The student performs assigned tasks and is responsible for assessing own progress in the acquisition of motor skill. This is facilitated through the use of task and criteria sheets.
Inclusion	This style is very similar to the self-check style, but varies in that it is more developmentally geared as the students select performance levels geared to their own ability.
Guided discovery	This style focuses on the sequence of the learning process as the teacher presents a sequence of questions that bring about corresponding responses by the student.
Divergent	The emphasis within this style is for students to be able to generate alternative solutions to learning problems—all of which are acceptable alternatives to a given problem. The focus is on the students' ability to create rather than replicate.

behavioral objective is predetermined as the transition point to another objective. This approach has the advantage of systematically determining time allotment for each objective and specific transition points. It also enables teachers to be held accountable for student learning. However, this approach also possesses such shortcomings as inflexibility, emphasis on rigid thought (there are other ways to think), and attention to individual differences only in the learning process, not in the required final product (i.e., achieving the behavioral objective).

Once again, you are faced with some choices—in this case, whether to treat time in a more or less structured way. Each way has both benefits and drawbacks.

Feedback

Rink (1985) states that "one of the most significant functions teacher behavior serves during activity is to provide clear feedback to learners on their performance" (p. 241). Feedback, which may be descriptive, corrective, or evaluative, provides information to the learner about the appropriateness or inappropriateness of her or his behavior. Certainly, the learner will be able to discern whether the ball went into the hoop or the bar stayed on the high-jump standard or she or he hit the perfect landing off the beam, but when the quality of performance is less than that desired, what kind of information is the student given? Feedback reinforces behavior (through praise, encouragement, and simply describing correct behavior) as well as provides information (through corrective statements) that allows students to make adjustments. Although a student might get feedback from an outcome itself, feedback related to the quality of performance is usually provided by others (the teacher or a classmate) or produced with technical assistance (e.g., videotaping).

Finally, the student isn't the only one receiving feedback; the teacher also receives feedback throughout a lesson, in constant reminders about the effectiveness or ineffectiveness of a lesson. Through student performance, the teacher gets information about which teaching methods work, which don't work, and what adjustments might or must be considered. The teacher cannot avoid reflection, unless he or she retreats to the confines of the bleachers or the safety of the office. Will you be amenable to feedback, and hence self-reflection, during your Monday-morning lesson? (For more on feedback, see chapter 5.)

Teacher and Student Roles in Planning

We believe the teacher should take an active role in lesson planning and implementation, but not necessarily to the total exclusion of students from the decision-making process. As you ready yourself for your Monday-morning lesson, ask yourself about the roles you will assume in the conduct of the lesson and those assumed by your students. Will the lesson be entirely teacher-centered, or will students have a voice in what happens while they are in the gym? Will students be empowered, or will they be totally controlled by your decisions for them? What will your specific roles be during the beginning, middle, and end of a lesson? What will your students be expected to do? Will you be the only person to model or demonstrate skills, or will students also demonstrate? Will you be the only one to provide feedback, or

will students observe one another and provide feedback? (See the responsibility model in chapter 4 for other empowerment suggestions.)

Finally, as will become clearer in the final chapter of this book, you might consider what will be expected of you by your school. We have yet to see a school that doesn't spell out some very specific set of role expectations for teachers and students in the teaching–learning process.

Organizational Patterns

How are activities, and as a consequence, students, to be arranged in your lesson? There are a multitude of possibilities. Remember the infamous green line? Or was it red? Either way, you remember that line the PE teacher asked you to stand on when she or he took attendance, addressed the class, selected teams, or broke the class into groups. That line served to organize the class. You can select any organizational pattern for any purpose as long as it facilitates easy access to information and opportunities for physical activity. Whether you have students organized in circles as an entire group or break down your class of 30 into six groups of five circles to practice a certain activity, you have to ask yourself whether your choices are promoting the elements of teacher effectiveness. A long line of 30 students waiting to shoot lay-ups at one basket is not nearly as effective as 10 groups of 3 shooting at 10 different baskets.

The way you use space and organize your tasks and your students within those tasks may make a huge difference in the number of turns each individual student gets and ultimately in what students learn. Consider, for example, how you would arrange students while you take attendance, during calisthenics, during drills in a given activity, during lead-up or regular games, or while lecturing to the class. Certainly, at times, space or equipment limitations, as well as an activity itself, may make it difficult to maximize students' opportunities to learn, but it is your role to make every attempt to promote maximum opportunity.

Continuity and Progression

This element is related to the relationships within and among lesson tasks and between your Monday morning lesson and the lessons that follow throughout the week. It is important that within a task (e.g., setting a volleyball) the progression of movements within the task are understood and practiced. For example, what series of movements contributes toward the refinement of that skill? Here, a developmental or qualitative analysis of a skill would be important for the teacher to conduct and translate into the teaching act. If you were to analyze the volleyball set, would your analysis look like the following or something different?

1. The student should face the direction in which the ball is intended to go.
2. The student's feet should be comfortably apart, and one slightly in front of the other.
3. The student's knees should be comfortably flexed.
4. The student's wrist should be cocked back as much as 60 degrees from the line of the forearm.
5. The student's fingers should be spread in a cupped manner.
6. With wrists cocked and fingers spread, the student should form a triangle with the thumbs and index fingers of both hands. The elbows should be flexed so that the hands are 6 to 8 inches above the forehead.
7. As the ball approaches, the entire body should spring gently into the ball.

8. The ball should be contacted with the pads of the thumb and first two fingers on each hand.
9. The relaxed wrist should act as the pivot of a springboard, allowing the ball to force it downward and then restoring force plus rebounding force, and the entire push of the uncoiling body should send the ball into its path.
10. The entire motion of the body should be through the ball and not away from it.

Whether your analysis is similar to this or not, it is important to conduct a task analysis and ascertain the developmental level of your students in relation to each step of your analysis. Of course, some students may be very advanced, whereas others may need to start from ground zero in learning a new skill.

Equally, consider what tasks or activities could be included within a lesson that would lead to the formal execution of a skill. Would the following help one to serve a volleyball from the baseline?

1. Serve 25 times from a distance of 10 feet against the wall.
2. Serve 25 times to a partner standing 20 feet away from you.
3. Serve 25 times to a partner standing on the other side of the net from a distance of 15 feet.
4. Repeat step 3 from 20 feet and then from the baseline.

The point is that there is probably a series of tasks that would help students acquire the skill, and the teacher must reflect on the usefulness of such progressions. Certainly, such variables as time, distance, space, and the number of people involved are but a few factors that would help in varying tasks and contributing to learning progressions and to the flow and momentum of a lesson.

Finally, will your lesson on Monday have continuity with the rest of the week's lessons? Will one lesson flow into the next? Will the activities on Tuesday connect with those presented on Monday? Will students benefit from these connections? Lessons must take continuity into account if the teacher expects students to return to their next class with a positive predisposition toward physical education, and, most important, if students are to learn.

EVALUATION

We have already suggested that the feedback process enables the teacher to assess student learning and the extent to which the lesson plan has been effective. You may believe that if your Monday morning lesson has numerous behavioral objectives, your evaluation may be easier; that is, student behavior may be easily assessed according to each behavior you expect of your students. This may or may not be the case, depending on the number of behavioral objectives you have for your 30 students. In fact, your ability to assess each and every student's progress toward each and every objective may be very difficult indeed. It would appear to be somewhat difficult to assess student progress toward each objective through mere observation, and a lesson geared toward formalized testing would appear to be the natural alternative for assessing behavioral objectives. However, this, too, may be a rather tedious and unexciting process for evaluating student learning. Formal testing is time consuming and may or may not be the best option in evaluating student progress. Nonetheless, should one elect to formally test students, there are countless instruments for assessing students' performance in the psychomotor, cognitive, fitness, and personal–social domains (Safrit, 1986).

Let's suggest an alternative evaluative strategy that may be linked to one or two goals for your Monday class. For example, let's say you would like your 30 students to perform a set in volleyball, and you would like them to demonstrate teamwork by passing the volleyball five times before it is set and then hit over the net. How would you evaluate your students? How would you evaluate the goals and procedures of your lesson? How would you evaluate your teaching? How would you evaluate your program? We now examine these questions.

Evaluating Your Students

Let's stay with the same example. Observing your students in practice and during a game will help you assess their progress. You can record each student's setting ability by noting the quality of performance as you scan the class in activity. In a game situation you can evaluate each student's contribution to the team concept. And you can give feedback to students while you record information about their performance. Your performance assessments can be in either qualitative terms (What did the student look like in performing the set?) or quantitative terms (How many times did the student perform the set? How many times was the student successful?)

You can also assess each student's performance with respect to the personal–social goals of the class (How did the student get along with others? What effect does the lesson have on the student's attitudes or feelings toward activity and his or her sense of self in PE?) This may be accomplished by observing students or by asking students to respond in writing or verbally to questions that focus on their affective reaction to each lesson. You might gain some very useful information about each student's likes or dislikes regarding the lesson, as well as suggestions as to how a lesson might be changed.

Finally, if you wish to gain insight into a student's cognitive gains (i.e., understanding movement concepts or principles, game strategy, rules, etc.), this again may be assessed through observation or through written or oral exercises. Does the student follow the rules? Does the student know what to do in a particular offensive or defensive strategy? Can the student explain a concept, principle, rule, or strategy verbally or in writing?

Naturally, it is unlikely that you could assess each student every day for every goal. Nonetheless, attempt to formatively evaluate students over time (throughout a unit of activity) rather than depending entirely on summative evaluations (whereby a student is usually tested at the end of a unit of activity). Understanding students over time seems to be much more reasonable than a one-shot, "show me what you got, kid" approach to student evaluation. Evaluation doesn't always have to be geared to the individual student. Notes and feedback may be recorded or presented in relation to small groups of students with similar entry characteristics and goals or to a class in total.

Evaluating Your Teaching

How do you know you have been an effective teacher? How do you know when the behaviors you exhibit in your class have influenced your students in a positive or negative direction? What evaluation techniques could you employ to assess your teaching? Do you even care about assessing your instruction, and why? What would you do with information about

your daily instruction? These questions all center around the assessment of your teaching and your willingness and ability to observe, analyze, and make decisions about your teaching.

In the last decade, the evaluation of teaching has received widespread attention (Wittrock, 1986). Research on teaching effectiveness has provided many answers about which teacher behaviors promote student learning in physical education (Graham & Heimerer, 1981; Harrison, 1987). These answers have resulted primarily from rigorous systematic observation of teaching and, in many cases, very complex research designs. Although we wouldn't suggest that you should seek to win the Nobel prize through the study of your teaching, we do think you can become a serious student of teaching by examining your instruction—by trying to better understand what you're doing on Monday morning! How do you do this?

First of all, as in the development of a good lesson, you'll need a plan to assess your teaching. This plan will center around your general interest in knowing how you teach or in the identification of a problem or issue you would like to assess and resolve. For example, do you want to assess the type of feedback you present to students or the extent to which you provide feedback on a daily basis? How do you deal with pupil control issues? Does your involvement in settling discipline problems consume too much time? Do you ask questions? How thoroughly do you explain lesson content? What do your students think of your instruction and your lessons?

These are just a few questions one might pose. Naturally, the next question is how to go about answering them—the methods and possible instrumentation involved. First, there are countless observational systems that one can employ. In fact, the text edited by Darst, Zakrajsek, and Mancini (1989) offers teachers and researchers a variety of instruments specific to physical education settings. These instruments are primarily quantitative and can assist you in gaining a descriptive picture of your teaching behavior. You can videotape your lesson and then code and analyze the behavior, or have another person (a teaching colleague or school administrator) trained in the use of a system collect and analyze the data.

You might opt to use a qualitative approach (Griffin & Templin, 1989; Locke, 1989; Templin, 1979). Again through the use of a video- or audiotape or through the assistance of others, you can develop a narrative of class events from which you might gain a better understanding of your teaching. Research using qualitative approaches has provided excellent insight into life in the gym for physical educators and physical education students (Griffin, 1981, 1984, 1985a, 1985b; Locke, Griffin, & Templin, 1986; Templin, 1989). The following illustrates a narrative collected during a 1-minute observation in a secondary school (Templin, 1979).

The students, each bouncing or tossing a utility ball, stood in specified spots on the gymnasium stage. The boys were dressed alike in white shirts, white shorts, white socks, and sneakers of various colors. The student teacher walked in front of the students against the back wall of the stage, stopped and stared at the students who were conversing with one another. One of the students noticed that the student teacher was staring at the class, and began

You can use a videotape of your class to quantitatively or qualitatively evaluate your teaching.

to "shh shh" the others. The entire class became quiet as the student teacher spoke as the students stood erect. They were at attention. The student teacher said, "Pay attention and don't bounce the balls until I tell you. If you do, you will have to sit out the remainder of the period." As the students listened, a boy dropped his ball and the student teacher noticed this as the boy regained possession of the ball. The student teacher then directed the boy to sit down. The boy walked to the side of the room where the student teacher stood and sat down next to the wall.

If you were the teacher, what would your response be to this portrait? Is this information useful to you in reflecting upon your behavior and your future interaction with your students? Can you imagine what an entire class might look like in narrative form? A few words can be very meaningful if you take the time to paint your classroom picture and analyze its meaning.

Finally, the use of surveys, questionnaires, and interviews may provide you with further data about your instruction. These tools may range from brief one- or two-question surveys (How was class today? How did I [the teacher] do today?) to more extensive assessments of one's teaching. Of course, day-to-day communication with students is important. Your students will give you lots of information if you just take the time to ask and if it is perceived as a genuine solicitation. Infrequent surveys and interaction with students to assess your teaching may not give you the objective and reliable data you are looking for.

Of course, the purpose of all of this is to develop reflective teaching. Being sensitive to what and how you are doing as a teacher is important. It will lead to personal and profes-sional growth and as a consequence will likely benefit your students as well.

Evaluating Your Lesson

As suggested earlier, the assessment of student progress toward goals will give you a great deal of insight into the success of your Monday-morning lesson. Equally, the examination of your teaching will provide feedback that will further help to assess and refine your lesson. The important point to remember is that you reflect upon both evaluation processes if your lessons are to improve and benefit your students. Your joy and satisfaction in teaching will depend to a great extent not only on your students' growth within physical education, but on your growth as well. This translates into having the best lessons possible for your students.

Posner (1989) presents a series of questions you may find useful when conducting a post-mortem of your Monday-morning lesson (see Figure 12.2). These questions should suggest ways to maintain what was positive about your lesson and to alter whatever didn't seem to work. In essence, the postmortem is a way to reflect upon and improve your lesson.

Evaluating Your Program

Program evaluation ranges beyond lesson evaluation in asking whether or not progress is being made toward the curriculum model's program goals. Of all the dimensions of evaluation, this question is the *least* likely to be asked. Most of the above suggestions could help determine the extent of progress toward program goals, but for the sake of simplicity we have divided program evaluation into three questions:

- Have student behaviors, whether or not stated as behavioral objectives, progressed in the direction of program goals?

1. Did the activity you planned actually occur? If not, why not?
2. Were the objectives realistic? Did other ones emerge during the lesson?
3. Did the learners' actual knowledge and skills correspond to your expectations? Did any discrepancies cause you to modify the lesson?
4. Did you cover what you planned? Did you plan too much or too little content to cover?
5. Did the procedures work? If not, what went wrong?
6. Did the results you anticipated occur? If not, what went wrong?
7. Did you provide sufficient resources? What else was needed?
8. Did you get adequate feedback during the lesson? What did you learn from the feedback? Did the learners get sufficient feedback?
9. Was the time adequate? Was the time used efficiently?
10. Were the follow-up activities done? Were they effective?

Figure 12.2. A lesson plan postmortem. *Note.* From *Field Experience: Methods of Reflective Teaching* (pp. 136-137) by George J. Posner. Copyright © 1989 by Longman. Reprinted with permission.

- Have instructional strategies that are clearly related to the implementation of program goals been employed on a daily basis?
- What are the teachers' and students' perceptions, thoughts, and feelings about the program?

By asking these three questions, you can detect not only behavioral changes but also your intentions and the affective and perceived impact of the program. For example, in relation to the concepts-based curriculum model, we would want to know (a) Did the students' conceptual knowledge base grow as the result of the program? (b) Were concepts taught to students on a daily basis? and (c) How did the teacher and students feel about this approach, and what did they perceive to be happening in the program?

In the end, these questions return us to the very first chapter of the book and to the question, "Is it worth doing?" Your students may be able to do a zillion sit-ups or set world records in track, but in the end both you and the students must decide whether these experiences are meaningful to teach and meaningful to learn

and do. And it is up to teachers to reflect upon the personal meanings they and their students attach to PE in determining, ultimately, what needs to be changed.

WRAP-UP

Mosston and Ashworth (1986) state that "successful teaching results from congruence between what was intended and what actually occurs in the lessons. To reach congruence, the teacher must know and capably manage a number of factors that can either enhance or hinder this potential congruence" (p. 1). This chapter has addressed those factors critical to the planning, organizing, and evaluation of a physical education class.

We have provided some data related to effective lesson planning, and we have examined lesson elements that must be reflected upon in the decision-making process. The relationships among lesson and objectives and tasks were discussed, as well as a number of lesson dimensions that influence the impact of the lesson plan. Basically, three questions must be posed in preparing and analyzing a lesson: What are you trying to achieve? How will you accomplish your goals and objectives? How will you know that you have accomplished your goals and objectives?

This chapter has provided ways of approaching each of these questions, as well as some strategies for evaluation of your instruction and your lesson. We then returned to the question "Is it worth doing?" in the overall examination of preparing, implementing, and evaluating your lesson.

THE EXPERTS RESPOND

Robin: I'm ready for Monday morning. I know what the goals for my class are, and so do my students—in fact, they determined many of their own goals. These kids are engaged in activities geared to their own developmental level, and I make sure that when they leave the gym, they share their feelings and perceptions with me in the last few minutes of class. Also, I keep a journal of my thoughts and feelings. To me, this is the essence of evaluation.

Chris: Lesson plans? Behavioral objectives? Individualized instruction? Formative evaluation? Give me a break! You think I have time for all this stuff? Give them a few games, and they'll be happy. What was that "busy, happy, and good" research? For once, I agree with it. Hey, I've been around a long time, and I know what is best for these guys, and it sure isn't the reciprocal style of teaching or conducting some task analysis! Furthermore, I know how I teach. Why would I want to study my teaching?

Lynn: Chris, as usual, you never cease to amaze me. Look, we know what it takes for kids to achieve—for teachers to be effective. Yes, once in a great while it may be appropriate to roll out the ball and not to prescribe their every move, but if you really care about your kids, you have to plan for each and every lesson in a systematic way. Where is your accountability? You've got to have goals, keep students on task, observe and give feedback to kids, and study your teaching. What's wrong with keeping records, charting kids' behavior, and using the data to everyone's benefit? What's wrong with being a little scientific about planning and teaching? What's wrong with studying how you teach? You may learn a little about yourself. Where I disagree with this chapter is in giving teachers a choice about using behavioral objectives. They are essential to good teaching; without them, goals remain fuzzy and teachers remain unaccountable.

Pat: I agree, Lynn—to a point! It seems like we agree pretty much on being organized, running drills, and all that good stuff. But I don't think I need a written lesson plan. Heck, as I walk down the hall into the gym, my plan comes to me just as well as if I spent hours writing everything down. I do wonder about all this record-keeping and behavioral-objectives business—your so-called scientific approach. As far as I can tell, the teacher can do only so much. It sounds like you're a robot in the way you teach.

Robin: Pat, you've hit upon a good point here. The technical or scientific approach to teaching has a very important place in our schools, but not at the expense of reducing kids to little machines responding to each command. What about the human touch? What about uncovering what's inside the teacher and what's inside kids through our lessons? Where's the art of teaching versus just the science? Life is not just a behavioral objective.

SELF-REFLECTION

It's not surprising that our experts differ to some degree on their approaches to planning and conducting a class. As suggested throughout this text, physical education has a very different meaning to each person, and as a consequence teachers have very different interpretations of what is worth doing as a teacher.

We thought it might be interesting to see where our experts fall on the continuum presented earlier (Figure 12.3). Lynn's approach is primarily technical, and Chris seems to operate on intuition and whatever seems to be easiest at the moment; Lynn follows a linear model of instruction that is prescriptive in nature à la Hunter (1984) and Posner (1989), whereas Chris plays everything by ear. Robin believes in an integrative approach to teaching that seeks a balance between the technical and scientific and the artful and humane aspects of the teaching–learning process. Robin is rather

mobile on our continuum. Finally, Pat is the traditionalist who leans toward the technical and follows the straight-and-narrow approach to teaching.

Where do you wish to fall on this continuum? Will your answer to this question benefit your students?

Although it is easy to stereotype individuals the way we have done with our experts, our intent was not simply to label a diverse group. Our intent was to help you think about your philosophy, attitudes, and behavior in relation to the various concepts and strategies illustrated in this book. This is no less true for this chapter. Again the question is, what's worth planning for your students? How will your teaching perspective influence your daily approach to teaching—your approach to Monday morning? Where will you fall on the continuum of lesson planning, implementation, and evaluation (Figure 12.4)?

To assess how much structure real teachers

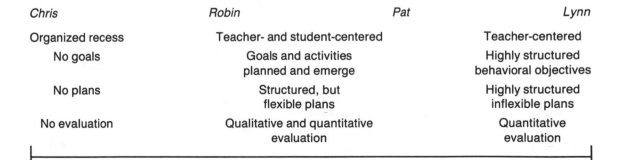

Chris	Robin	Pat	Lynn
Organized recess	Teacher- and student-centered		Teacher-centered
No goals	Goals and activities planned and emerge		Highly structured behavioral objectives
No plans	Structured, but flexible plans		Highly structured inflexible plans
No evaluation	Qualitative and quantitative evaluation		Quantitative evaluation

Figure 12.3. A continuum of teaching methods and lesson planning: The experts.

Where are you?

Organized recess	Teacher- and student-centered	Teacher-centered
No goals	Goals and activities planned and emerge	Highly structured behavioral objectives
No plans	Structured, but flexible plans	Highly structured inflexible plans
No evaluation	Qualitative and quantitative evaluation	Quantitative evaluation
	Where are you?	

Figure 12.4.   A continuum of teaching methods and lesson planning: Where are you?

in real PE settings put into their lesson planning, visit three secondary schools and observe a physical education lesson. Analyze each lesson using Posner's (1989, p. 51) structured (the far-right side of the continuum) set of questions and strategies for analyzing a lesson (which are based on Hunter's [1984] work):

1. **Anticipatory set.** What has the teacher done to get the students' attention, to relate the lesson to what the students have done previously, and to engage them in the lesson? Look for how the teacher communicates to students that the lesson is about to begin, whether the teacher reviews previous lessons, how the teacher tries to stimulate interest, and what the teacher does to lay the groundwork for the lesson.

2. **Objective and purpose.** What has the teacher done to communicate to the students what they are supposed to get out of the lesson and why that is important?

3. **Input.** What knowledge and skills necessary to achieve the lesson's objective does the teacher make available to the students, and how does the teacher provide them? Look for the specific methods employed.

4. **Modeling.** How does the teacher show the students what they are expected to produce or learn to do? What kinds of demonstrations are employed?

5. **Checking for understanding.** How does the teacher monitor the students' understanding of concepts and proficiency in skills during the lesson? How does the teacher adjust the lesson on the basis of feedback? Look for ways the teacher invites questions, how the teacher asks and answers questions (including the amount of time the teacher waits for an answer), how many students the teacher involves in questioning, and what the teacher does with a student's answer, especially when it is wrong.

6. **Guided practice.** How does the teacher give the students opportunities to practice using their new knowledge or skills under direct teacher supervision?

7. **Independent practice.** How does the teacher provide opportunities for students to practice using their new knowledge or skills independently?

Design and implement two lessons using the models illustrated in Figure 12.1 and Tables 12.1 and 12.2. After teaching each lesson, answer the questions in Figure 12.2 as a means of analyzing and judging the effectiveness of your lesson.

Finally, videotape or observe a lesson by a secondary teacher or yourself and quantitatively and qualitatively study the teaching process. Select a systematic observation system of your choice, code your tape, and then describe your results. Follow this with recommendations for the teacher. Repeat the process qualitatively.

SUGGESTED READINGS

The following texts provide additional insight into curriculum and instruction processes:

Hellison, D. (1986). *Goals and strategies in teaching physical education*. Champaign, IL: Human Kinetics.

Lawson, H., & Placek, J. (1981). *Physical education in the secondary schools: Curricular alternatives*. Boston: Allyn & Bacon.

Mager, R. (1962). *Preparing instructional objectives*. Palo Alto, CA: Fearon.

Mosston, M., & Ashworth, S. (1986). *Teaching physical education*. Columbus, OH: Merrill.

Rink, J. (1985). *Teaching physical education for learning*. St. Louis: Times Mirror/ Mosby.

Siedentop, D., Mand, C., & Taggart, A. (1986). *Physical education: Teaching and curriculum strategies for grades 5-12*. Palo Alto, CA: Mayfield.

The following readings may be useful in the evaluation of your students, lessons, teaching, and programs:

Anderson, W. (1980). *Analysis of teaching physical education*. St. Louis: Mosby.

Darst, P., Zakrajsek, D., & Mancini, V. (1989). *Analyzing physical education and sport instruction*. Champaign, IL: Human Kinetics.

Kirkendall, D., Gruber, J., & Johnson, R. (1987). *Measurement and evaluation for physical educators*. Champaign, IL: Human Kinetics.

Locke, L. (1989). Qualitative research as a form of scientific inquiry in sport and physical education. *Research Quarterly for Exercise and Sport,* **60**(1), 1-20.

Safrit, M. (1986). *Introduction to measurement in physical education and exercise science*. St. Louis: Times Mirror/Mosby.

Chapter 13

The Art of Teaching

Teaching involves artistry, qualities that defy precise measurement; these talents can be sensed but not pinned down very accurately when an excellent teacher is being observed. Comments such as these are typical: "She has a nice touch with kids" or "There's good chemistry in his gym" or "She just seems to know when to do what to whom" or "Her students sure work hard for her" or "He has eyes in the back of his head." Many terms have been used to try to capture the essence of this artistry—*intuition, creativity, personality, love*, and so on. As one teacher told a researcher who wanted to evaluate her teaching:

> You know, when I teach it's like an act of love. Between me and my students, there's a relationship that creates a current that explains whether they learn something or not. You won't be measuring that current because you or your damn instruments can't see it and probably don't even think it's there. (Huberman, 1987, p. 11)

The same researcher got a similar message about the complexity and mystery of real-world teaching from another teacher: "My model of instruction and learning was, as [the other teacher] diplomatically put it, just a little undercomplicated" (Huberman, 1987, p. 11).

THE ART AND SCIENCE OF TEACHING

With the advent of research on teaching, scholars have argued about and struggled with the relationship between the science of teaching and the art of teaching. Sometimes, scholars of the science of teaching in physical education point out that such seemingly artistic qualities as chemistry or charisma are in reality specific behaviors that can be taught to teachers. As one such researcher commented during a presentation on the measurement of effective teaching: "I'm confident that someday we'll be able to calibrate charisma!" Other times, these scholars tend to argue that a scientific basis for effective teaching exists but that teachers must modify these findings to meet the needs of their students and settings—that is, they must apply some artistry to the scientific findings. On the other end of the science–art spectrum, Alan Tom (1984), in arguing for teaching as an art and a craft, states that teachers must create their own styles and strategies rather than replicate others' blueprints, scientific or otherwise. Somewhere in the middle, Cronbach (1982), a social scientist, points out that social science research can offer insights into particular situations and settings but will never reach the point of developing laws for teaching. Or, as Shavelson (1988) puts it:

> Professional competence lies in the translation of scientific theories and "facts" into practical, goal-directed actions. Because the set of potential applications is indefinitely large—and therefore so is the set of "novel" situations encountered by the practitioner—practice must involve the art of translating scientific knowledge into actions applied to novel situations, even constructing new knowledge on the spot from experience when surprising situations arise. (p. 6)

In large part, the debate over the art and science of teaching can be explained by the conflicting assumptions, conceptions, or paradigms held by the debating scholars. Zahorik (1986) identifies three different conceptions of good teaching—science–research, theory–philosophy, and art–craft—which can serve to label scholars in the art–science debate. Henderson (1988) suggests five paradigms of teacher education that are both overlapping and conflicting "frameworks for describing the complex nature of teaching" (p. 14): (a) efficient promotion of student achievement, which is similar to Zahorik's science–research conception; (b) expression of personal theory and belief, which is similar to Zahorik's theory–philosophy conception; (c) moral craftsmanship and critical theory, which is similar to Zahorik's art–craft conception; (d) pedagogical reasoning and action, which emphasizes teaching knowledge; and (e) pedagogical presence, as described in van Manen's work (1986). The point is that teaching can be viewed from a number of perspectives, each of which emphasizes certain aspects of teaching and ignores others.

Teaching is neither pure art nor pure science, but we believe, along with the critic of the researcher cited above, that scientific models are "undercomplicated," that artistry not only exists but is a crucial factor in effective teaching. Although it is by its very nature somewhat inexplicable, we believe that it can be conceptualized, at least to a point, and that by so doing, physical education teachers will be able to make at least some small improvements in their artistry. It may well be that some of you are, by your socialization and perhaps even your heredity, better at artistry than others; good teachers may in some sense be born, not made. However, all of us can improve our artistry, and that is the goal of this chapter.

We have conceptualized artistry into three general components, each with a number of subcomponents. Please keep in mind that these concepts lack a certain degree of precision, that conceptual fuzziness is inherent in the definition of artistry. The three general components are

- personal qualities and style,
- intuition, and
- self-reflection.

PERSONAL QUALITIES AND STYLE

Our conceptualization of the personal qualities and style component of artistry includes a number of subcomponents:

- The therapeutic triad, buttressed by exceptional approachability, enhancing student dignity and worth, enthusiasm, commitment, and teaching by example
- The development of credibility involving the augmented therapeutic triad as well as

creative, relevant teaching and persistence and confrontation
- A playful spirit

The Therapeutic Triad

Perhaps the most influential treatment of personal qualities is that of Carl Rogers (1983). Rogers applies the therapeutic triad originally designed for therapists to teaching. This triad consists of

- concern,
- empathy, and
- genuineness.

Concern refers to teachers' caring about students' welfare and development and being able to communicate a feeling of warmth. Empathy refers to teachers' ability to put themselves in their students' place (in their gym shoes), to feel what they feel. Genuineness refers to teachers being themselves rather than phonies. These components of the therapeutic triad sound straightforward, but they are difficult to put into practice. Lots of students are impossible to love and difficult to like. Empathy is extremely difficult even with one's closest friends. Genuineness not only flies in the face of much of what teachers are "supposed to be" with students, but being genuine could mean sharing one's anxieties and vulnerabilities, thus opening up a whole new set of problems.

Still, the therapeutic triad makes some sense, especially if a few interpretations and modifications are added. Kids do need to know that their teacher cares about them, not necessarily that they are loved but that their welfare and development are major concerns. Empathy is difficult, but listening, hypothetically at least, is not (although most of us don't do it very well). By listening, teachers can see more of the student's

side and can convey the impression, hopefully a genuine one, that they are trying to understand and, in connection with the previous discussion, that they care. Some related strategies also convey these messages: active listening or paraphrasing in which what the student says is repeated back (e.g., "You're saying that you don't like gymnastics"); teachers reporting their own inner feelings; teachers offering alternatives without prescribing correct solutions; or teachers sharing ways they have dealt with similar situations without implying that these ways are correct for the student.

By listening, teachers can convey concern and empathy.

The concept of genuineness is complex. The literature on effective teaching emphasizes modeling and other specific teacher behaviors, suggesting that teachers should indeed do things that aren't genuine for them. And of course, these scholars are right—to a point. That a teacher is having a bad day and feels like being nasty does not justify being nasty. On the other hand, it may be appropriate for teachers to share their feelings; after all, they are human, too (they don't sleep in the back of the gym), and students need to know that. In most instances it would be inappropriate to share with students a shattered romance; but teachers who communicate their own vulnerability—that they don't know some fact or don't perform some skill very well, that they are human and do make mistakes and aren't always "up"—seems to us to be preferable to teachers who present themselves as authorities who have all the answers.

Other Personal Qualities Related to the Therapeutic Triad

In Csikszentmihalyi and McCormack's (1986) study of the influence of teachers, "teenagers [saw] influential teachers as exceptionally approachable—'easy to talk to' and ready to listen" (p. 418). Exceptional approachability is another way to state the case for concern and empathy. Wigginton (1986) put it yet a different way:

> The one sin that is unforgivable is to diminish a student's sense of dignity and worth. The corollary is that it is equally wrong not to work to enhance that sense of dignity and worth. And many students, having turned from their parents temporarily, want it from us. (p. 235)

Enthusiasm has been implicated in many discourses on effective teaching and as a result has been studied in an effort to identify behaviors that can be taught to teachers. In the study of the influence of teachers cited above, "teenagers described influential teachers in terms of their ability to generate enthusiasm for learning through personal involvement with the subject matter and skill in teaching it . . . teachers who communicate a sense of excitement, a contagious intellectual thrill" (Csikszentmihalyi &

McCormack, 1986, p. 418). From our perspective, attempting to copy enthusiastic behaviors misses the point. First of all, we all have our own ways of enthusing. Second, enthusiasm ought to be genuine. (How do you act when you are genuinely enthusiastic about something?) As the above quote suggests, teachers who were identified as being influential communicated a "sense of excitement . . . a contagious . . . thrill." We strongly suspect that no teacher can communicate such excitement and contagion without personally feeling it, especially day in and day out (whether anyone can do it day in and day out is another question). Third, the above quote refers to personal involvement and skill in teaching. From these teenagers' point of view, enthusiasm manifested itself in much more than some "rah rah" expression of enthusiasm. We believe that in order for teachers to be enthusiastic, they must be genuinely committed. Once again, choice of curriculum model is crucial. Further, choice of subject matter (e.g., badminton versus volleyball) can make the difference in a teacher's enthusiasm (to which anyone who has taught can attest).

In the above quote, teenagers referred to the personal involvement of teachers. John Rustin said this about teaching: "[It] is a painful, continual and difficult work, to be done by kindness, by watching, by warning, by precept and by praise, but—above all—by example" (cited in Nolte, 1988). Part of what being genuine as a teacher means is to be what one stands for, to do what one preaches. The popular indictment of teaching—"Those who can, do; those who can't, teach"—needs to be rebutted by deeds rather than words. Teaching by example, along with enthusiasm and commitment, strengthens a teacher's genuineness.

Developing Credibility

Wigginton (1986) states that

> Teachers have to build up credibility like money in the bank. Each act with a student, carried through to successful completion, is like a deposit. The student's reaction, communicated to peers through that elaborate grapevine of theirs, is like interest. (p. 232)

Credibility, like trust, needs to be earned, and the process is often a slow one. The therapeutic triad, augmented as we have suggested, is essential to this process. So are some other things. Teachers must "take the trouble to express their message in unusual, memorable ways" (Csikszentmihalyi & McCormack, 1986, p. 418) and to connect their subject matter to students' lives in meaningful ways. Of course, making a handstand meaningful to a bunch of kids whose hormones are in high gear is no easy task. Creative teaching will help, and so will finding some relevance for the task in student lives.

In the long run, credibility is also enhanced by persistence. What we mean by persistence is the commitment of teachers to outlast their students! It is clear that students have their own hidden (or perhaps not-so-hidden) goals that often conflict with the teacher's goals (see chapter 2). Teachers sometimes give up their goals: "The kids seem to want to play bombardment, so that's what I better give them." One of our experts, Chris, seems to be making this argument. Anything new is likely to be met with various gestures of derision ("Boy, is this dumb!"). Adjusting and modifying one's plans is certainly important, as we shall argue shortly, but so is having the courage to stick to

them in the face of hostility. We call that quality persistence.

Grant (1988) pushes this concept further:

> The teacher must have the . . . ability to engage in the creative confrontation that is at the heart of all good teaching. The teacher must have the courage to make demands on a student, to insist that the student . . . do work that is often difficult . . . and sometimes boring. (p. 7)

The development of credibility and trust requires balancing creative, relevant teaching with persistence and confrontation, all within the context of concern, empathy, and genuineness. This is a two-part balancing act—the teacher trying to determine how much to push students, what he or she "can get away with," while trying to entice students in creative, relevant ways; and the teacher trying to show concern and empathy while mustering the courage to confront and be persistent and true to her or his goals. Both the qualities themselves and this balance of qualities require considerable artistry on the part of the teacher. There is no formula for determining the ratio of, say, relevance to confrontation, and there is no set of specific behaviors that will produce any of these qualities for all students in all settings. A key to the implementation of personal qualities and style is intuition, which we will discuss shortly.

A Playful Spirit

A playful spirit is essential to physical education. Certainly not all of our activities are playful; fitness isn't necessarily play-oriented nor is, for example, self-defense instruction. But we believe that a playful spirit on the part of the teacher creates an enjoyable environment for learning. Self-defense can be taught playfully (it's certainly serious enough by its very nature not to need a boost of seriousness), and so can fitness. Playful spirit means feeling and expressing the fun of the activity in a way that is personally genuine. A teacher who doesn't like a particular activity but must teach it can share a short story of his or her own ineptness; learning to laugh at oneself is an important part of developing a playful spirit. Teachers can look for fun and humor in the students' interaction with the activity, sharing what they see as well as what students say. Student humor is often priceless. Of course, students are good at laughing at others' foibles rather than their own. They need to learn that being playful excludes laughing at others but very much includes laughing at oneself.

There is a fine line in some of this. For example, one of us, in teaching self-defense, has told students after they tried to do a round kick that they look like birds trying to take off, that they need to keep their arms down to protect themselves. They laughed and seemed to get the point. However, there is nothing playful about this comment if students perceive the teacher to be making fun of them.

INTUITION

Some teachers seem to have a second sense. They sense that their plan is not going to work before they try it out, so they change it. They sense that certain kids who are usually friends aren't going to be able to work together on this particular day, so they separate them. They sense that one of their favorite activities or drills, one they really enjoy in their own leisure time, just won't work with this group of students. These teachers possess what we call intuition. By intuition we simply mean the ability to predict what is going to work accurately most of the time, based on a few clues (Rubin, 1985). There is nothing paranormal, mystical, or magical about this kind of intuition. It's a matter of paying attention to clues, drawing conclusions based on an extension of these clues, and then acting on these conclusions. For example, a teacher who has planned to start a new unit in volleyball but notices that most of her students are using the volleyballs to try the basketball challenges of the previous unit may decide to stay with basketball for a couple more days or even just ask her students if they want to stay with basketball a while longer. An observer might think that this teacher had not planned very well and then, after watching the class, wonder what secret this teacher possesses that enabled her to get such cooperation from her class.

You might have noticed that the teacher in the example just given possesses another quality in addition to intuition: flexibility. Intuition is useless for teachers who are rigid, whose

A teacher's playful spirit creates an enjoyable environment for learning.

plans are going to be executed no matter what, because they won't make the necessary changes no matter what clues they observe. Plans that are "etched in stone" cannot be modified, adapted to a changing situation, or scrapped. Intuition, as we have defined it, is necessary to sense what changes need to be made; flexibility is necessary in order to make the changes.

Because we have already made a case for persistence, the question of conflict between persistence and flexibility arises. Both are important. Persisting in one's commitment to one's values is central to good teaching in our view, but so is being insightful enough and flexible enough to change when change is necessary. Commitment is essential; rigidity is problematic. A rule of thumb we have used in our own teaching is to ask "How much can I get away with on this particular day with these kids?" by which we mean: How closely can I adhere to my plan and my goals? How much do I have to modify just to get something I deem important across today?

It takes more than flexibility to come up with an alternative plan, strategy, or activity; it often takes on-the-spot creativity. Too often, creativity is perceived as a genetic talent that only few of us possess, so most of us don't try to cultivate it. In reality, being creative means thinking of as many alternative ways of doing something as one can—in other words, loosening up one's thinking. For example, if a teacher's goal is to promote fair play in her or his class, one way to do this is to lecture students about the importance of playing fair. That's one way (and not a very effective way at that). What are some other ways? The teacher could assign points for specific fair-play behaviors that would be part of the score of the game. The teacher could ask students to fill out a brief questionnaire after the game concerning the ex-

tent of their effort and success at playing fair. The teacher could have students rank playing fair, winning, and playing as well as they can (Webb, 1969) and discuss the results. And so on. As we have said, everyone can be creative, at least to some extent. But it takes practice.

One way to help develop intuition, flexibility, and creativity is an adaptation of Orlick's (1990) solutions bank. Before a particular class period the teacher thinks about, and writes down, the various things that could go wrong with or interfere with the day's plan. For each of these problems, the teacher writes down a couple of solutions: if such-and-such happens, then. . . . After a while, this kind of thinking will become automatic, and the teacher won't need to go through the process in such a structured manner. The whole idea is to help the teacher become mentally prepared for the variety of disruptions and interruptions that may be encountered in the day's lesson; in this way, the unforeseen becomes part of the teacher's awareness. We think that the solutions-bank exercise helps teachers tune into clues related to various potential problems, to be more flexible in their planning, and to practice creative solutions.

THE ARTISTRY OF SELF-REFLECTION

Perhaps the key to the art of teaching is the central theme of this book: self-reflection. The simplest form of self-reflection is to take a couple of minutes at the end of a class or a day to think about what worked, what didn't, and what might have worked better. The goal is to derive as much insight as possible from the day's experiences, to learn from one's successes as well as one's mistakes, to become just one "click" better at teaching. The insight that

The key to the art of teaching is self-reflection.

comes from such reflection contributes significantly, perhaps immeasurably, to the teacher's artistry.

Conceptualizing Self-Reflection

Every quality we have discussed so far in this chapter—concern, empathy, genuineness, playful spirit, enthusiasm, creativity, intuition, flexibility—would benefit from reflective thought. How caring did I appear to my students today? How much listening did I do? How much fun did I have? How could I have done these things better? Did I pick up any clues and modify my plans as a result? If so, did it work? If not, what am I missing in my observations?

However, self-reflection extends beyond a daily analysis of one's artistry. It pervades (or ought to pervade, from this perspective) every aspect of teaching. The teacher becomes a problem solver, analyzing every situation that didn't work well, as well as every situation that did. The goal is to gain as much insight into one's teaching as possible and to build on these insights, because, as Schon (1983, p. 140) puts

it, "artistry hinges on the range and variety of the repertoire that the teacher brings to an unfamiliar situation."

In addition to reflecting upon one's artistic qualities and problem-solving specific situations, self-reflection requires that the teacher reflect upon the application of theoretical and scientific teaching principles to determine whether they really work with specific students in a specific setting as applied by that specific teacher. Everything the teacher tries needs to be evaluated. For example: Does a predetermined ratio of positive to corrective comments apply to all students? Do all students need to meet the minimal criteria for aerobic development in order to experience aerobic development? Do any of the individualized instruction approaches work? If not, why not? Do hustles and prompts help create a more positive environment? Does the sit-out option work? Do game modifications work? Do lab days work? Do moral education discussions work? And so on.

Of course the larger reflective question is, What's worth doing? Am I *trying* to make the kind of contribution that I really value, that I want to stand for? Whether they are working or not, if your pursuits are not worth doing, changes need to be made, either in your job or, more modestly, in the curriculum model or goals. We have discussed this in chapter 1 and at some length throughout this book and will continue to do so, for we believe that this question is closely related to commitment and lies at the heart of good teaching. A related question is what students need, what's worth doing for them. Both of these questions—what's worth doing in relation to the teacher's values and what's worth doing in terms of the kids' needs—are central to the reflection process.

Self-reflection can also facilitate a deeper self-study. How defensive am I when things go wrong? Who or what do I blame? Am I really exploring alternative ways of getting the job done? One's self-esteem can be examined as part of this self-study. Do I feel competent as a performer? Am I fit enough? Do these things matter to me or affect my attitude about myself as a teacher? How do I feel about myself as a teacher?

Doing Self-Reflection

Perhaps the best way to discipline oneself to reflect on a regular basis is to keep a journal, at least until self-reflection becomes a habit. We have given the journal-keeper much to reflect upon. It might help, at least at first, to limit journal entries to reflections on the two questions we raised earlier: What's worth doing? and Is it working? Sometimes it helps to start the daily entry with a grade (A-F) or score (10-1) of one's perceived satisfaction in these two areas, followed by a brief explanation of the reasons for the grade or score. Eventually, reflections on one's artistry, on specific problems, on generic teaching principles applied to a specific setting, and on oneself as teacher can be undertaken. The important thing is for teachers to take time to think about what they did, whether they could have done better, and what they might do the next day to improve.

In the daily press of activities not only is it easy to skip a journal entry—after all, who else cares?—but even when journal entries are diligently made, the what's-worth-doing question is often ignored. This is not surprising; daily incidents (e.g., a fight, a lesson gone wrong, overhearing a comment critical of one's teaching) take precedence over more abstract philosophical matters. However (and this is a big however), the reflective teacher is one who rises above these daily incidents, as important as they are, to evaluate the purpose and under-

lying values of the program, to be certain that they continue to hold up in the face of new experiences. If not, changes at a more fundamental level are required, changes that cannot be captured by gaining insight into how to stop a fight or better prepare a lesson.

Reflecting About Your Hidden Curriculum

Some of the messages teachers send to students are not part of the planned curriculum. The most common example is the out-of-shape physical education teacher who preaches fitness (this is, of course, a violation of the teaching-by-example principle). However, how teachers treat students—for example, whether they pay more attention to boys than girls, whether they respect student opinions—and the values teachers bring to their gyms—for example, that winning is very important or that taking a shower is more important than helping another student—permeate every lesson and may not be consistent with the teacher's intended message. Research (Dodds, 1983) suggests that conflicting messages reduce the impact of the planned curriculum, that what students learn is often not what teachers intend, and that teachers are often totally unaware that this hidden curriculum is operating.

One of the roles of self-reflection is to look at one's hidden curriculum, at the messages hidden in the organization of the class, in the inclusion and exclusion of students as participants and leaders, in the comments made to students. This is difficult, because much of this activity is deeply imbedded. A Chicago teacher recently reported his struggle with competitive achievement in directing a basketball program for students in a residential boys' home (Georgiadis, 1990). He found himself wanting to win and as a result only playing certain players and screaming at the officials (who volunteered just so that the students could have a game). On his own, he recognized the disparity between his goals (the responsibility model) and his behavior and, in a journal, began to keep track of the extent to which his behavior matched his goals.

Once again, science can help to identify the problem (i.e., that most programs have a hidden curriculum) and its impact (e.g., that the hidden curriculum interferes with the objectives of the planned curriculum), but teachers are left to figure out how to detect their own hidden messages and how to get these messages into line with their planned curriculum. We believe that cultivating the art of self-reflection is the best hope for reducing the hidden curriculum. (Of course, a trained observer would help, but that's not very likely in most settings.) Self-reflection focuses the teacher's attention on what is being communicated to students by word and deed and the relationship of these messages to the teacher's goals.

WRAP-UP

Whether teaching is more an art form or more a science continues to be debated. It is clear, at least to us, that teaching is in large part artistry and that many components of that artistry can be described without reducing them to science. We have attempted to describe these artistic components: certain personal qualities—among them caring, empathy, genuineness, enthusiasm, persistence, and a playful spirit; intuition supported by flexibility and creativity; and self-reflection. If they can be conceptualized, teachers can become more aware of them, can pay more attention to their presence or absence, and can explore ways of becoming more artistic. That has been the goal of this chapter.

THE EXPERTS RESPOND

Chris: First you make a big deal about the importance of science in teaching, and now you make a big deal about artistry. I don't think either one is very important in good teaching! Teaching just isn't as difficult as you make it sound—you make a mountain out of a molehill. There is hardly one idea from this book that I use in my teaching, yet I get along fine, and my students are happy.

Robin: That's because you don't teach! It doesn't take much to supervise a recess! I think teaching is mostly an art, and I like the idea of being given the authority to create my own goals and strategies, to be able to be myself in my gym rather than trying to act out some predetermined list of behaviors.

Lynn: I see two problems with your approach. First of all, we do know a lot about what effective teachers do. It seems foolish to me not to try to replicate those behaviors in my gym. Second, most of the "qualities" described in this chapter can be tightened up to the point that they become specific behaviors, despite what the chapter says about the necessity of being fuzzy. Listening is certainly a behavior. Caring can certainly be transformed into a short list of specific behaviors. Enthusiasm consists at least in part of prompts and hustles. Even self-reflection is a behavior.

Robin: I notice you've left out genuineness, creativity, and intuition; hmm . . . . But more to the point, do you really think that caring or empathy or genuineness or a playful spirit can be reduced to a set of specific behaviors, taught to teachers, and then, when those teachers emit (isn't that the word you use?) those behaviors, that anything vaguely resembling the original concept is *felt* by the kids? I think that those of us who need to improve in these areas would do better to first decide whether we want to be better, whether these qualities are important to our teaching, and then, if we do, to do a serious analysis of our teaching, what we need to improve, and how to take the first step. For example, I need to improve my intuition. My intentions are wonderful and I love my kids, but I try to force my lessons on my kids too much rather than modifying my plans in response to what is going on in my gym. I need a more flexible attitude about my plans, and I need to key on what the kids are doing and saying. It's not that I don't notice; it's that I act like a steamroller—it's my way or the highway, to quote Pat.

Pat: Speaking of Pat, I have two cents' worth, too. What I'm uncomfortable about in this artistry business is that it seems so lovey-dovey, so soft. Let's care, let's be vulnerable, let's make adjustments if the kids aren't happy, let's be sensitive. . . . Oh, I know. There was a little bit in there about confronting and outlasting students. But most of it was trying to get kids to trust us and learning how to adjust to kids. What ever happened to the old-fashioned notion that teachers are in charge, that they know something, that students need to toe the

mark, that if you "spare the rod, you spoil the child" (and I'm not referring to corporal punishment here; even I don't believe in that, except in extreme cases). Yes, Robin, it is my way or the highway. We're not here to please students; we're here to educate them!

Lynn: The problem with your approach, Pat, is that kids aren't the same as they were in the "old days." They face more social problems, have more choices, are more aware, and so on, as was described in chapter 2. We do have some responsibility to motivate them, to educate them. We do have to be artists, even though I believe that science offers a better way to become artists.

Robin: I struggle with your point, Pat. Because one of my major goals is self-responsibility, I want my students to begin to take charge of their own lives, to see how their intentions and actions have consequences for themselves and for others. One choice they have is whether to bear down in school, whether to take school seriously. Of course, to make this choice they have to fight through peer pressure and, because they have been raised on the electronic media, they also have to accept the idea that they won't be entertained in the manner to which they are accustomed. That's where our artistry comes in. We have to make it attractive enough for them that they will give it a try. I guess fear also works, at least to a point; if kids are scared they will bear down to survive. But I'm not sure that the highway isn't a preferable alternative to fear-based education.

Pat: Let's talk results. There are a lot of older folks still around who were educated in what you call fear-based education, and they seem to have done just fine, thank you!

SELF-REFLECTION

We hate to break up this little tea party, but the experts' critique of artistry seems to be shedding more heat than light on the subject. The following are the artistry concepts we have described in this chapter; on a separate sheet of paper, write out your responses to the questions that follow the list.

- Concern/caring
- Empathy/listening
- Genuineness
- Exceptional approachability
- Enhancing student dignity and worth
- Enthusiasm/commitment
- Teaching by example
- Creative, relevant teaching
- Persistence
- Confrontation
- A playful spirit
- Intuition
- Flexibility
- Creativity
- Self-reflection

1. Which of these seem most important to you in being a successful teacher? Least important? Why?

2. For each of these qualities, can you identify one coach or teacher whose values, attitudes, or behaviors exemplify the quality? For each, give a specific example to support your choice.

3. Think of the most influential physical education teacher or coach in your life. How many of these qualities, if any, did he or she possess? How important were these qualities in this teacher's or coach's influence on you?

4. In your view, how many of these qualities could be conceptualized and taught scientifically—that is, how many could be reduced to specific behaviors that could then be taught to, and practiced by, teachers?

5. As you read over this list, is your artistry sufficient to face the 30 hypothetical students we have assigned you? Your own inventory of your artistic qualities as we have discussed them can serve as the basis for whatever changes you need to make.

If you are teaching or coaching now, do this exercise on yourself. If not, observe a teacher or coach. Select a specific incident (e.g., an argument, a disruptive student, a game or drill that doesn't work), make a judgment on how it was handled (well, not very well, very poorly), and try to analyze what went right or wrong and why. Try this a few times. It will take some practice to get better. Compare this focused analysis with your usual evaluations of situations in your life. Any differences?

SUGGESTED READINGS

Csikszentmihalyi, M., & McCormack, J. (1986). The influence of teachers. *Phi Delta Kappan*, **67**, 415-419. (An excellent discussion of the characteristics of influential teachers.)

Rogers, C. (1983). *Freedom to learn in the 80's*. Columbus, OH: Bell & Howell.

(Detailed description of the therapeutic triad and its application to education; includes a review of studies that support his ideas.)

Rubin, L. (1985). *Artistry in teaching*. New York: Random House. (Devoted entirely to the art of teaching; includes a discussion of intuition.)

Schon, D. (1983). *The reflective practitioner: How practitioners think in action*. New York: Basic Books. (An in-depth treatment of the art of reflection as applied to several professions.)

Tom, A.R. (1984). *Teaching as a moral craft*. New York: Longman. (An influential argument for teaching as an art and craft.)

Wigginton, E. (1985). *Sometimes a shining moment: The Foxfire experience*. Garden City, NY: Anchor Books. (A refreshing analysis of teaching based on one teacher's experiences; supported by wonderful anecdotes.)

Zahorik, J.A. (1986). Acquiring teaching skills. *Journal of Teacher Education*, **37**, 21-25. (Shows how one's conception of good teaching influences one's perception of the role of art and science in teaching.)

Chapter 14

Confronting the Real World

In each chapter we have tried to keep our discussions tied to real-world situations. We have asked you to do your own reflection as well as tolerate the reflections of our invited experts. Equally, we have asked you to reflect throughout this text about what its content may mean for teaching your 30 students. This final chapter will be no different as we look at the real world of schools, teaching, and physical education from another perspective, through a more descriptive lens. So we ask you to start reflecting about your past school and physical education experiences as a student. Try to recall your former teachers in PE and in other subjects. Think about the political and social environments that prevail in schools. Finally, reflect about the type of school and PE program you would like to teach in and about whether or not the issues we have presented in this book are relevant to the real world. What is the real world like, from your perspective?

Again, use a critical perspective in asking why schools and PE programs are structured and operate in certain ways. Rather than presenting detailed analyses, we will be more descriptive than analytical in our presentation of the real world. We call on you to ask why things are the way they are—why the norms of schooling and physical education in one setting may be so very different from those in another setting.

Certainly, there has been much written of late about realities of teaching physical educa-

tion, and it is important that you read the case studies that provide insight into others' experiences (Evans, 1989; Graham, 1982; Locke et al., 1986; Locke & Massengale, 1978; Sage, 1989; Sikes, 1988; Templin, 1983, 1987, 1988, 1989; Templin & Schempp, 1989).

A few words of caution, however. Some profiles or case studies do include very positive experiences of physical education teachers, but others provide the harsh reality of the dark side of teaching PE—a side that some have suggested is the prevailing norm within our public schools. Again ask why some PE programs seem so good but others seem so ineffectual, and ask what you would do in the situations described in this literature. Ask yourself what strategies you should employ in responding to

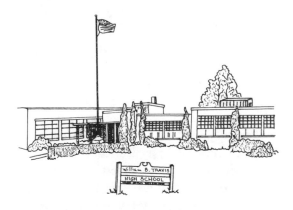

How will you respond when you confront the real world of teaching physical education?

both the positive and the negative. Ask how you would challenge the dominant views that exist in relation to how others (including physical educators) view physical education. Be critical and attempt to gain as much insight as possible about our schools and physical education programs today.

THE CONDITIONS OF TEACHING

Perhaps the best way to examine the real world is to understand the various factors or workplace conditions that may influence you. These are also called the agents or agencies of teacher socialization. You are familiar with many of these factors or workplace conditions because of the countless number of hours you have spent in schools serving "an apprenticeship of observation" (Schempp, 1989); that is, the time you have spent observing the teaching–learning process. Lawson (1989) addresses political, organizational, situational, and personal–social factors that influence the teacher's world. You are reminded that the magnitude of the influence of these factors will be tied to the idiosyncratic nature of the school in which you teach. Let's examine what we mean by this.

Political and Economic Factors

Think about the equipment and facilities available to students in physical education settings. What is the budget of most physical education programs? What about the requirement that students must take physical education—every day, twice a week, one semester a year? What type of contract must teachers work under? Do teachers have professional development opportunities? Who is the chair of the physical education department? Why was this person selected?

What type of support does the school administrator give to the PE department? These are just a few economic and political questions one might pose.

As a teacher you will be confronted with the political and economic realities of the schooling process. Politically, you will (or should) become knowledgeable about federal, state, and local policies related to how school and physical education programs operate. You will be expected to enforce school and program policies related to a variety of factors: curriculum, discipline, evaluation, and attendance, among others. These policy areas are directed not only at students, but at you the teacher as well. It may seem ironic, but the yardstick of success for you as a teacher may be not your students' achievements but the degree to which you are able to uphold school and program policy.

Another political consideration is your involvement in professional organizations. When you join a school district, it is likely that you will be invited to join a local teachers' union that is linked to either the National Education Association or the American Federation of Teachers. This invitation will reflect representation by an organization that is geared to assure favorable employment and work conditions for you. Whether you join a union or not will be a big decision for you. Of course, the presence of unions in most organizations is controversial, particularly when an organization such as a school corporation believes it is, or is actually, providing a positive work situation for its employees.

Another decision with political overtones is related to your membership in professional organizations specifically organized for physical education teachers. The American Alliance of Health, Physical Education, Recreation and Dance (AAHPERD) is the national organization that provides opportunities and resources for your professional development. This organization sponsors national and regional conferences and develops literature designed to benefit the practitioner. Each state and region in the country has affiliate organizations also organized to help you. The specific influence of these groups is usually related to the extent to which the practitioner becomes involved in an organization and seeks professional development experiences and resources (Kneer, 1989).

Economically, you may be grasping at financial straws in your role as a teacher. Traditionally, physical education budgets are rather meager; it is rare that PE is on an equal funding basis with other subject areas. Again, context may make the economic differences for you. The typical affluent suburban school fares much better than the typical inner-city school. Of course, the question is, what are the consequences of school or program funding? Does affluence translate into teacher or program effectiveness? Certainly economic resources help, but money isn't always the bottom line to success (or to teacher or student satisfaction). What are you willing to do with or without resources? Can you create an effective program without great resources? If you can't, how will you lobby for support from others to gain those resources?

Organizational, Situational, and Personal–Social Factors

All of this relates to the organizational, situational, and personal–social climate established within a school system, school, or subject area, and this climate depends to a great degree on the social order present. Joyce, Hersh, and McKibbin (1983) state:

Within every human group there soon develops a social order. That is, interaction becomes less random and more patterned so that coherent sets of values, norms, and roles develop to make relationships predictable and relatively stable. . . . The people who create the social system are, in turn, affected by it. It prescribes their behavior and imbues them with its values. It specifies how decisions will be made and status accorded. It delineates the kinds of relationships people will have—whether they be cooperative or unilateral, austere or loving, honest or dishonest. (pp. 108-109)

One concern you will face upon entry into a school (and even after years of service) relates to the nature of the social order of the school and the physical education program. You will need to know what kinds of relationships exist in your school and program and what kind of role you will be accorded as a teacher of physical education. You will need to know the status of physical education within the school curriculum and how much power and authority you will have in shaping the future of the curriculum and your own teaching destiny.

Although you are referred to the recommended readings at the end of this chapter for further insight into these questions, we would like to give you a little insight into the social world of physical education teaching. Historically (and we see no bright future on the horizon without your help), PE and PE teachers have had a peripheral status with the school curriculum and faculty. Parents, students, school administrators, and even some PE teachers (like Chris!) see our subject as moderately important at best. As Goodlad (1983) found, PE is well liked, but it is perceived as being low in relevance. Such a perception is an outgrowth of a point of view that characterizes PE as supervised recreation, a criminal waste of time, or a setting in which embarrassment, humiliation, discomfort, noninvolvement, and student conformity appear to be the norm. PE teachers are perceived as being more interested in their coaching roles than in their teaching roles, and they are physically and psychologically separated from teaching colleagues and administrators alike. In essence, PE seems superfluous to student learning, and the PE teacher's occupational status is marginal at best. This setting has provoked ridicule and, most recently, a call for reform due to the unfitness of American youth (Sullivan, 1989). These perceptions of the roles and values of physical education are quite opposite to the picture we have tried to communicate in this book.

How does this characterization fit your picture of physical education or the portrait of the settings you have observed or even instructed in? Unfortunately, more positive characterizations are difficult to come by, although we do know that the social order in some settings makes physical education a very good place to be for both students and teachers. Again, the fate of each program, student, and teacher is situational. For example, let's look at two situations representative of profiles of excellence (see Templin, 1983) and of struggle (see Locke et al., 1986):

a local doctor were granted $30,000 by two private foundations to obtain equipment, student aides, clinical assistance, and needed research tools. . . . A local family donated money to purchase Nautilus machines. . . . the booster club purchased floor coverings. . . . Duane and Anita recognized that group instruction failed to provide adequately for the unique needs of the students. . . . Students were preassessed and given a personalized program which was agreed upon by the student and the teacher. . . . Duane and Anita found that instruction time could be saved with an audio-visual tool to introduce students to the unit. . . . Duane decided to produce short instructional videotapes to illustrate how to use each station correctly, safely, and efficiently. . . . The school superintendent encouraged Duane and Anita to develop a special physical education class to accommodate the needs of physically handicapped students. . . . An evening adult fitness program draws almost 600 participants. . . . Developing a quality strength and fitness program for their high school students, athletes, and community was not an impossible dream. (Kneer & Grebner, 1983, pp. 20, 22)

Duane and Anita

They envisioned an ideal weight training facility and program to develop the strength and fitness of all their students, athletes, and members of the community. . . . Duane and Anita forged a collaboration that made their dream come true . . . Duane solicited donations. . . . Duane convinced administrators to approve knocking out basement walls adjacent to his present space. . . . Duane and

Kim

Kim privately mulls over lyrics which foreshadow her destiny—"And another one bites the dust". . . . Though she lacks a gymnasium and designated field, Kim's concerns focus on her students' needs and other teachers' discomforts. . . . Kim is limited by her environment. . . . her school is situated on a very small lot surrounded by barbed wire fences and busy streets. . . . she must share the grounds with classroom teachers who take their students outside for breaks. . . . she now believes "teachers are so caught up with saving themselves—the law of preservation," that they can no longer risk creativity or being spontaneous. . . . Kim has felt her sense of integrity being eaten away by the seemingly arbitrary demands of new rules. . . . [Although Kim has a great relationship with her principal] Kim fears losing such rapport to the demands and pressures resulting from the recent educational reforms. She believes teachers and principals are now embarking on two different career paths and their previous opportunities for camaraderie will be sacrificed. . . . Kim is also distressed by the image of teachers now battling for limited numbers of merit pay raises. . . . As a result of the reforms, Kim believes that teachers will have to change their focus from student needs to more personal concerns. . . . Kim fears the new demands will force teachers to stand alone before representatives of depersonalized structures charged with the responsibility of evaluating teachers' effectiveness and economic value. It is a specter which haunts her, and leaving teaching seems to be the only way to escape. (Faucette, 1986, pp. 44-46)

A CONSPIRACY OF ONE (AND MANY)—CHANGING THE SOCIAL ORDER

The difficulty that Kim and others experience lies in changing the social order of those schools and programs in which PE is peripheral. What can you or anyone do to make physical education a better place? This is a difficult question to answer, but it most likely depends on your commitment to teaching effectiveness and your ability to carry out a "conspiracy of one" to provoke change. This is not to suggest that you take the risk alone. Having a support network of colleagues, administrators, students, parents, and others to help you in your efforts is important. However, there are no guarantees about the extent to which others will join you. You may face a lonely fight in attempting to maintain quality instruction and resist those barriers that inhibit your teaching and program effectiveness. This suggests that while others are rolling out the ball, you are engaged in instruction. While others are silent, you are speaking out for what you believe. While you are planning for the future, others may be quite content with the way things are in the present. There are many challenges, but we recommend that you take the risk and invite others to join your efforts to make physical education the best it can be. Don't be content. You will probably find out that engaging in change strategies can be messy business, but the rewards will outweigh the hassles in your pursuit of excellence.

If you want to change the social order, you may need to speak out for what you believe.

Strategies

What we have just said suggests that there are a variety of ways in which you will respond to the norms of the setting in which you teach. Just as you will attempt to socialize students, so do schools (administrators, teachers, students, parents, and others) socialize teachers to execute their roles in a certain way. You must be prepared for this socialization process; various social strategies are useful for coping with its demands. For example, Lacey (1977) presents three strategies for facing the socialization process. First, for those expectations and demands that are uncomfortable for you or those that seem inappropriate to you, one may *strategically comply*. That is, one meets the demands of a situation, but retains reservations about them. This may be called "playing the game." You may be asked to teach certain activities, grade in a certain way, or discipline students in prescribed ways, but at the same time you have reservations about doing so. This is difficult for all teachers, but particularly for beginning teachers. What will you do if someone asks you to do something that runs contrary to your own beliefs or training?

Another strategy suggested by Lacey is *internalized adjustment*. You may find that others' expectations are quite appropriate and that you have no reservations whatsoever in their application. The skills and attitudes you bring to a setting may be readjusted in a way that you feel is best for you and for your students. You will continue to learn new ways of teaching as you mature as a practitioner. This is healthy for your professional development, but remember that your growth must be linked to the subsequent growth of your students.

Finally, *strategic redefinition* is one's attempt to redefine the norms of the work situation. As Griffin (1986) points out, this strategy is most risky, in that an individual or group may become alienated and be perceived as a threat to others. Trying to change curricular and instructional processes may not be easy and calls for a careful assessment of what is possible and what is not possible. Yet again, with the conviction to promote teacher effectiveness (and hence student achievement), attempts at redefinition seem admirable.

One point to consider: Even if this is a result of neglect and low status, most physical education teachers have the freedom, we believe, to define their own settings. Redefinition may not be as risky as we or others might suggest. The conspiracy of one may mean the teacher would have to establish covert norms or modes of operation inside her or his own turf; that is, the conspiracy actually resides between the teacher and her or his own students in the day-to-day routines within physical education. It is their own empire. For example, norms related to attendance, attire, participation, leadership, game playing, and grading may be quite different from what is expected by school administrators and others.

Finally, we should note some of the strategies presented by Griffin (1986, pp. 58-59) in examining possible responses by teachers when confronted by systemic barriers:

Compromising: Teachers compromise by making a conscious decision to cut their losses, give up on unattainable goals, and focus on achieving what they perceive to be possible in their contexts. Where teaching motor skills and maintaining a sequential curriculum seem impossible, teachers may lower expectations to creating classes in which children have fun and are highly active—achievable goals in all but the most dismal settings.

Ignoring: Some teachers respond to systemic impediments by ignoring them. Despite several constraints in critical areas such as class size, instructional time, equipment, schedule, facilities, or administrative policy, these teachers go through the motions of teaching.

Tinkering: Some teachers respond to systemic obstacles by tinkering—directing their creative energies into making numerous small-scale changes in their teaching. Having recognized what they feel powerless to change, these teachers zero in on those things they do control: a new method of taking attendance, an innovative unit, special privileges for well-behaved students, or a different approach to a familiar unit. In the face of the professional isolation with which so many teachers live, it is probable that they tinker with their teaching as much for their own stimulation and need to avoid routine as to improve their students' programs.

Challenging: There are teachers who challenge the systems they work in by filing grievances, applying outside political pressure, or repeatedly voicing individual complaints. The risks, both personal and professional, are high for challengers. Both the stress of being a "troublemaker" and the time and energy required to follow through with formal or informal challenges are considerable. In addition, system change comes in small steps and takes more time than most teachers have the patience to endure. Finally, to be a successful challenger requires a political savvy many teachers have not acquired. A naive challenger in a school system that values compliance may be in for a rude awakening to the realities of school politics.

Overcoming: There are teachers who, even in the face of systemic barriers that would defeat most teachers, manage to create and nurture excellent programs. Through uncommon dedication, persistence, and vigilance, these teachers sustain both their own enthusiasm for teaching and their students' respect, interest,

and engagement. Maximum use is wrung out of every minute of class time, every corner of the gym or locker room, and every piece of equipment. This excellence, however, is achieved in spite of the system, not because of the encouragement or support offered.

These strategies suggest that the real world may be harsh at times, but it is not unbending. Its flexibility may depend to a great extent on whether you choose to work with it, learn from it, or at times, tinker with, challenge, or overcome it. Whether you are passive or overtly proactive in your interaction with the system of schooling will determine your satisfaction and achievement in that setting. If you decide to be proactive, be prepared to articulate and justify your needs and the curricular and instructional options you wish to promote. We acknowledge that more responses such as ignoring, giving up, and quitting certain situations (Griffin, 1986) may be among the behavioral responses one may elect in contrast to those suggested above, but we hope you elect a different route—one that suggests a fight. Whether you fight covertly inside your gym walls or publicly for what you think is best, you can feel good about the fact that you aren't necessarily content with a business-as-usual mindset, and that you are trying to do that which is best for your students. You can feel good about making an effort to better your program and the education of your students.

GOOD SCHOOLS

You may find your work life to be most satisfying in "good schools." Duane and Anita teach in a good school. Although the challenges of maintaining the excellence of these schools is never-ending, social strategizing to overcome constant barriers will undoubtedly be less of a problem for you. This is because good schools have characteristics that will nurture your success.

Good schools are committed to teaching excellence because they have set the appropriate conditions to breed excellence (Frymier et al., 1984): They have clear academic and social goals; they have order and discipline and pervasive caring, and they promote trust and support; they provide public rewards and incentives for teachers; they have community support; they encourage risk taking; they embrace cooperative decision-making; they encourage the study of teaching; and they provide opportunities for student responsibility. This is the type of setting from which a teacher in any subject area will benefit. The social order here is healthy, as teachers, administrators, students, and parents work side by side to promote student achievement. Teaching is perceived as a valuable occupation, and teachers are encouraged to grow professionally and are rewarded for growth. It is a setting that is collegial and one in which the teacher can mentor and be mentored.

Finally, good schools are oriented to the future and to possibilities, rather than to the present and to problems. They are goal oriented and see impermanence as central to everyday life; that is, good schools don't rest on their laurels, but seek constant improvement in their structures. Good schools and good teachers go hand in hand to the benefit of their students. Good physical education programs should be no different.

WRAP-UP

This chapter has asked you to examine the "real world" of teaching public-school physical education. We have suggested that you maintain a critical perspective in the analysis of the factors that help shape the norms of schooling and physical education, and we have pointed out that any analysis of our schools, physical education teachers, and physical education programs will reveal the idiosyncratic nature of the real world; that is, every school context has its own unique characteristics and ways of influencing those who live in those settings, including PE teachers and students. In discussing those factors, we have provided two examples of how two different settings have had positive and negative impact upon its teachers.

Further, we discussed social strategies for coping and becoming a proactive agent in the promotion of what we have called "a conspiracy of one." Teachers do not have to be passive zombies, compliant to the dictates of others; teachers can influence what goes on in their gymnasiums.

Finally, we addressed good schools as a way to provide you with a comparative standard. Many factors have been identified as essential to the composition of an effective school setting, and those factors that make schools good are no different than those that make physical education good.

Schools are, in fact, complex organizations that influence each and every inhabitant. Your experience as a former public- or private-school student has provided a protracted apprenticeship of observation, but that apprenticeship was just the beginning. What you have learned in teacher training opens your vision to a whole new understanding of life in schools and in the gym. You face many challenges ahead as a teacher, but perhaps none so great as that of figuring out how we can make schools and programs of physical education positive for all.

THE EXPERTS RESPOND

Most certainly our experts have their opinions about the nature of the real world and how they might set about to change it. Let's listen to what they have to say and see whether you agree with them.

Chris: Look, what's the big deal—it's just PE. We aren't talking about the Super Bowl or nuclear physics here, are we? Look, whatever they want I'll give them, even if it means just playing games. I'm not going in there to create waves!

Robin: Does this mean that if they expect a lot out of you, you'll give them that, as well? I don't believe my ears, especially after your first comment about the Super Bowl. If it's not a big deal, why did you go into PE in the first place? We have to promote a setting in which the kids learn and see PE as being a meaningful school experience—one in which they feel good about themselves and the subject matter.

Pat: Chris, I'm sorry you have been the whipping boy throughout our discussions, but once again, don't you think we owe our students everything we've got? And what about our own sanity? Don't we deserve to work in a healthy situation? I'm sick of everyone putting PE and PE teachers down. I know I am pretty stuck in my traditional ways, but tradition isn't all that bad, and I think I'm contributing to our field.

Chris: You are darn right I feel like the whipping boy! Give me a little slack, won't you?

Lynn: Sorry, big guy. You don't deserve it. Look, we know that if we are given the opportunity, we have the knowledge and skills to affect our students' lives positively. All we need are the right conditions to do the job. I come from a school where the academic and social order is excellent for every subject area and every teacher. I get to observe how the science of teaching works and how effective a teacher can truly be.

Chris: Enough of the personal testimonies. We aren't going to make that much of an impression on the field. We'll be 6 feet under before something might change.

Robin: Enough yourself. I've seen caring teachers, students, parents, and administrators. I've seen good lessons and fair and decent treatment of students. I've also been to a couple of conferences—there's so much we can do, and what's wrong with trying to make things better?

Lynn: Absolutely nothing—but again, we have to have standards, and everyone has to follow them. As far as I can tell, that's part of the problem. No one cares. That's what we need—someone to care—and it's got to start right at home with our own teachers who have the courage to fight for a better deal for PE. This will translate into a better and more meaningful experience for our students. Hopefully, someone will listen.

SELF-REFLECTION

We have asked you to examine physical education settings to assess what's going on in the gym in relation to the topics presented throughout this book. This final chapter has been similar, and the upcoming exercises represent a synthesis of all that you have been asked to reflect upon. It's time to open your mind in seeing what this book is all about and to examine some of the workplace factors that influence the teacher's satisfaction and effectiveness on a daily basis. It's time to be critical and to ask yourself how you would respond to systemic barriers and just what type of setting is most desirable for you. Go out and study the real world and see if what we have been saying makes any sense. See if this world is as diverse as we suggest, and assess whether physical education and physical educators are providing the type of education their students deserve.

1. Interview two secondary school physical education teachers—one male and one female—at both the junior high and senior high school levels. Before interviewing the teachers, construct an interview schedule that focuses on the factors discussed in this chapter. Conduct your interview (use a tape recorder) over as many sessions as necessary, and then transcribe and analyze your interviews.

Your task is to analyze the context in which each teacher works and to assess

- if the teacher is satisfied in his or her work setting,

- the key factors that promote or constrain the success of the teacher and the PE program,

- the strategies the teacher uses to cope with or change her or his setting,

- what you believe the future holds for the teacher and the programs in which he or she teaches, and

- what you would do to change or maintain the setting.

2. What will be your personal strategy for change when you enter a workplace that is less than desirable? What will you do to maintain a good work setting?

3. Based on your research, what do you see as the key ingredients for change and for a brighter future for school physical education?

SUGGESTED READINGS

Evans, J. (1988). *Teachers, teaching, and control in physical education*. Lewes, England: Falmer Press. (An edited British text that gives the reader a cross-cultural view of school physical education.)

Goodlad, J. (1983). *A place called school*. New York: McGraw-Hill. (A book based on Goodlad's study of schooling, which provides insight about the status of America's schools, the occupation of teaching, and various curricular areas.)

Graham, G. (Ed.) (1982). Profiles in excellence: Processes and teachers in children's physical education. *Journal of Physical Education, Recreation, and Dance*, **53**, 37-54. (Various profiles of excellent elementary physical education teachers and their schools and programs.)

Locke, L., Griffin, P., & Templin, T. (Eds.) (1986). Profiles of struggle. *Journal of Physical Education, Recreation, and Dance*, **57**(4), 32-63. (Seven profiles of physical education teachers caught in the struggle to maintain effective programs and to persevere as teachers under difficult workplace conditions.)

Rosenholtz, S. (1989). *Teachers' workplace: The social organization of schools*. New York: Longman. (An examination of the effects of social organization on school climate and performance.)

Templin, T. (1983). Profiles of excellence: Fourteen outstanding secondary school physical educators. *Journal of Physical Education, Recreation, and Dance*, **54**, 15-36. (Fourteen secondary school physical educators are profiled and illustrate the range of possibilities in supportive school environments.)

Templin, T., & Schempp, P. (Eds.) (1989). *Socialization into physical education: Learning to teach*. Indianapolis: Benchmark Press. (An edited text geared toward examining socialization into physical education. Those chapters related to the influence of the school setting and other related socialization agents [chapters 8-16] are highly recommended.)

Closing Thoughts

This is our last chance to badger you about reflecting on your teaching. It's also our last chance to ask you what you're going to do with your 30 hypothetical students (we'll skip doing that; you've heard it enough). And it's the last time our experts will have a shot at you.

One of the things we've emphasized is having some kind of program evaluation. Turnabout is fair play: How ought we evaluate the effectiveness of this book? We opened by arguing that, at least from two left-handers' perspectives, teaching physical education is more about principles than about prescriptions, more a moral activity than a mechanical one, more idiosyncratic than generalizable. We went on to say that teachers need to be empowered to become the chief decision makers, problem solvers, and evaluators of their own programs. Therefore, one way to evaluate our effectiveness is to see just how well we lived up to our own billing.

We have raised four questions and followed each with a number of concepts, ideas, and options, emphasizing time and again the linkages among values, program purpose, teaching and management strategies, and program planning and evaluation. We have not prescribed very much in all of this, except in saying that you ought to be reflective in making your decisions and that the decisions are interrelated.

We have also argued that teaching physical education is a moral activity, both because any decisions teachers make affect students' lives and because teachers are in the business of helping kids become certain kinds of human beings. For the most part, we have used reflection to make these points, coming back again and again to the question of what's worth doing and pointing out all along the way the implications of various models, strategies, and ideas. Although we did not take a direct stand on the issues, except to argue in response to our first question that reflection makes more sense to us than other approaches to teaching, we do plead guilty to citing several examples that reflect our own values and to spending more time on those issues and ideas that we find more attractive or interesting.

We tried to focus on you as an individual in this process, and in so doing we not only emphasized the decisions you need to make but also that no linear step-by-step mechanical process is likely to fit all of you. Perhaps those of you who need a lot of structure will be uncomfortable with our approach; if so, feel free to develop a step-by-step process that best meets your needs. The best advice we can give is to learn your own idiosyncrasies and work within them, perhaps even getting them to work for you.

Another way we could evaluate this book's effectiveness is by checking in on you in a few years, not so much to see if your students are stretching slowly and if you are giving brief, visual cues (by then research will no doubt have found some better ways), but to see if you are routinely reflecting on your teaching and making changes based on this reflective activity. If you are, we might just take some of the credit!

It wouldn't be fair to end without a final word from our experts, even though that can be dangerous (as you have seen).

Pat: My final words to you are to be very certain before altering tradition. It has held up very well over time. Also, don't be afraid to be the boss. The last thing today's kids need is to be mollycoddled. Good luck!

Robin: I'd just like to say that teaching is a moral activity; what you do matters in kids' lives, not just to their bodies or their leisure time, but to how they feel about themselves, their goals, how they relate to others. You—all of us—can make a difference beyond skill and fitness development if we choose to do so.

Lynn: The thought I'd like to leave with you is to have some evidence to back up what you do. Too often, PE teachers do what they were taught, whether they can support it or not. Be able to give reasons, and hopefully some supporting data, for what you teach. Also, keep up-to-date. Research is constantly changing our knowledge base. If you don't stay informed, your students will suffer.

Chris: I can't believe I have the last word! I just want to wish you the best in your teaching career. I guess I hope you don't burn out like I did, but most of all I hope, whether you burn out or not, that you have some fun along the way!

SELF-REFLECTION

No, Chris. We get the last word. True to our format throughout the book, our last word is in the form of a self-reflection exercise. We want to leave you with the challenge of developing a personally relevant curriculum and instruction model that can be refined endlessly throughout your career, so we finish up with these questions:

1. How satisfied are you with the current social and cultural trends in the United States? Do you want to perpetuate these trends in your physical education program? To the extent that you don't, what can you do in your program to help alter these trends? How do you plan to deal with the heterogeneous group of students in your gym? Will equity be an important value in your gym?

2. What are your value priorities in teaching physical education? What purpose, what program goals best represent your commitment to your students? Can you justify your choices?

3. What physical education subject matter is most likely to help you fulfill your purpose as a physical education teacher? Fitness activities? Motor skills? Seasonal sports? Games? Cooperative games? Concepts? Outdoor pursuits? The martial arts? (Other activities?) How can you teach this content in a way that helps students make progress toward your program goals? The motor skill progression? Fitness concept labs? Games for understanding? (Other models?) How ought you plan and evaluate your lessons to ensure that your program purpose becomes a reality?

4. What strategies and activities other than physical education subject matter are necessary to put your values and purpose into practice? Prompts and hustles? Reciprocal teaching? Individualized instruction? Counseling time? The inner game? (Other strate-

gies?) How can they be integrated into your lessons? Can you develop and implement a lesson plan based on your reflective thinking?

5. What are you going to do about discipline and motivation problems in your gym? Do you want some strategies that will help prevent these problems from interfering with your teaching, or are you more interested in helping your students with their personal and social development as a primary program goal? What are you going to do about your students' many physical, social, and emotional differences? Do you have some strategies ready to put into practice? Are you going to try to help students "get along" as a primary program goal?

6. What is your own assessment of your teacher artistry? If it needs some work, how do you propose to go about getting better?

7. Are you prepared to "confront reality"? What do you need to do to get prepared?

Some of our colleagues bemoan the current state of physical education, citing the confusion, lack of standards, and endless options in subject matter, goals, and strategies. As you might guess, we applaud the diversity as an opportunity for each of us to develop more fully, more uniquely, as a physical education teacher. It is up to each of us to seize this opportunity. However, the way is not without difficulty. As Sheldon Kopp (1972, p. 6) once commented: "It will cost you your innocence, your illusions, your certainty." But we believe this is far preferable to having our values, purposes, implementation processes, and perhaps even our styles dictated by someone else.

References

American Alliance for Health, Physical Education and Recreation. (1978). Mainstreaming. *Practical Pointers*, **1**, 4-5.

American Alliance for Health, Physical Education, Recreation and Dance. (1988). *Physical best: The American Alliance physical fitness education and assessment program*. Reston, VA: Author.

Almond, L. (1983). Games making. *Bulletin of Physical Education*, **19**, 32-35.

Bain, L.L. (1986, June). *Present status and future directions in research on teaching and teacher education in physical education*. Paper presented at the International Conference on Research on Teaching and Teacher Education in Physical Education, Vancouver, BC.

Bain, L.L. (1988). Curriculum for critical reflection in physical education. In R.S. Brandt (Ed.), *Context of the curriculum: 1988 ASCD yearbook* (pp. 133-147). Washington, DC: Association for Supervision and Curriculum Development.

Bandy, S.J. (1987). Editorial. *Philosophy Academy Newsletter*, pp. 2-3.

Barrett, K.R. (1979). Observation for teaching and coaching. *JOPERD*, **49**, 22-31.

Becker, E. (1973). *The denial of death*. New York: Free Press.

Berliner, D. (1985). Does ability grouping cause more problems than it solves? *Instructor*, **94**, 14-15.

Breinin, C.M. (1987). A complaint and a prediction. *Phi Delta Kappan*, **68**, 15-16.

Brophy, J. (1988). Educating teachers about managing classrooms and students. *Teaching and Teacher Education*, **4**, 1-18.

Bunker, D., & Thorpe, R. (1986). *Rethinking games teaching*. Loughborough, England: University of Technology.

Carey, J., & Taylor, R.A. (1987, March 2). Battling the bulge at an early age. *U.S. News and World Report*, pp. 66-67.

Carlyon, W. (1984). Reflections: Disease prevention/health promotions—bridging the gap to wellness. *Health Values*, **8**, 27-30.

Casperson, C.J. (1987). Physical inactivity and coronary heart disease. *Physician and Sports Medicine*, **15**, 43-44.

Children's Defense Fund. (1989). A vision for America's future: A children's agenda for the 1990's. Washington, DC: Author.

Coakley, J.J. (1986). *Sport in society* (3rd ed.). St. Louis, MO: Times Mirror/Mosby.

Cooper, K.H. (1968). *Aerobics*. New York: Evans.

Corbin, C.B. (1987). Youth fitness, exercise, and health: There is much to be done. *Research Quarterly for Exercise and Sport*, **58**, 308-314.

Corbin, C.B., & Lindsey, R. (1980). The conceptual approach to teaching physical fitness. *The Physical Education Newsletter*.

Corbin, C.B., & Lindsey, R. (1985). *Fitness*

for life (2nd ed.). Glenview, IL: Scott Foresman.

Corbin, C.B., Whitehead, J.R., & Lovejoy, S.A. (1988). Youth physical fitness awards. *Quest*, **40**, 200-218.

Cronbach, L.J. (1982). Prudent aspirations for social inquiry. In W.H. Kruskal (Ed.), *The social sciences: Their nature and uses* (pp. 61-81). Chicago: University of Chicago Press.

Csikszentmihalyi, M., & McCormack, J. (1986). The influence of teachers. *Phi Delta Kappan*, **67**, 415-419.

Darst, P., & Armstrong, G.P. (1980). *Outdoor adventure activities for school and recreation programs*. Minneapolis: Burgess.

Darst, P., Zakrajsek, D., & Mancini, V. (Eds.) (1989). *Analyzing physical education and sport instruction*. Champaign, IL: Human Kinetics Books.

deCharms, R. (1976). *Enhancing motivation: Change in the classroom*. New York: Irvington.

Dewey, J. (1933). *How we think*. Chicago: Henry Regnery.

Dodds, P. (1983). *Consciousness raising in curriculum: A teacher's model for analysis*. Paper presented at the 3rd Physical Education Curriculum Theory Conference, Athens, Georgia.

Dotson, C. (1988). Health fitness standards: Aerobic endurance. *JOPERD*, **59**, 26-31.

Drew, N. (1987). *Learning the skills of peacemaking*. Rolling Hills Estates, CA: Jalmer Press.

Duckett, W. (1988). Using demographic data for long-range planning. *Phi Delta Kappan*, **69**, 166-170.

Evans, J. (1989). Moving up and getting out: The classed and gendered career opportunities of physical education teachers. In T. Templin & P. Schempp (Eds.), *Socialization into physical education: Learning to*

teach (pp. 235-248). Indianapolis: Benchmark Press.

Faucette, N. (1986). Educational reform—enough is enough. *JOPERD*, **57**(4), 44-46.

Fenstermacher, G.D. (1986). Philosophy of research on teaching: Three aspects. In M.C. Wittrock (Ed.), *Handbook of research on teaching* (3rd ed., pp. 37-49). New York: Macmillan.

Fernandez, R.R. (1988). School dropouts: New approaches to an enduring problem. *Education and Urban Society*, **20**, 363-386.

Fox, K.R. (1988). The self-esteem complex and youth fitness. *Quest*, **40**, 230-246.

Fox, K.R., & Biddle, S.J.H. (1988). The use of fitness tests: Educational and psychological considerations. *JOPERD*, **59**, 47-53.

Freischlag, J. (1977). Cultural pluralism. *Journal of Physical Education and Recreation*, **48**(5), 22-23.

French, R., & Jansma, P. (1982). *Special physical education*. Columbus, OH: Merrill.

Frymier, J., Cornbleth, C., Donmoyer, R., Gansneder, B., Jeter, J., Klein, M., Schwab, M., & Alexander, W. (1984). *One hundred good schools*. West Lafayette, IN: Kappa Delta Pi.

Gallwey, W.T. (1976). *Inner tennis*. New York: Random House.

Georgiadis, N. (1990). Does basketball have to be all W's and L's? An alternative program at a residential boys' home. *Journal of Physical Education, Recreation, and Dance*, **61**, 42-43.

Glasser, W. (1977). Ten steps to good discipline. *Today's Education*, **66**, 61-63.

Goodlad, J. (1983). *A place called school*. New York: McGraw-Hill.

Goodlad, J. (1988). Studying the education of

educators: Values driven inquiry. *Phi Delta Kappan*, **69**, 105-111.

Gore, J.M. (1987). Reflecting on reflective teaching. *Journal of Teacher Education*, **38**, 33-39.

Graham, G. (Ed.) (1982). Profiles in excellence: Processes and teachers in children's physical education. *JOPERD*, **53**, 37-54.

Graham, G. (1987). Motor skill acquisition—an essential goal of physical education programs. *JOPERD*, **58**, 44-48.

Graham, G., & Heimerer, E. (1981). Research on teacher effectiveness: A summary with implications for teaching. *Quest*, **33**(1), 14-25.

Graham, G., Holt/Hale, S.A., & Parker, M. (1987). *Children moving* (2nd ed.). Palo Alto, CA: Mayfield.

Grant, G. (1988). The teacher's predicament. *School Safety*, **3**, 5-10.

Greene, M. (1986). Philosophy and teaching. In M.C. Wittrock (Ed.), *The handbook of research on teaching* (3rd ed., pp. 479-504). New York: Macmillan.

Griffin, P. (1981). One small step for personkind: Observations for sex equity in coeducational physical education classes. *Journal of Teaching in Physical Education*, Introductory issue, 12-17.

Griffin, P. (1984). Girls' participation patterns in a middle school team sports unit. *Journal of Teaching in Physical Education*, **4**, 30-38.

Griffin, P. (1985a). Teachers' perceptions of and responses to sex equity problems in a middle school physical education program. *Research Quarterly for Exercise and Sport*, **56**(2), 103-110.

Griffin, P. (1985b). Boys' participation styles in a middle school physical team sports unit. *Journal of Teaching in Physical Education*, **4**, 100-110.

Griffin, P. (1986). Analysis and discussion:

What have we learned? *Journal of Physical Education, Recreation, and Dance*, **57**(4), 57-59.

Griffin, P. (1989a). Gender as a socializing agent in physical education. In T. Templin & P. Schempp (Eds.), *Socialization into physical education: Learning to teach* (pp. 219-232). Indianapolis: Benchmark Press.

Griffin, P. (1989b). Assessment of equitable instructional practices in the gym. *CAHPER Journal*, **55**, 19-22.

Griffin, P., & Templin, T. (1989). An overview of qualitative research. In P. Darst, D. Zakrajsek, & V. Mancini (Eds.), *Analyzing physical education and sport instruction* (pp. 399-409). Champaign, IL: Human Kinetics.

Hales, S. (1985). The inadvertent rediscovery of self in social psychology. *Journal for the Theory of Social Behavior*, **15**, 237-282.

Harrison, J. (1987). A review of the research on teacher effectiveness and its implications for current practice. *Quest*, **39**, 36-55.

Harter, S. (1986). Processes underlying the construction, maintenance, and enhancement of the self-concept in children. In J. Suls & A.G. Greenwald (Eds.), *Psychological perspectives on the self* (Vol. 3, pp. 137-181). Hillsdale, NJ: Erlbaum.

Heitmann, H.M. (1988). Supervising the secondary school physical education program. *NASSP Bulletin*, **72**, 86-93.

Hellison, D. (1973). *Humanistic physical education*. Englewood Cliffs, NJ: Prentice-Hall.

Hellison, D. (1978). *Beyond bats and balls: Alienated (and other) youth in the gym*. Washington, DC: AAHPERD.

Hellison, D. (1985). *Goals and strategies for teaching physical education*. Champaign, IL: Human Kinetics.

Hellison, D. (1986). Cause of death: Physical education. *JOPERD*, **57**, 27-28.

Henderson, J. (1988). A curriculum response to the knowledge base reform movement. *Journal of Teacher Education*, **39**, 13-17.

Herrigel, E. (1953). *Zen in the art of archery*. New York: Pantheon.

Hoffman, S.J. (1987). Dreaming the impossible dream: The decline and fall of physical education. In J.D. Massengale (Ed.), *Trends toward the future in physical education* (pp. 121-135). Champaign, IL: Human Kinetics.

Horrocks, R.N. (1978). Resolving conflict in the gymnasium. *JOPERD*, **4**, 61.

Huberman, M. (1987). How well does educational research really travel? *Educational Researcher*, **16**, 5-13.

Hunter, M. (1984). Knowing, teaching, and supervising. In P. Hospord (Ed.), *Using what we know about teaching* (pp. 169-192). Alexandria, VA: Association for Supervision and Curriculum Development.

Hustler, D., Cassidy, A., & Cuff, E. (Eds.) (1986). *Action research in classrooms and schools*. London: Allen and Unwin.

Ingham, A.G. (1985). From public issue to personal trouble: Well-being and the fiscal crisis of the state. *Sociology of Sport Journal*, **2**, 43-55.

Institute for Aerobics Research (1987). *Fitnessgram*. Dallas: Author.

Jewett, A.E., & Bain, L.L. (1985). *The curriculum process in physical education*. Dubuque, IA: Brown.

Joyce, B., Hersh, R., & McKibbin, M. (1983). *The structure of school improvement*. New York: Longman.

Katch, F.I., & McArdle, W.D. (1988). *Nutrition, weight control, and exercise*. Philadelphia: Lea & Febiger.

Kirk, D. (1986). A critical pedagogy for teacher education: Toward an inquiry-oriented approach. *Quest*, **5**, 236-246.

Kneer, M. (1989). The influence of professional organizations on teacher development. In T. Templin & P. Schempp (Eds.), *Socialization into physical education: Learning to teach* (pp. 123-143). Indianapolis: Benchmark Press.

Kneer, M., & Grebner, F. (1983). Teamed for excellence. *JOPERD*, **54**, 20, 22.

Knutson, M. (1977). Sensitivity to minority groups. *Journal of Physical Education and Recreation*, **48**(5), 24-25.

Kohn, A. (1986). *No contest: The case against competition*. New York: Houghton Mifflin.

Kopp, S.B. (1972). *If you meet the Buddha on the road, kill him!* Palo Alto, CA: Science & Behavior Books.

Kopperud, K. (1986). An emphasis on physical fitness. *JOPERD*, **57**, 18-22.

Lacey, C. (1977). *The socialization of teachers*. London: Metheun.

Lampert, M. (1985). How do teachers manage to teach? Perspectives on problems in practice. *Harvard Educational Review*, **55**, 178-194.

Lather, P. (1985, April). *Empowering research methodologies*. Paper presented at the meeting of the American Educational Research Association, Chicago.

Lawson, H. (1989). From rookie to veteran: Workplace conditions in physical education and induction into the profession. In T. Templin & P. Schempp (Eds.), *Socialization into physical education: Learning to teach* (pp. 145-164). Indianapolis: Benchmark Press.

Lawson, H., & Placek, J. (1981). *Physical education in the secondary schools: Curricular alternatives*. Boston: Allyn & Bacon.

Leonard, G. (1974). *The ultimate athlete*. New York: Viking.

Leonard, M.L., & Reyman, J.E. (1988). The odds of attaining professional athlete status: Refining the computations. *Sociology of Sport Journal*, **5**, 162-169.

Liemohn, W. (1988). Flexibility and muscular strength. *JOPERD*, **59**, 37-40.

Locke, L. (1989). Qualitative research as a form of scientific inquiry in sport and physical education. *Research Quarterly for Exercise and Sport,* **60**(1), 1-20.

Locke, L., Griffin, P., & Templin, T. (Eds.) (1986). Profiles in struggles. *JOPERD*, **57**(4), 32-63.

Locke, L., & Massengale, J. (1978). Role conflict in teacher–coaches. *Research Quarterly*, **49**(2), 162-174.

Lockhart, A., & Mott, J. (1981). An experiment in homogenous grouping and its effect on achievement in sports fundamentals. *Research Quarterly*, **22**, 58-62.

Martinek, T. (1981). Pygmalion in the gym: A model for the communication of teacher expectations in physical education. *Research Quarterly for Exercise and Sport*, **52**, 58-67.

Martinek, T. (1989). The psycho-social dynamics of the pygmalion phenomenon in physical education of sport. In T. Templin & P. Schempp (Eds.), *Socialization into physical education: Learning to teach* (pp. 199-219). Indianapolis: Benchmark Press.

Mertens, S., & Yarger, S.J. (1988). Teaching as a profession: Leadership, empowerment, and involvement. *Journal of Teacher Education*, **39**, 32-37.

Miller, D.M. (1984). Philosophy: Whose business? *Quest*, **36**, 26-36.

Miller, R.F., & Jarman, B.O. (1988). Moral and ethical character development—views from past decades. *JOPERD*, **59**, 72-78.

Minkler, M. (1983). Health promotion and elders: A critique. *Generations*, **8**, 13-15.

Morris, G.S.D., & Stiehl, J. (1989). *Changing kids' games*. Champaign, IL: Human Kinetics.

Mosston, M., & Ashworth, S. (1986). *Physical education: From intent to action*. Columbus, OH: Merrill.

Nixon, J., & Locke, L. (1973). Research on teaching in physical education. In R. Travers (Ed.), *Second handbook on research on teaching* (pp. 1210-1243). Chicago: Rand McNally.

Nolte, M.C. (1988). The root of all good. *School Safety*, **3**, 11-13.

Oliver, B. (1988). Educational reform in physical education. *JOPERD*, **59**, 67-68.

Orlick, T. (1978a). *Winning through cooperation*. Washington, DC: Hawkins.

Orlick, T. (1978b). *The cooperation book of games and sports*. New York: Pantheon.

Orlick, T. (1990). *In pursuit of excellence*. Champaign, IL: Human Kinetics.

Paffenbarger, R.S., Jr., & Hyde, R.T. (1980). Exercise as protection against heart attack. *New England Journal of Medicine*, **302**, 1026-1027.

Pangrazi, R.P. (1987). Effective class management skills. *JOPERD*, **58**, 13.

Pease, D.A. (1978). *Teaching model for skill acquisition*. Unpublished manuscript.

Placek, J. (1983). Conceptions of success in teaching: Busy, happy, and good? In T. Templin & J. Olson (Eds.), *Teaching in physical education* (pp. 46-56). Champaign, IL: Human Kinetics.

Placek, J. (1984). A multi-case study of teacher planning in physical education. *Journal of Teaching in Physical Education*, **4**, 39-49.

Porter, A.C. (1988). Understanding teaching: A model for assessment. *Journal of Teacher Education*, **39**, 2-7.

Posner, G. (1989). *Field experience: Methods of reflective teaching*. New York: Longman.

Ravizza, K. (1973). *A study of the peak experience in sport*. Unpublished doctoral dissertation, University of Southern California at Los Angeles.

Raywid, M.A., Tesconi, C.A., & Warren, D.R. (1984). *Pride and promise: Schools of excellence for all people*. Westbury, NY: American Educational Studies Association.

Rink, J. (1985). *Teaching physical education for learning*. St. Louis: Times Mirror/Mosby.

Roberts, M. (1988, February). School yard menace. *Psychology Today*, pp. 53-56.

Rogers, C. (1983). *Freedom to learn for the 80's*. Columbus, OH: Merrill.

Rohe, F. (1974). *The zen of running*. New York: Random House.

Romance, T.J., Weiss, M.R., & Bokoven, J. (1986). A program to promote moral development through elementary physical education. *Journal of Teaching in Physical Education*, **5**, 126-136.

Ross, E.W., & Hannay, L.M. (1986). Towards a critical theory of reflective inquiry. *Journal of Teacher Education*, **37**, 9-15.

Ross, J.G., & Gilbert, G.G. (1985). Summary of findings for national children and youth fitness study. *JOPERD*, **56**, 45-50.

Rubin, L. (1985). *Artistry in teaching*. New York: Random House.

Ryan, K. (1970). *Don't smile until Christmas: Accounts of the first year of teaching*. Chicago: University of Chicago Press.

Safrit, M. (1986). *Introduction to measurement in physical education and exercise science*. St. Louis: Times Mirror/Mosby.

Sage, G. (1989). The social world of high school athletic coaches: Multiple role demands and their consequences. In T. Templin & P. Schempp (Eds.), *Socialization into physical education: Learning to teach* (pp. 251-266). Indianapolis: Benchmark Press.

Schempp, P. (1989). Apprenticeship-of-observation and the development of physical education teachers. In T. Templin & P. Schempp (Eds.), *Socialization into physical education: Learning to teach* (pp. 13-37). Indianapolis: Benchmark Press.

Schon, D. (1983). *The reflective practitioner: How professionals think in action*. New York: Basic Books.

Schubert, W.H. (1986). *Curriculum: Perspective, paradigm, and possibility*. New York: Macmillan.

Schunk, D.H. (1987). Peer models and children's behavioral change. *Review of Educational Research*, **57**, 149-174.

Segrave, J.O., & Hastad, D.N. (1984). Future directions in sport and juvenile delinquency research. *Quest*, **36**, 37-47.

Shavelson, R.J. (1988). Contributions of educational research to policy and practice. *Educational Researcher*, **17**, 4-11ff.

Siedentop, D. (1980). *Physical education: Introductory analysis* (3rd ed.). Dubuque, IA: Brown.

Siedentop, D. (1983). *Developing teaching skills in physical education* (2nd ed.). Palo Alto, CA: Mayfield.

Siedentop, D. (1987). High school physical education: Still an endangered species. *JOPERD*, **58**, 24-25.

Siedentop, D., Mand, C., & Taggart, A. (1986). *Physical education: Curriculum and instruction strategies for grades 5-12*. Palo Alto, CA: Mayfield.

Sikes, P. (1988). Growing old gracefully? Age, identity and physical education. In J. Evans (Ed.), *Teachers, teaching and control in physical education* (pp. 12-40). Lewes, England: Falmer Press.

Slavin, R. (1987). Ability grouping and student achievement in elementary schools: A best evidence synthesis. *Review of Educational Research, 57*, 293-350.

Sternberg, R.J. (1990). Mental self-government. *Phi Delta Kappan, 71*, 366-371.

Sullivan, R. (1989, March). The unfitness boom. *Sports Illustrated*, p. 13.

Swisher, K., & Swisher, C. (1986). A multicultural physical education setting: An attitude. *Journal of Physical Education, Recreation, and Dance, 57*(7), 35-39.

Templin, T. (1979). Taking the blinders off. *The Physical Educator, 36*, 123-126.

Templin, T. (Ed.) (1983). Profiles of excellence: Fourteen outstanding secondary school physical educators. *JOPERD, 54*, 15-36.

Templin, T. (1987). Some considerations for teaching physical education in the future. In J. Massengale (Ed.), *Trends toward the future in physical education* (pp. 51-67). Champaign, IL: Human Kinetics.

Templin, T. (1988). Settling down: An examination of two women physical education teachers. In J. Evans (Ed.), *Teachers, teaching and control in physical education* (pp. 57-82). Lewes, England: The Falmer Press.

Templin, T. (1989). Running on ice: A case study of the influence of workplace conditions on a secondary school physical educator. In T. Templin & P. Schempp (Eds.), *Socialization into physical education: Learning to teach* (pp. 165-195). Indianapolis: Benchmark Press.

Templin, T., & Schempp, P. (1989). *Socialization into physical education: Learning to teach*. Indianapolis: Benchmark Press.

Thomas, C.E. (1983). *Sport in a philosophic context*. Philadelphia: Lea & Febiger.

Tinning, R. (1985). *Student teaching and the pedagogy of necessity*. Paper presented at the AIESEP International Conference on Research in Physical Education and Sport, Adelphi University, Garden City, NY.

Tom, A.R. (1984). *Teaching as a moral craft*. New York: Longman.

Torbert, M., & Schneider, L.B. (1989). A safe hockey game. *JOPERD, 60*, 19.

Trotter, R.J. (1985, September). Muzafer Sherif: A life of conflict and goals. *Psychology Today*, pp. 55-59.

Tyler, R. (1949). *Basic principles of curriculum and instruction*. Chicago: University of Chicago Press.

Updyke, W. (1984). *Planters-AAU physical fitness program annual report of results*. Bloomington, IN: Indiana University Press.

U.S. Department of Health and Human Services. (1980). *Promoting health/preventing disease: Objectives for the nation*. Washington, DC: U.S. Government Printing Office.

Valli, L., & Tom, A.R. (1988). How adequate are the knowledge base frameworks in teacher education? *Journal of Teacher Education, 39*, 5-12.

van Manen, M. (1977). Linking ways of knowing with ways of being practical. *Curriculum Inquiry, 6*, 205-228.

van Manen, M. (1986). *The tone of teaching*. Richmond Hill, Ontario: Scholastic-TAB.

Veal, M.L. (1988). Pupil assessment issues: A teacher educator's perspective. *Quest, 40*, 151-161.

Vertinsky, P. (1985). Risk benefit analysis of health promotion: Opportunities and threats for physical education. *Quest*, **37**, 71-83.

Vogel, P., & Seefeldt, V. (1988). *Program design in physical education*. Indianapolis: Benchmark Press.

Wang, B. (1977). *An ethnography of a physical education class*. Unpublished doctoral dissertation, University of North Carolina at Greensboro.

Webb, H. (1969). Professionalization of attitudes towards play. In G.S. Kenyon (Ed.), *Aspects of contemporary sport sociology* (pp. 161-178). Chicago: Athletic Institute.

Weiss, M.R. (1987). Self-esteem and achievement in children's sport and physical activity. In D. Gould & M.R. Weiss (Eds.), *Advances in pediatric sport sciences* (Vol. 2, pp. 87-119). Champaign, IL: Human Kinetics.

Weiss, M.R., & Bredemeier, B.J. (1986). Moral development. In V. Seefeldt (Ed.), *Physical activity and well-being* (pp. 373-390). Reston, VA: American Alliance for Health, Physical Education, Recreation and Dance.

Werner, P. (1989). Teaching games: A tactical perspective. *JOPERD*, **60**, 97-101.

Wigginton, E. (1985). *Sometimes a shining moment: The Foxfire experience*. Garden City, NY: Anchor Books.

Wildman, T.M., & Niles, J.A. (1987). Reflective teachers: Tensions between abstractions and realities. *Journal of Teacher Education*, **38**, 25-31.

Wilson, N. (1976). *The frequency and patterns of selected motor skills by third and fourth grade girls and boys in the game of kickball*. Unpublished master's project, University of Georgia.

Wilson, W.J. (1988). *The truly disadvantaged*. Chicago: The University of Chicago Press.

Winnick, J. (Ed.) (1990). *Adapted physical education and sport*. Champaign, IL: Human Kinetics.

Wittrock, M. (Ed.) (1986). *Handbook of research on teaching*. New York: Macmillan.

Wolfgang, C.H., & Glickman, C.D. (1980). *Solving discipline problems*. Boston, MA: Allyn & Bacon.

Zahorik, J.A. (1986). Acquiring teaching skills. *Journal of Teacher Education*, **37**, 21-25.

Index

Z

KING ALFRED'S COLLEGE

LIBRARY